# Victoria's Legacy

## Judith Lynch Waldhorn
## &
## Sally B. Woodbridge

### Drawings by
## Wendy Wheeler

101 Productions
San Francisco

San Francisco photographs by Michael Boedeker.
Bay Area photographs by Sally Woodbridge.
Maps designed and executed by Joan Levi-Kring.
Text for Chapters I and II by Judith Waldhorn.
Text for Chapters III and IV by Sally Woodbridge.
Cover drawing: Haas-Lilienthal house, San Francisco.

Copyright © 1978 Judith Lynch Waldhorn and Sally Byrne Woodbridge
Drawings copyright © 1978 Wendy Wheeler

Printed in the United States of America.
All rights reserved.

Published by 101 Productions
834 Mission Street, San Francisco, California 94103

Distributed to the book trade in the United States by
Charles Scribner's Sons, New York.

*Library of Congress Cataloging in Publication Data*
Waldhorn, Judith Lynch.
   Victoria's legacy.

   Bibliography: p.
   Includes index.
   1. Architecture, Domestic--California--San Francisco
Bay region--Guide-books. 2. Architecture, Modern--19th
century--California--San Francisco Bay region--Guide-
books. 3. Architecture, Victorian--California--San
Francisco Bay region--Guide-books. 4. San Francisco--
Dwellings--Guide-books. I. Woodbridge, Sally Byrne,
joint author. II. Title.
NA7238.S35W34   917.94'6'045   78-18350
ISBN 0-89286-139-8

# CONTENTS

# ABBREVIATION KEY

Each entry in the tours in this book is followed by the building date and an abbreviation providing information on the style of the house. Abbreviations providing information on the origin of the house are included when available. For a discussion of the styles listed in this key, see Victorian House Styles, pages 196 to 205. For further information on the evolution of the house styles and a discussion of the roles of the contractor, architect and owner-builder, see Victorian Home Building in San Francisco, pages 7 to 32.

**House Styles**
C    Combination of styles
I    Italianate
IB    Italianate with bay windows
IF    Italianate with a flat front
M    Mixed: A block of houses that vary in style because they were built at different times
O    Other: Less common styles such as Colonial or Classical Revival, Gothic Revival and Old English or Elizabethan, as well as house designs that do not fit into any category
QA    Queen Anne
QT    Queen Anne with a tower
SFS  San Francisco Stick

**Building Information**
A    Architect
AB    Architect-builder
B    Builder
C    Contractor
D    Developer
OB    Owner-builder

In this book the term "Victorian" is not used to designate a particular style of architecture or interior design, but as a general term to indicate a period more or less bracketed by the reign of Queen Victoria, 1837 to 1901. Though the buildings described here were built far from England, the influence of that country and its culture stretched easily to the West Coast of the United States. In fact, it would be nearly impossible to find a term so rich in American associations as "Victorian."

# Victorian Home Building in
## San Francisco

*2527 Washington Street (entry 87, Pacific Heights West)*

# VICTORIAN HOME BUILDING IN SAN FRANCISCO

## Architecture That Delights the Eye

At first they all look alike, those skinny wooden houses perched on hills, the creations of San Francisco's nineteenth-century entrepreneurs, the Victorian tract builders. The fronts presented to the passerby are laden with wood and plaster details, their surfaces interrupted by bay windows—decorative bravura hiding the plainest clapboard backsides. Their ebullience is stunning at first, and the eye is overwhelmed.

Survivors of that first visual onslaught begin to look more closely. Now, houses that looked alike at first, are not alike at all. When subjected to more discriminating vision, most are quite distinct from one another. In fact, the hasty judgement of *all alike* quickly reverses, and suddenly it seems that all are *different,* with variations as major as a roofline and profile, and as minute and almost imperceptible as the different piercing of a cornice bracket.

Some of the causes of this seemingly infinite variety are already known: abundant coastal redwood, easily turned, pressed, and sawn to keep pace with the most fertile imaginations of the millwrights; the development of a new technology for the working of wood, particularly the power-driven jigsaw and lathe; local millworks, whose annual trade catalogs might feature scores of doors, each slightly different from the next; and an abundance of house-plan books, which only hinted at the many ways to combine the variety of embellishment available. There were also magazines published for architects and the building trades (including one that originated in San Francisco), which provided house plans, inspirations for new varieties of "trim and fancywork," and editorials about new products, styles, paint and interior treatment.

Yet these factors are not sufficient to account for the enormous array of individual Victorian details or the way in which these details were combined into totally different patterns of decorations. Newly discovered historical information, however, has provided a clue: In the 1880s and 1890s, the two major decades of home construction of the century, more than fifteen hundred individuals were building, moving and remodeling houses in San Francisco!

The discovery of this information—twenty-one years of "building intelligence" from the *California Architect and Building News* cross-referenced by architect, contractor or builder—is especially timely, since these furiously embellished buildings are now the focus of a wave of public affection. Those so inclined and financed are buying the Victorians and restoring to all of us some of our heritage of the nineteenth century. Since the remaining homes number in the mere thousands and their fans are legion, not all are able to own or rent one. Luckily, the Victorian revival includes many thousands of people who enjoy just looking. Even schoolchildren are learning to appreciate Victorian exuberance, described as "designful" by one enthused second grader.

One of the joys of learning to look is being able to recognize the work of some of the more prolific architects, contractors and owners, many of whom "signed" their creations with "signature details": standard or custom

*Cameo face over the entry of 263 Dolores Street,*
*designed by architect Charles Devlin and built in 1892*

millwork, a characteristic house profile, or a consistent combination of individual parts. These details make Victorian viewing as addictive as bird-watching, because you can actually learn to identify Nelsons, Andersons, Einsteins and others as you walk through each neighborhood.

## The Early Days, from Pueblo to City

Perhaps it's a marvel that San Francisco ever developed at all. The early settlers found a raggedy peninsula of sand and built upon it a great metropolis. What began as Yerba Buena, a pueblo of huts, shacks and tents huddled on the cove, became a city within a few decades after the Gold Rush. Its shoreline was tidied up with fill and its tracts of sand dunes were tamed with plantings and transformed into sites for thousands and thousands of "fancywork" houses.

Spanish land grant confusion, various annexations and squatters' claims rendered City land titles cloudy and confused during the 1850s and early sixties. Numerous suits moved ponderously through the courts, and titles were finally cleared in the late sixties.

As the *Alta California* newspaper commented March 29, 1869, "Land speculation has greatly increased in San Francisco during the last five years, and it has now become one of our chief branches of business." The shortage of homes was attributed to a vastly increased migration to California of "working men" who were attracted to California's climate, agriculture and trade, and whose movement here was inevitable, "as the railroads have made access convenient and cheap."

This influx of population, combined with the limited amount of land available in San Francisco, caused the price of land to rise, and the *Alta* editor feared that the demand for affordable lots would soon exceed the supply:

> The greatest profits in property south of Mission Creek have been made mostly by men who were comparatively poor and began with small investments, against the advice of their friends, and against the general opinion, which was that prices were too high, and could not be maintained. The seekers after cheap homesteads, if the present rate of progress continues, will in a short time have to make up their minds to go out 20 miles or more, or cross on the ferry and build up a new town at Saucelito, after the manner of Oakland and Alameda.

The institutional intermediary between the salable land and the buyer was the homestead association, a corporation that bought land, subdivided it into parcels and then transferred the titles to the lots to its shareholders. Each share entitled the holder to one parcel of property. Some bought only one, but many of the Victorian-era tract builders bought up whole blocks for later development. In 1869, the *Alta* estimated that there were eighty to one hundred homestead associations buying land in and about the City. To illustrate the rising value of property, the *Alta* cited the example of the Pioneer Race Track, the City's first raceway. Bounded by 24th, 26th, Capp and Alabama streets, the racetrack land was located about four miles from City Hall in the Inner Mission neighborhood, and was purchased by the San Francisco Union Homestead Association for $500 per acre in 1859. Ten years later it was valued at $20,000 per acre.

The search for profits led some of the associations to feature the low prices of their parcels as the prominent part of their advertising brochures. For example, the City Homestead Association offering was billed as "The 90 Dollar Lots." A closer examination showed that their location was out at the southern boundary of the City, near Lake Merced. This association advertised "lots of 25-feet front by 100 feet in depth" for $4 payment per month. Another homestead association offered 400 lots, at $510 each, "in payments of $10 per month, no interest." Although much of the land was still marshes out in the Bayview when it was sold, the advertisement brochure depicted prospective homeowners strolling tree-lined streets.

More than a hundred homestead associations covered the "suburbs" of the City with a patchwork quilt of land for sale. They provided an institutional mechanism that made possible the relatively inexpensive purchase of standard-sized lots, and helped set the stage for the major decades of Victorian-era home building in San Francisco.

### The Decades of Building
The years from 1870 to 1906 produced the bulk of San Francisco's Victorian buildings. Although there was much overlapping in style trends— and a great many remodelings, additions and alterations during the era— each decade can be roughly associated with a characteristic pattern of structural profile, details and decorative materials: what the hindsight of history calls "style." Some architects and builders helped set the style that characterised each decade, others followed and "jumped from one style to the other with surprising alacrity."[1]

The vitality and the ferment of that time is expressed in the thousands of Victorian-era homes that still line the streets of San Francisco. Their astonishing richness of detail and variety of shape was described in 1887 by the *San Francisco Chronicle* as "houses with no two sides alike, houses of chaste and rigid outline, and houses all angles and florid garniture, houses eccentric and scrappy as a crazy quilt, apparently pieced together from the leavings of other houses."[2]

*"Donuts" and "drips" on a portico
at 725 Castro Street*

A local weekly categorized the City's architecture as "latitudinarian " and emphasized the "striking variety" of the houses: "It would be difficult to classify these residences as belonging to any one style of architecture, for all the different orders have been reproduced with what might be termed a free treatment."[3]

While styles, shapes and details varied, the homes shared a common construction method, balloon-framing, a technique developed in Chicago in the 1830s. Standard lumber sizes and machine-made wire nails were the two essential ingredients that enabled rapid building of inexpensive wood frame homes, whose seeming insubstantiality contributed to the "balloon" nickname.

Both the underlying structural members and much of the decoration on San Francisco Victorian homes are redwood, a local material that had many advantages. It was cheap and plentiful; it resisted rot, termites and fire; and it was easily worked into different shapes, whose possibilities were limited only by the imaginations of the designers. Thus it was the perfect material to express the buoyant optimism of the nineteenth century.

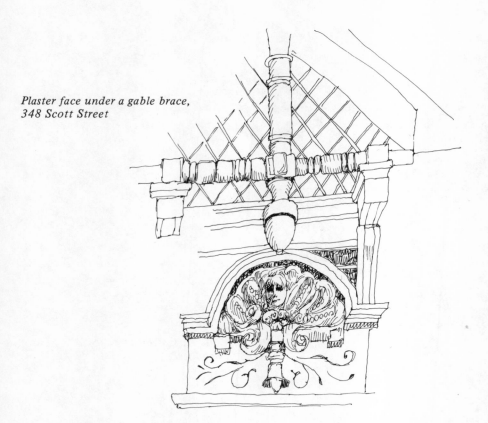

*Plaster face under a gable brace,*
*348 Scott Street*

The common theory that wood frame construction was necessary in San Francisco because its flexibility would enable it to withstand earthquakes was disagreed with in 1887 by George Wolfe, a local architect:

> The earthquake theory, so often propounded, is simply absurd, for we have never had a shock here that was strong enough to seriously affect a properly constructed building. . . . The reason for our wooden houses is easily enough found and is too sensible to need ficticious support. . . . Here there are no extremes of climate, and a wooden residence supplies every need for comfort. . . . That is to say, with a very slight outlay for fuel, we can keep thoroughly warm during the winter, while the slight structure of our wooden houses permits an amount of window glass space that would be utterly impracticable in heavier buildings.[4]

### The 1870s

"Chaste, noble, simple and stately" are words often used to describe the Victorian houses of the 1870s, now called the Italianate style. Some of their simplicity undoubtedly resulted as much from lack of complex milling machinery as from any nobility or restraint on the part of builders or buyers. Trade catalogs of the time offered a relatively simple exterior

12

treatment, often rooted in the Classical decorative tradition: flat window hoods, squeezed pediments, entryways supported by fluted columns with Corinthian capitals. On top was a bracketed cornice that was usually a false front—a clever masquerade for the less impressive peaked-roofed building behind. The flat-fronted house was ideal for the San Francisco of the 1870s. Its decorative elements could be mass-produced by the simple millwork machinery available at the time, and its tall false front made the house look more imposing on its narrow twenty- or twenty-five-foot lot.

One of the earliest versions of the flat-fronted city rowhouse was published in 1862 in a house-plan book prepared by Hinkle, Guild and Company of Cincinnati, Ohio. It was twenty-one feet wide with details described later by *Sloan's Architectural Magazine:* "The windows are of varied forms, some flat, others have the half-round arch. . . . The deep shadow is produced by the heavily projecting cornices and brackets, so charming, so inexpensive and so easily applicable."[5] Those same details appear on San Francisco's flat-front Italianates as redwood replicas of house parts produced in other areas of the country in brownstone or cast iron.

The five-sided slanted bay window became a popular addition to the flat front, creating a variant with the same details that characterized the earlier version: wooden replicas of stone door and window hoods, bracketed cornices and quoins, or corner blocks, such as might be found on European stone or brick buildings.

The bay window, which was also called "bow," "oriel," and "swell," proved so popular in both its slanted version and its later rectangular and round shapes, that San Francisco was dubbed "the city of bay windows." One architect tried to analyze the phenomenon: "'Bow' windows are almost universally popular, and we hold it as evidence of good sense on the part of thousands of owners who would not build a house without them. They are invaluable adjuncts, furnishing increased convenience, comfort, sunlight and protection to health."[6]

Many City homes of the 1870s were the products of The Real Estate Associates (TREA), a development company that built more than one thousand houses before declaring bankruptcy in 1881. An enormous operation for the time, TREA was San Francisco's first major tract builder. According to their claims, between 1870 and 1875 they had produced "more detached houses than any other person or company in the United States in a similar time span." They paid wages of up to ten thousand dollars a week to employ three to four hundred men to produce their houses, many of which still stand, eloquent testimony to the virtues of mass production. TREA was responsible, for example, for the handsome trio of

Italianates at 120-26 Guerrero Street and also for their more modest companions around the corner at 226-36 Clinton Park.[7]

Critics sharpened their pencils and attacked these homes of the seventies. First, the mansions, such as those built on Nob Hill of Classical designs with so-called "Frisco-American" variations:

> Imagine the incongruities of honest outlines being concealed upon the principal facade by a classic cornice, balustrading and ribbed parapets, porticoes supported by massive columns, these in turn borne by concealed 2x4 and 4x4 posts, all of these adornments consisting of wood and with the ingenuity of the house painter so dyed as to represent the clearest white marble or the exquisite sandstone and as such appears until the sun has left its guage [sic] marks in the nature of warps, checks, etc., a glaring condemnation and advertisement of sham.[8]

Unfortunately the 1906 fire destroyed the Nob Hill examples mentioned by that critic. One magnificent example of an Italian villa remains in Pacific Heights, however, the Casebolt mansion at 2727 Pierce Street. This official landmark, which may have been built as early as 1865, has much of the large-scale embellishment associated with the grandiose castles that once could be found on Nob Hill.

The more modest Italianates, such as those built by The Real Estate Associates, were also criticised: ". . . the insultingly plain house with its hall and side rooms, its narrow staircases leading up to the front door, the inevitable bow window, the cheap and nasty scrollwork of the planing mill, all built upon a uniform model."[9]

### The 1880s
The mid-1880s were boom years for San Francisco; construction started on at least four new buildings each working day. More cable car lines were extended to outlying neighborhoods, creating a flurry of land sales and auctions. Sellers were criticized for having their properties "fixed up for sale with all the cheap preliminaries of white-washed fences and trees, a flag pole floating a big flag, and other such devices as will add superficial attractiveness and tune purchasers' minds up to the highest pitch of appreciation."[10]

The most popular house style of the eighties was a vertical-looking rowhouse with a three-sided rectangular bay window, whose ninety-degree angles were much easier to mass-produce than the five-sided bay of the seventies with its complex mitering and molding. The surfaces of the homes of this decade, now called "San Francisco Sticks," were laden with an abundance of wooden enrichment. The promise of redwood was fulfilled as

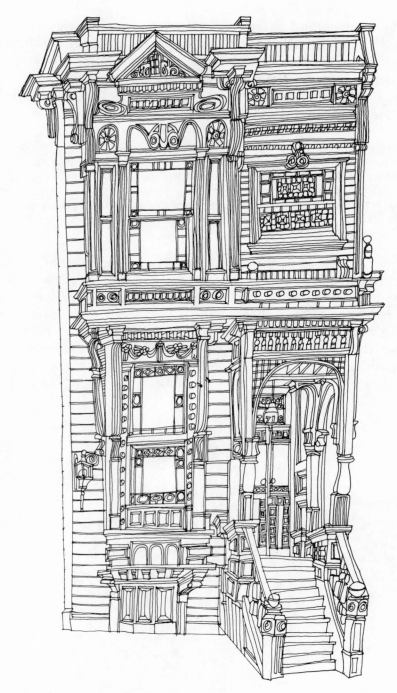

*San Francisco Stick, 2781 Clay Street*

local millwrights pushed the material to its limits, turning, sawing, carving, pressing and incising. The basic house shape was similar to the Italianate; the difference was in the type and degree of ornamentation.

This change in decorative treatment was called for in 1875, in an article by W. N. Lockington in the *Overland Monthly,* a local magazine that may have helped set the tone for the eighties:

> That [San Francisco] is a city of wood would be no reproach were the wood properly treated; but the wooden houses lie, like a man with a false shirtfront —they try to hide their material. They imitate stone; their fronts are channeled into blocks and sanded over, and quoins, windowsills, cornices and other details are copied from those of the brick and stone dwellings of other modern cities. There is no need for this. . . . A wooden building should not ape a stone one, but should show its material and delight in it.[11]

No longer was wood used to mimic stone details or to faithfully reproduce Classical embellishment such as quoins or Corinthian columns. Breaking away from more traditional residential adornments, architects, contractors and owners could choose from a bewitching assortment of such details as geometric strips, waffles, leaves, drips, holes and sunbursts.

By the late 1880s, entire catalogs were devoted to seemingly infinite variations on just one item of embellishment. For example, the 1891 catalog offering of the Joseph Hafner Manufacturing Company of St. Louis,

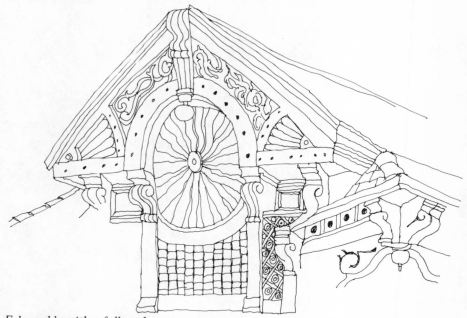

*False gable with a full sunburst,*
*2845 Greenwich Street*

Missouri, contained a lengthy series of "cottage doors," whose names shed light on the "styles" of the time. Number 253, "The Cleveland," and 254, "The Queen Anne," were identical, from incised lower panel to a sunburst over the window, except for one detail: the "Queen Anne" door had a window with marginal panes; the "Cleveland" a single pane. One suspects the names were assigned almost capriciously. A glance through the rest of the catalog shows doors named for states and cities: "Winnebago," "Nashville"; and doors named for people: "the Garfield panel," "the Jenny Lind marginal"; there is even a door called "The Mikado."

Some catalogs featured different kinds of windows and their decorative finish. The shape of the window opening itself could vary from rectangular to circle-topped to segmented. The finish used to frame the window opening could be a simple flat hood or a concoction of mass-produced wooden embellishment.

Floral decorations also took up whole pages in trade catalogs. These gentle and ephemeral manifestations of nature, on which the Victorians doted, were produced in vast quantities by machines, even though they look like the delicate and unique products of individual handcrafting. Most of these floral decoratives were made by carving machines or stamped out by the thousands as designs were wrought from damp wood with hydraulic presses.

San Francisco boasts few buildings with entire cast-iron fronts, but decorative iron details were used by the builders and architects of the eighties in a variety of ways. The most novel application of decorative ironwork is readily apparent in any old photograph of a San Francisco residential neighborhood. Spear-tipped rows of iron cresting used to bristle from the tops of most homes built here during the 1880s. House plans in catalogs and in architectural magazines of that decade frequently showed iron cresting on the roof; sometimes it also guarded the entryway. The former extent of these rooftop fences seems startling today, because virtually all are gone, the victims of weather, wartime scrap metal drives, or anti-Victorian modernizers.

The exuberant transcending of traditional building details in the eighties was echoed by a new attitude toward paint colors. In the 1870s, the houses of the tract builders tended to be painted all one color, usually white, beige or gray, sometimes with the trim black or dark green. Some of the Nob Hill and Van Ness Avenue mansions of the wealthy during that decade were actually painted to masquerade as stone or marble, while others were painted in dark colors.

By 1887, enough people were painting their houses in lighter, brighter colors for the *San Francisco Chronicle* to notice and comment: "Just when

*Queen Anne rowhouse, 3919 20th Street,*
*built in 1893 by C. T. Emmons*

the present esthetic movement began, it would be hard to determine, but it first manifested itself in a growing aversion to grey paint. Cautiously at first, and then more and more boldly, houses appeared in browns, yellows, greens and even reds, all sorts of unorthodox colors."[12]

## The 1890s

This decade of building brought a radical change in house style, a trend that in San Francisco appears to have started during the eighties. In 1884, the *California Architect and Building News* held a nationwide contest and invited architects to submit plans for residences. The prizes ranged from a check for fifty dollars to "a box of drawing instruments." The magazine received several hundred entries, virtually all submitted by Eastern architects. The four winners were all similar: All were completely different from the vertical, rectangular-bayed false-gabled rowhouses of the eighties. These "premium" homes had towers and true gabled roofs, with attic space behind them. They featured horizontal lines—plaster garlanding, frieze bands and belt cornices—rather than the vertical lines of the eighties. Plaster, not wood, was the predominant material recommended for embellishment.[13] These structural and decorative elements define the style that today we call the Queen Anne; in the Victorian era that name was only one of many given to the same general style.

Windows with leaded panes, or glittering faceted round "jewels" and colored glass in mosaic patterns were found in most homes of the nineties. Decorative glass is one of the happiest characteristics of this decade. On gray days, the colored windows brighten the view of the outside world. On bright days, the sun invades with glowing hues, splashing the parlor with patterns, slipping through a bevel to make a rainbow in the hallway. Art glass creates a private, shimmering interior garden, its designs and locations trailing the movements of the sun.

The whimsical house of the nineties was a favorite target of the critics, one of whom decried its "inconsistencies, absurdities, oddities and extreme fanatical tendencies."[14] Another critic attacked the gabled rowhouse:

Why the fantastic curved piece with its radiating spindles over the porch? Why the meaningless little columns to the attic window which we know support nothing at all, and why so much cheap detail on the frieze and in the gable's peak? All of this we know costs the owner dollars while it has not even added cents to the effect. Our only answer to these questions is that Man, as exemplified in the everyday American citizen, wishes an exceedingly active quality in his architecture. He wishes all parts of his building to be on the move—to be doing something—and he objects to the dignified surface and simple opening.[15]

19

By the 1890s, the decorative elements of the towered Queen Anne—plaster enrichment, steep gable, broader main hallway and horizontal demeanor—were embraced wholeheartedly by Victorian tract builders, who eliminated the tower but kept the rest.

## "Building Intelligence" from 1880 to 1901

The fire that was the aftermath of the 1906 earthquake destroyed the million-dollar extravaganzas built for the silver bonanza kings and the railroad barons on Nob Hill and Van Ness Avenue. Unfortunately for twentieth-century researchers, the blaze also consumed many official building records, leaving most Victorian homes anonymous, undated and unclaimed by any architect or builder. But information that will help reveal the secrets of most of the era has recently been uncovered.

The *California Architect and Building News* was published in San Francisco from 1879 until mid-1901. Its architectural renderings, descriptions of local trends and often apoplectic denunciations of the profession would be enough to render it both delightful to read and invaluable for research. Each issue, however, also ends with a section called "Building Intelligence," that is the key to solving the fire-shrouded mystery of thousands of San Francisco buildings.

The method of arranging the information varies. During the initial years of publication, addresses were listed randomly and contained minimal facts: approximate location, size, construction cost, the name of the original owner, and the architect or contractor responsible for the building. But by the late 1880s, each listing was entered alphabetically by street and often contained additional information about the terms and amounts of contracts with individual tradespeople such as the plumber, plasterer, painter and cement layer. Each of the 246 monthly lists contains from 50 to 150 items, depending on the liveliness of the building industry that month.

All kinds of structures are listed, including commercial buildings, but the bulk of the information concerns residences. A surprisingly large proportion of that information describes changes to existing homes, making those decades seem like a ferment of alterations—and helping to account for some of the immense variety of homes that remains.

For example, the mansard-roofed home at 2460 Union Street was, according to the magazine, pieced together from several other houses. This "moving and alterating [sic] old buildings" was done by the architectural firm of Mooser and Cuthbertson in 1892 for $2,200. The magazine even offered a plan to "modernize" an 1876 Italianate built by The Real Estate Associates by adding a Queen Anne wing, complete with a tower. This alteration was actually carried out by the Boone family on their Mission District home, which used to stand at 21st and Bartlett streets.

While the range of construction costs was broad—from a few hundred dollars to the admittedly low $250,000 estimate for the Flood mansion—the majority of the houses are listed at $10,000 or less. From $3,500 to $5,000 seemed a standard price for a two-story dwelling throughout all twenty-one years of the listings.

The procedure for translating an individual listing from "Building Intelligence" into the current address of a Victorian house is intricate and sometimes extremely frustrating. Here is an example:

> Location: South side Pine Street, between
>     Octavia and Laguna
> Size: 2-story, brick basement, stable
> Architect: Wolfe & Son
> Cost: $10,000
> Owner: Capt. Thos. G. Taylor
> Date of listing: August, 1880

*Cast iron handrail,*
*770 Treat Avenue*

Since the listings do not give the house number, the next step is to look up the owner in *Langley's City Directory,* under a date a year or two after the original listing date, and hope that he or she is listed in the same approximate location—which would not be the case if the owner built the house to rent or sell. But Thomas Taylor is there: "Thos. G. Taylor, mining supt." is listed in the 1882-1883 *Directory* at "1911 Pine St."

Many City street names are now different, so the next step is to check the booklet, *Changes in San Francisco Street Names.* The next and last step, verifying the house number, can be extremely time-consuming and annoying: Approximately two-thirds of the Victorian-era house numbers have been changed. The changes, however, were not always predictable ones: Sometimes the numbers would be reorganized only on one block, often in an apparently arbitrary way; at other times all the numbers along the entire length of a street would be raised or lowered. Another reason this step is potentially frustrating is that no regular City records have been kept of how, when, or what numbers were altered. Sometimes the new number was entered by a conscientious inspector in a set of 1906 *Block Books* kept by the Central Permit Bureau, so each listing must be checked there. This final research procedure is crucial; unfortunately, too many researchers expect to be able to go from the nineteenth-century *City Directory* straight to the same address. That error has resulted in much misinformation about who built and lived in what house.

When the listing approximation is finally transformed into a 1970s street address, the last step is the most suspenseful: rushing out to the site to see if the house is still there. Captain Taylor's home, our sample listing, still stands intact, meticulously maintained by the Catholic teaching nuns who live there.

**Contractors**

While the architectural profession tends to receive the credit for home designs, contractors were actually the most important force in shaping Victorian San Francisco. More than seven hundred were building throughout the City, constructing some individual homes, but most often producing clusters of two or more alike. Their names reflect the cosmopolitan population of the time: John Keneally, J. F. Le Bourveau, Emmanuel Picasso, Hyde and Cox, Ingerson and Gore, Daniel Einstein, Jacques and Company.

Contractors were the major builders of the "suburbs," as the outlying neighborhoods of the City were then known. But before their construction activities could begin, a major impediment had to be overcome, the steep grade of many streets in those hilly neighborhoods.

*Door knob detail with birds,*
*1713 Green Street*

The grid pattern was a conventional town layout often used in the United States, adopted from early Roman planners who found that it used land most efficiently. In flat areas, that grid system makes eminent sense; in San Francisco, however, it resulted in streets being laid out straight up and down the hills, rendering many of the grades too steep for horses to haul construction materials.

The steep streets of the "suburbs" were redeemed, however, by a device that has since become synonymous with San Francisco:

> When the cable car became a certainty, a demonstrated fact, hills were no longer a foreboding aspect. When it was made sure that the ascents up steep grades could be made with the same ease and personal comfort, and a great deal more of scenic and romantic luxury, than on level roads, the hilltops soon gained favor and advanced in value more than double within a single year. [16]

As contractors and others began to decorate the hills with homes, the local press responded with justifiable smugness: "It must be concluded that great things have been achieved in San Francisco, that with all the vices, immoralities and cosmopolitanisms permitted within her borders ... she presents a record in fact unequalled by but few cities in the Union."[17]

William W. Rednall was the most prolific contractor of the two decades. His hundreds of homes were usually low in price, ranging from a $695 farmhouse to a $3,000 cottage on Potrero Hill. Cranston and Keenan produced several of the rare tower-house clusters left in the City. They also built a cluster of alternating rowhouses and tower houses that still stands in the 700 block of Broderick Street.

But not all contractors built cheap homes or clusters of identical ones. In 1881, the Moore Brothers built a $22,000 mansion for Mrs. Dominga de Goni Atherton, at 1990 California Street. When less than a year old, the house was described as "quaint" in a society column reporting on Mrs. Atherton's February 9, 1882 housewarming, when the house was "dedicated, so to speak." According to the newspaper, "Mrs. Atherton sought to model its outlines after the plan of her former South American residence ... her intention being to have a house that would suit her tastes and her predilections."

The reporter made an attempt to describe the home: "It is, properly speaking, two stories high ... and belongs to what might be termed a modernized Elizabethan order ... picturesque in its outlines, original and extraordinary ... looking as if a restored relic of the medieval days had been dropped down into the midst of things of the nineteenth century." The writer was less receptive to the interior: "The rooms are so low as to have a depressing effect on a stranger entering the house. ... The whole structure looks as if the builder had a *carte blanche* with regard to ground to be covered ... but was restricted in the matter of height."[18]

The contemporary old-house watcher would find this description confusing, since the house is now definitely three stories high, looks unrestricted in height and has a large corner tower not mentioned in the newspaper description, but which is surely too imposing to be overlooked.

An answer may be found by searching the "Building Intelligence" listings of the *Building News.* Maybe Mrs. Atherton was miffed by the society column. In any case, six months later she hired yet another contractor, Charles Tilden, to make "additions," which cost $3,000. Perhaps the tower and the front room with the brooding clipped gable were added then.

## Architects

About a quarter of the fifteen hundred builders of the eighties and nineties were practicing architects. One of the most productive was Henry Geilfuss, who came to San Francisco from Germany in 1876, when he was twenty-six. He worked as a draftsman the first two years, then began his own

*Bay-windowed Italianate,*
*2040 Union Street*

25

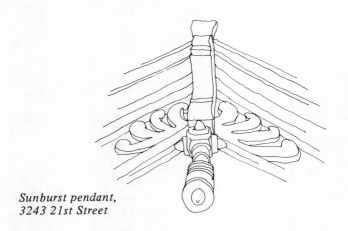

*Sunburst pendant,*
*3243 21st Street*

firm. Geilfuss is credited with several renowned Victorian homes: the Westerfeld villa on Alamo Square, 1198 Fulton Street, which he designed in 1887; and the Dietle house, 294 Page Street, which he designed in 1888 for $7,740. But Geilfuss was also responsible for hundreds of buildings in all price ranges. Many are gone, but others await discovery by the walker, such as 102 Guerrero, 881-93 Fulton and 824 Grove. A favorite Geilfuss embellishment was a floral corner cover like the one gracing the cottage he built for himself in 1882. The cottage still stands at 811 Treat Avenue in the Mission District, nestled in the shadow of the John McConnell school.

Two works of architect W. H. Lillie illustrate how his profession contributed to the wide variety of Victorian houses. For Edward Coleman, president of the Pacific Rolling Mill Company, Lillie designed a tower house with lavish bands of ornament in a torch and garland pattern. The home was built in 1896 at a cost of $13,640 and still stands at 1701 Franklin Street, an official landmark recently refurbished for law offices. Lillie also worked for the Rountree Brothers, tract builders of the 1890s. For them he designed a block of seven Queen Anne rowhouses, for $3,200 each, with a winsome variety of fronts below typical peaked roofs with archways, plaster garlands and decorative shingles. The houses still stand at 108-24 Lyon in the Haight Ashbury, although their "misguided" facades are scarcely recognizable as Lillie's charming concoctions.

The architectural profession in San Francisco was quite proud of its accomplishments:

> Our city can boast of many talented men, men who have lent to the city of today their creative talents and in the handsome, massive and magnificent buildings which line our streets, and in the palatial residences in every section, we see evidences of their skill which would reflect credit on any city in the country.[19]

Some architects, such as Joseph Cather Newsom, published brochures about their houses. In the introduction to his *Artistic City Buildings, Flats and Residences,* published around 1895, Newsom admonished those about to build: "Having over 2500 different designs and photographs of buildings, erected under my supervision in the Free, Queen Anne, Ann Hathaway, Spanish, Knickerbocker, Renaissance, Eastlake and Picturesque style, I can suit almost any taste." Newsom attempted to justify both himself and his profession in his brochure:

> WHERE DOES NEWSOM GET HIS IDEAS? Well, that's good. I don't get them in my dreams, like some architects, but by solid study and work. Having a large and valuable library full of good books, thousands of latest Eastern and European photographs—it is from these that I combine my new features, taking a feature here and there, and making a happy result. There is no disgrace to copy, but the brains have to be extended to know where to put what you have copied.... It has been my chief object to produce designs and examples entirely foreign from those that appeared in any of my former works. . . . The different styles, etc., are intended to meet all tastes and pockets. . . . The artisan can have as artistic a home as the merchant, if he so desires, for little money.

## Owner-Builders

Owner-builders were the third important influence on Victorian construction, and several hundred people so described themselves. The majority built only the houses in which they lived, but a few became real estate developers. For example, Dr. C. C. O'Donnell hired "daywork" to build five slightly peculiar homes in 1887 for four thousand dollars. Perhaps he also designed them, for the cluster at 1328-46 York Street in the Inner Mission neighborhood looks like none other in the City! George Edwards scattered his houses throughout the Mission District, and Joseph Comerford and Frederick Kleebauer built distinctive clusters of cottages in Noe Valley. Fernando Nelson constructed clusters in Noe Valley, the Inner Mission, Eureka Valley and the Duboce Triangle, and many houses of the Hinkel family still stand in the Western Addition.

The tract developer operated in a very different manner from the architect. For example, when P. B. Berge, a well-to-do San Franciscan, asked architect B. E. Henriksen to design a home for his lot on the northeast corner of Webster and Pine streets, he received a custom house design with floor plans and elevations drawn on linen, and a handwritten thirty-page set of specifications wherein virtually everything in the house was detailed; the architect received a payment of $260. A home buyer of more modest means would probably go to a developer such as Fernando

Nelson, who built some four thousand homes in a career that spanned almost a century. His signature details of donuts, drips and button boards abound in the Inner Mission, Eureka and Noe valleys and the Mint Hill neighborhood. Buyers of his houses had little choice; they bought what he was building that year. Nelson carried a leather receipt book in his hip pocket for on-the-spot transactions. The prices were right, however; an entire Nelson home could be purchased for $750, just about three times the design fee for the home above planned by architect Henriksen.

Initially the developers built all the houses within a cluster to look alike. This similarity was soon felt to be undesirable, however, causing "confusion and trouble to the dwellers therein," and soon the builders began to employ alternating designs, and houses were painted in different colors. In the final stage of the evolution of the cluster, all the houses were varied in design.[20]

In *Artistic Country Homes,* 1895, Joseph C. Newsom published a rendering of what he called "Three Modern Homes," all on the same block. The "Classic Colonial," at $2,800, features a hip roof, a tall chimney on each side, two Palladian windows, a frieze band of plaster swags and a columned entryway topped with a turned balustrade. His "Mexican-American Home" has a corner entryway with three stout columns. The tiled roof has extra dormers on either edge. Two oval windows peer out near the front door, bordered with ornate cartouche frames. Next door is his $2,800 "Queen Anne," which has little in common with the homes we now assign that name. Newsom's stucco and half-timbered "Queen Anne" would today be called Tudor.

Not everyone approved of this variation. One critic said of such a cluster:

> [It is] one of the ugliest rows of houses that can be found anywhere. It is as weird an aggregation of grotesque forms as the most motley line-up of the Chinese soldiery. Each one of its fifteen fronts is towered and minareted, arched and twisted into such shapes that the effect of the whole is that of a perfect labyrinth of unreason ... [they are] aggressively uninteresting. Yet all of this might be somewhat overlooked, were it not for the fact that the whole row was designed by one man, who seems to have taken himself seriously and to be entirely unconscious of the singular though unenviable distinction he has attained.[21]

### The Decades of Neglect

The carefree extravagance of the Victorian house has always had its detractors. One critic decried the builders and their methods: "Many scarcely give a thought to the manner of construction, their sole aim being

*San Francisco Stick with a French cap,*
*built in 1885 at 207 Day Street*

*Landing newel post,*
*4331 20th Street*

to present a showy house. This they accomplish by a liberal plastering on of 'gingerbread' work and by engaging the services of painters who are expert in the mixing of fancy colors. . . ."[22] In the *Overland Monthly,* W. N. Lockington complained:

> . . . especially conspicuous in San Francisco is the misuse of ornament . . . we have a front loaded with endless repetitions of the same detail; the same scrawny scroll looking at us from a hundred window-heads; the same little panels stuck in every corner; strings of vegetables, all alike, hanging from every column; and wreaths and cornucopias, badly carved, dangling between every projection, as if to leave a bit of plain surface anywhere were to break an eleventh commandment. . . .[23]

Thousands of the Victorians that survived the fire were demolished during the decades that followed. Several thousand were removed in a frenzy of publicly planned and funded urban renewal that plucked the heart from the Western Addition, once the location of the most lavish collection of pre-1906 homes in San Francisco.

Many more Victorians were located in neighborhoods zoned for high-density housing, a factor that often resulted in the land's being worth more than the building on it. Many fell victim to the wrecking ball, to be replaced by apartment buildings ranked in dreary sameness. Houses that escaped destruction were threatened by the development of successive waves of products that were used to strip, smother and alter Victorian buildings into distorted versions of their former selves. After the turn of the century, asbestos shingles were heralded as fire retardant and maintenance free. Many home owners succumbed, and millwork was discarded and redwood siding was hidden by unattractive sheets of fiber-flecked tweedy grey, green or pink shingles, and a dull shadow was cast over formerly spirited blocks of homes. Stucco, "cultured rock," aluminum siding and textured spray had their vogues as well, all justified as often by fashion as by economy.

## What is Left of Victoria's Legacy?
The 1906 fire, which destroyed the concentration of mansions, chalets and turreted castles on Nob Hill, left untouched the work of the contractors, architects and owners who had followed public transportation routes out to the "suburbs."

The burgeoning revival movement of the 1970s naturally raised the question of how many Victorians remain. A comprehensive survey of nine Victorian neighborhoods in San Francisco was sponsored by the National Endowment for the Arts in 1975 and 1976. Its results answer many revivalist questions and also reveal a vast reservoir of disguised Victorian homes awaiting restoration.

In the surveyed neighborhoods—Alamo Square, Bernal Heights, Eureka Valley, Glen Park, Haight Ashbury, Inner Mission, Mint Hill, Noe Valley and Potrero Hill—are 13,487 Victorian structures. The Queen Anne row-house, a design favored by the contractors of the 1890s, is the predominant style remaining: some 5,500 are left. The rectangular-bayed home of the 1880s, the San Francisco Stick style, is still represented by about 3,600 buildings. There are about 3,100 left from the 1870s: 1,900 flat-front Italianates and 1,200 with slanted bay windows. The Queen Anne tower house, the dramatic design most often associated with the Victorian building era, is the rarest, with only 385 left. The legacy of the "1,500 builders" is apparent in the survey results, because more than 700 homes could not be classified into any definite style category. There are more than 400 "clusters" of two or more identical homes, often bearing signature details.

The extent of misguided improvements is startling, because fifty percent of all the structures surveyed had been altered in some significant way. Thus, the revival potential is doubled, because fully half the remaining Victorians have been "disguised" as something else.

Stucco salesmen have had the most success: Some twenty-four hundred houses have been altered, modernized or otherwise defaced with that product. Asbestos shingles have been used to cover more than nineteen hundred homes, while about seven hundred buildings have been stripped of some important part of their architectural anatomy, such as the false gable, the tower, the entryway or the cornice.

## Learning to Look

The purpose of the walking-driving tours, indeed the purpose of this book, is to open eyes to detail and to open hearts to a reverence for our nineteenth-century legacy of embellished architecture. "Open your eyes!" was scrawled in foot-high capital letters on the ground floor of a Queen Anne in the Haight Ashbury in 1978. The spray can calligrapher had an important message, if a vandal's method of expressing it.

Only a handful of Victorians in a few neighborhoods can be mentioned here. But take your Bird Watcher's Guide, following, and explore beyond the maps that follow. Use our guide to help train your vision. Recognize and cherish what is old; love the giddy, whimsical, fantastical products of an era when embellishment was cause for celebration.

As you look up, around, through and behind, be sure to look down for a final clue to our Victorian-era heritage. Those small square sidewalk plates, with a round central insert, are sewer vents. They provide a link to the hundreds of builders and suppliers who helped construct and outfit the homes.

Unnoticed by hurried walkers on the 1300 block of Sanchez Street are three sewer grates that tell the story of the San Francisco Stick cluster built there in 1892. On one plate is the name of the builders, the Rountree Brothers, while "C.C.W. Haun, 413-28th St., Art Stone," is embossed on a second plate, telling who laid the cement sidewalk. The plumbing in the cluster was installed, according to the third vent, by "J. Dutton, 515 Hickory Ave., S.F."

Ideally, the walker should look in the spirit of this charmed critic of the era, writing in 1887:

> The architecture of San Francisco in our residence streets has no counterpart in the world, and we have no reason to be ashamed of it. It is light, airy and pleasing in style, and is to the architecture of Europe and the Eastern States as Spanish music is to the grand and heavier compositions of Wagner. It has improved wonderfully in tone during the past few years, and promises to still further improve in the future; and the results will be that our City will in the end become a model to the world for all that is beautiful in the way of lighter architecture.[24]

# A BIRD WATCHER'S GUIDE TO SAN FRANCISCO VICTORIANS

Because the 1906 fire consumed so many construction records, it is fortunate for contemporary walkers that San Francisco's builders often provided clues to help identify their houses. Many of the tract builders of the eighties and nineties used "signature details" to sign their houses, almost as an artist signs a painting. Learning these signature details adds to the enjoyment of looking at Victorians, as the walker (or driver) can identify houses as products of individuals.

### Jonathan Anderson

A. Jonathan Anderson was a carpenter who built several homes in Noe Valley and signed them with this indescribable but instantly recognizable piece of bandsawn redwood.

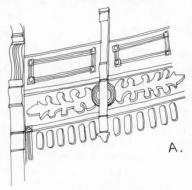

A.

B. Anderson also used a false gable decorated with a "tick-tack-toe" bargeboard and waffle pattern millwork.

### Jonathan Anderson

Many of contractor John Anderson's Queen Anne rowhouses still remain in Eureka and Noe valleys. Anderson put this vase of flowers underneath each gable end. As the decorations were made from pressed sawdust, they often deteriorated and had to be removed. The spaces where they have been, however, are usually still visible.

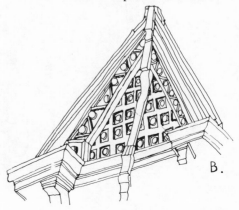

B.

## John Coop

A. Developer John Coop was also the head of the San Francisco Planing Mill. Perhaps he built his homes to showcase some of his millwork. Several of his clusters have these frieze panels with swags, and a row of shield-shaped sawn decoratives across the bay window.

B. Some Coop homes have different profiles or varied bay window shapes, but virtually all have this signature detail: a flat decorative shaped like an anchor with a piece of routed molding below.

### Cranston & Keenan
A few homes done by contractors Cranston and Keenan exhibit this sunburst with a face.

### Daniel Einstein

A. Contractor Daniel Einstein often "signed" his homes with a belt cornice that combined dentils on top, cove and fishscale shingles in the middle, and a row of small square floral decoratives on the bottom.

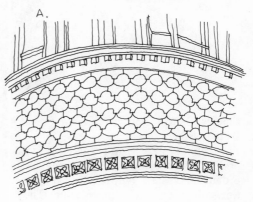

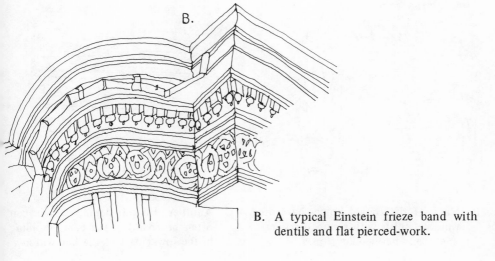

B. A typical Einstein frieze band with dentils and flat pierced-work.

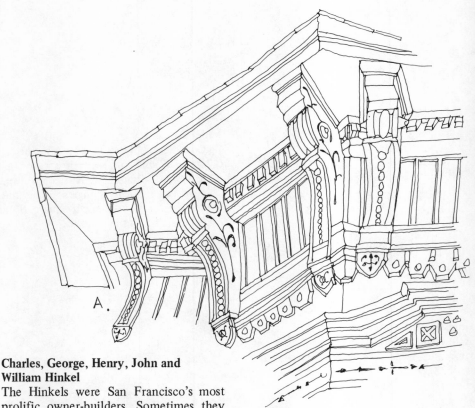

## Charles, George, Henry, John and William Hinkel

The Hinkels were San Francisco's most prolific owner-builders. Sometimes they produced clusters individually, at other times they worked in partnership. They seem to have shared many of the same signature details, regardless of whose name was on the property.

A. A typical Hinkel cornice, with brackets, strips and a row of shield-shaped decoratives pierced with holes.

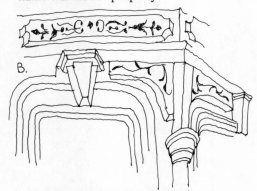

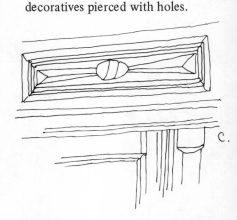

B. Many of the Hinkel homes have this window finish with rounded corners, shields and beveled keystones.

C. Another Hinkel detail, which can often be found in the panel molding in the lower part of the bay window.

A.

**Fernando Nelson**

Fernando Nelson designed and named several of his signature details. According to his son, Nelson would get an idea, scrawl it on an envelope or paper bag and take it down to the Townley Brothers mill. The details would be produced in great quantities, and Nelson would then have them hauled out to the construction site and nailed onto the houses.

A. Nelson used these three details on both San Francisco Stick and Queen Anne houses. He called the series of joined circles "donuts." The long, thin vertical millwork on the column he called "drips," since they looked like dripping paint. Above the donuts is a "button board," another favorite.

B. A wavy, stylized quarter-sunburst can be found in the arched entry of many of Nelson's Queen Anne houses.

C. A Nelson false gable. The half-round row of dentils also appears in the true gables of some of his Queen Anne rowhouses.

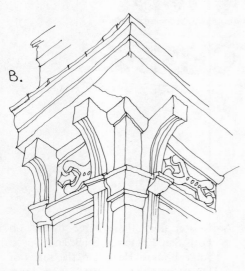

### John Weir

A. John Weir used these flat bandsawn decoratives on his clusters in the Inner Mission and Noe Valley neighborhoods. He alternated four-leaf clovers with flowers.

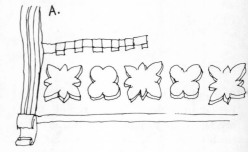

B. This unique detail may be found in the main cornice and across the middle of a Weir house.

38

# Walking Tours
## of
# San Francisco Victorians

The San Francisco section of this book is divided into ten tours, which are designed to be walked (maps are marked with U-turns and occasionally walks are routed in the opposite direction on one-way streets). Some tours are quite long, however, and you may want to use a car or public transportation on sections of tours having several blocks between houses.

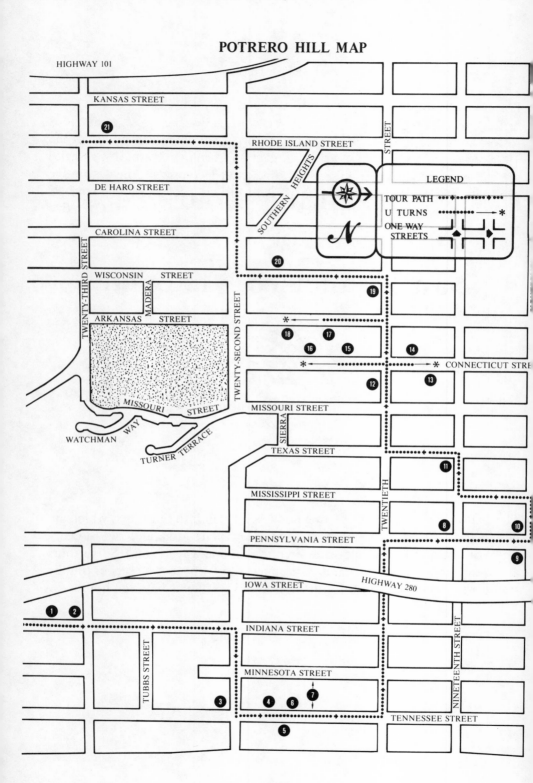

# POTRERO HILL MAP

# POTRERO HILL

Potrero Hill is an astonishing mixture, from splendid, elegant mansions to "cheap dwellings," from the shabbiest clusters to the most meticulous restorations. More than nine hundred Victorian buildings were found in the 1976 survey of the Hill. Half are misguided improvements; asbestos shingles are the most prevalent disguise. Asbestos and stucco prevail; the decorative products of the 1950s and 1960s have made few inroads. More than half the Victorians left on Potrero Hill are Queen Anne rowhouses. Over five hundred remain; most are the simple, inexpensive variety. When surveyed, almost one-fifth were categorized as "other," not fitting into any style category, eloquent testimony to the neighborhood's many owner-builders, who hired day labor to concoct their own versions of the popular styles of the day.

Walking on the Hill can be strenuous. The Victorians listed are often far apart, and the streets are steep. But the contrasts, the stunning vistas and the glimpses into the working world of the port make the pathways of Potrero Hill rewarding.

1. **1258 Indiana Street**
(c. 1865/0) An extremely simple house, with lap siding on the second floor and channel rustic siding underneath. Its high brick foundation and plain door and window hoods make it look like an early farmhouse.

2. **1200 Indiana Street**
(c. 1895/QA)

3. **1100 block of Tennessee Street**
(c. 1880/IF, IB) Entrance to the "Dog-patch" section of Potrero Hill. This block was the shabbiest found in the 1976 survey, but now it is being revived. On this dead-end, unpaved street are five Italian-ate homes, one with a bay and four with flat fronts.

4. **1060 Tennessee Street**
(1895/0) The Irving M. Scott school is a Classical Revival building with fluted corner pilasters. It was damaged by a fire, and in 1977 was declared surplus property and sold by the Board of Education.

5. **1045-49 Tennessee Street**
(1892/SFS) Both originally had delicate floral decoratives, but 1045 has been stripped and clad in asbestos shingles.

6. **1036-42 Tennessee Street**
(c. 1898/SFS, QA) Both structures first had water service connected in 1889, but 1036 is an SFS with a false gable and a garage addition, while 1042 is a QA with spindles and a sunburst.

7. **1002-14 Tennessee Street, 903-15 Minnesota Street**
(1887/SFS; Rees O. Davis, C) Thirteen remain of the seventeen cottages originally built in this cluster, probably versions of architect John C. Pelton's $585 "Cheap Dwelling" published in the *San Francisco Evening Bulletin*, April 3, 1880.

8. **400 Pennsylvania Street**
(1870/IF) Built for the Prentice Crowell family, until 1977 its front retaining wall sported bright blue paint and a large

white "YES." It still has its palm tree, characteristic of Victorian-era gardens.

## 9. 301 Pennsylvania Street
(1866/0) This Classical Revival home was built for the C. French Richards family. It now houses an ambulance service, and is dwarfed by the enormous radio dispatch transmitter on its roof. The simple entryway has fluted pilasters topped by Corinthian capitals.

## 10. 300 Pennsylvania Street
(1868/IB) Built for Captain Charles Adams, the well-to-do New England merchant and shipper who first developed this section of the Hill.

## 11. 1243 19th Street
(c. 1895/QT)
Unusual sunbursts on the tower. The decoration extends around the corner to Texas Street, where the gable has a sprightly bargeboard.

## 12. 1527 20th Street
(c. 1895/QA)

## 13. 415 Connecticut Street
(c. 1895/QA) This home was "misguided" with a facing of pressed brick, which was removed in 1977. The remodeler added a riot of spindles, finials, shingles and flat decorations.

*607 Arkansas Street (entry 18)*

## 14. 474 Connecticut Street
(c. 1890/C) This home combines the rectangular bay of the SFS with the true gable and bargeboard reminiscent of a QA.

## 15. 512-18, 524-26 Connecticut Street
(c. 1885/SFS) Six homes probably patterned after Pelton's $1,140 "Cheap Dwelling," which the *San Francisco Evening Bulletin* published June 26, 1880.

## 16. 520-22 Connecticut Street
(c. 1885/SFS)

## 17. 553 Arkansas Street
(c. 1895/QA) Built for Richard Pengelly, foreman and shipwright with the Union Iron Works, this house has deeply carved floral decoratives and a half-circle art glass window in the front bay.

## 18. 559-607 Arkansas Street
(c. 1885/IB, SFS) This cluster of cottages has several handsome sidewalk sewer grates; bring your children here to take rubbings from them. The bay windows in the cluster vary in shape; six cottages still have French caps.

## 19. 1745 20th Street
(c. 1885/SFS) Although this home has been disguised with asbestos shingles, the handsome shape can still be seen, with its double rectangular bays and arched windows. A spiral staircase swoops up to the door, which has a columned portico.

## 20. 760 Wisconsin Street
(c. 1890/C) Another Potrero Hill combination, with a false front, a rectangular bay, a waffle pattern below the cornice and a spindled arch in the entry.

## 21. 1176 Rhode Island Street
(1897/SFS; Fernando Nelson, D) This cottage resembles Nelson's Eureka Valley cluster at 546-72 Liberty Street.

# INNER MISSION

Although Spanish explorers claimed California in the early 1600s, they established no outposts here until 1776, when the Presidio was founded at the entrance to the Bay, an excellent military vantage point. The site for Mission Dolores was chosen soon after, in a sheltered sunny valley ideal for raising cattle and crops.

In the decade after the Gold Rush, many of the neighborhood's early residents were squatters. Halted by the sand dunes of the western half of the City, they moved south into the area around the mission and found it hospitable, with good weather and flat terrain.

In 1850, a private company was granted a franchise to construct a wooden plank road along Mission Street from 3rd Street to 16th Street. That road immediately opened up the northern part of the neighborhood as a recreation center, and soon San Franciscans were able to enjoy a race-track, restaurants, a zoo and the two-block "pleasure resort," Woodward's Gardens.

The 1976 survey found some 2,600 Victorian homes in an area bounded by Dolores, Army and Market streets and the James Lick Freeway. More than 900 are Italianate buildings of the 1870s, while another 800 are the Stick-style homes popular in the eighties. Only about 550 Queen Anne houses were found, for by the 1890s, most Inner Mission land was built on.

This neighborhood was one of the first to show signs of the Victorian revival movement, as whole blocks on streets such as Liberty, Fair Oaks, Hill and Guerrero were brightened with new paint and restored to their former elegance. Those streets are explored in the Inner Mission West walking tour. But even in the lesser-known "flatlands" of the neighborhood are clusters of Victorian homes that will gladden the hearts of walkers. That part of the area is the subject of the Inner Mission East walking tour.

# INNER MISSION EAST MAP

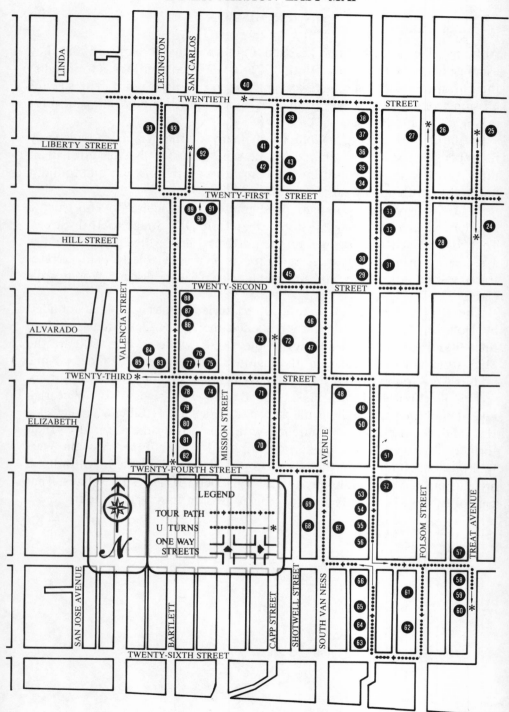

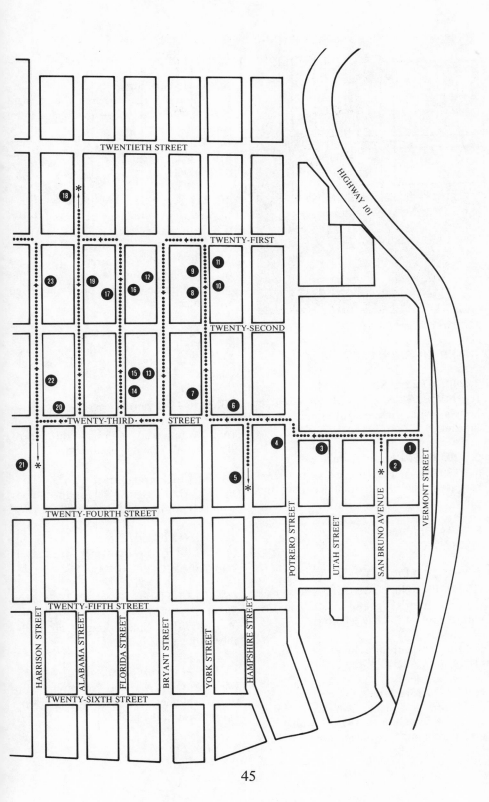

45

*939 York Street (entry 10)*

## INNER MISSION EAST

**1. 2403-07 22nd Street**
(c. 1895/QA) A group of three simple houses with rickrack-patterned corner brackets.

**2. 1205-07 San Bruno Avenue**
(c. 1895/QA) Two homes with wrens' havens in the plaster that decorates the gables.

**3. 2603 23rd Street**
(c. 1875/IB)

**4. 1106-16, 1122-36 Potrero Avenue**
(1889/SFS; John C. Weir, C) A cluster of six with Weir's signature details in the cornice and on the bay windows.

**5. 1168-70 Hampshire Street**
(1889/SFS; John C. Weir, C)

**6. 2758-70 23rd Street**
(1893/SFS; William Armitage, A) A group of four homes, two of which are intact and two "misguided."

**7. 1082 York Street**
(c. 1888/SFS; John Coop, D)

**8. 968-82 York Street**
(c. 1895/QA) The center house of these three has been remodeled with aluminum siding.

**9. 956 York Street**
(c. 1895/QA)

**10. 939 York Street**
(c. 1895/QA) An unusual arched entryway with latticework.

**11. 910, 917-35 York Street**
(c. 1895/QA) Four of these five are intact, but house 917 has been smothered with stucco.

**12. 2312-22 Bryant Street**
(c. 1895/QA) Five rowhouses. House 2312 has bargeboards and fishscale shingles.

**13. 2436-46 Bryant Street**
(c. 1895/QA) Three more of the peaked-roof rowhouses so common in this part of the Inner Mission neighborhood.

**14. 1059-61 Florida Street**
(c. 1895/QA) Two relatively simple homes with belt cornices of fishscale shingles.

**15. 1031-41 Florida Street**
(c. 1885/SFS) Three cottages with French caps and spindled porticoes.

**16. 905-17 Florida Street, 2773-75 21st Street**
(c. 1885/SFS) Nine cottages, all probably by the same builder.

**17. 918-44 Florida Street**
(c. 1895/QA) A cluster of seven, with finials, spindles, and unusual plaster embellishment in the gables.

### 18. 814-18 Alabama Street
(c. 1895/QA) Three homes similar to a cluster in the 900 block of the same street.

### 19. 937-51 Alabama Street
(c. 1895/QA) Four houses probably built by the same person responsible for 814-18 Alabama Street.

### 20. 2972-76 23rd Street
(c. 1885/SFS) Both have false gables with sunbursts over the windows in the second story.

### 21. 2710-12 Harrison Street
(c. 1880/IF) These two narrow houses resemble the "Cheap Dwellings" published in the *San Francisco Evening Bulletin* in the early 1880s.

### 22. 2661 Harrison Street
(c. 1880/IF) Unusual triangular bays make the front of this double house look like an accordian.

### 23. 2517-29 Harrison Street
(c. 1895/QA) Seven more of the peaked-roof cottages of the nineties.

### 24. 811 Treat Avenue
(1882/SFS; Henry Geilfuss, A) Architect Geilfuss built this home for himself. Originally it had a stable in back.

### 25. 725 Treat Avenue
(1883/SFS) This home was originally owned by Lydia Rebecca Beers, who later married Robert Hawks Cowan, a retired British soldier.

### 26. 2417 Folsom Boulevard
(c. 1895/QA)

### 27. 2442 Folsom Boulevard
(c. 1895/QA) A spritely paint scheme led neighborhood children to nickname this the "fruit salad house."

*Corner board at 811 Treat Avenue (entry 24) and fluted portico column with buttons, 725 Treat Avenue (entry 25)*

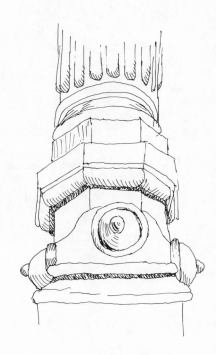

*Flat-front Italianate, 733 Shotwell Street (entry 31)*

**28. 2533 Folsom Boulevard**
(1891/SFS)

**29. 760 Shotwell Street**
(c. 1880/IB)

**30. 754 Shotwell Street**
(c. 1890/QA) A house covered with big daisies.

**31. 733 Shotwell Street**
(c. 1875/IF)

**32. 715 Shotwell Street**
(c. 1875/IB)

**33. 701-09 Shotwell Street**
(c. 1875/IB) Originally all in this cluster of five looked like house 701.

**34. 680 Shotwell Street**
(c. 1895/C) This house combines elements of both the flat-front Italianate and the Queen Anne rowhouse.

**35. 658 Shotwell Street**
(c. 1880/IB)

**36. 650 Shotwell Street**
(1889/SFS)

**37. 646 Shotwell Street**
(1884/SFS)

**38. 618 Shotwell Street**
(1898/SFS)

**39. 3441-45 20th Street**
(1891/QA, QT; Charles I. Havens, A) Late in the 1960s, an attic fire forced the removal of the top floors of these two homes. Originally the corner building had a tower with a witch's cap.

**40. 3466-76 20th Street**
(c. 1875/IB) A cluster of three houses.

**41. 544 Capp Street**
(c. 1875/IF) This home has an unusual L-shaped floor plan. It is now the home of the Community Music Center.

**42. 552-58 Capp Street**
(c. 1875/IB; The Real Estate Associates, D) Two Italianates.

**43. 521 Capp Street**
(c. 1890/QA)

**44. 571-81 Capp Street**
(c. 1875/IB; The Real Estate Associates, D) Four homes with cutwork balustrades over the entries.

**45. 3126 22nd Street**
(1900/O; Martens & Coffey, A) Originally the German Evangelical Lutheran Church, now St. John's.

**46. 1106-26, 1150-60,**
**1170-86 South Van Ness Avenue**
(1889/SFS; T. J. Welsh, A) Twelve houses, seven of which are intact. These and 703-09, 731-65 Capp Street, directly behind, were built for the Baroness Mary E. von Schroeder, a real estate developer.

**47. 1136-42 South Van Ness Avenue**
(1894/QA; Martens & Coffey, A)

**48. 1201 South Van Ness Avenue**
(c. 1885/SFS) Unusual brooding false gables on this commercial-residential building. The second floor was restored by San Francisco Victoriana after a fire in 1976.

**49. 910 Shotwell Street**
(c. 1875/IF)

**50. 926 Shotwell Street**
(c. 1875/IF)

*571-81 Capp Street (entry 44)*

### 51. 985 Shotwell Street
(c. 1875/IF) Originally built as four apartments with separate entrances.

### 52. 3149 24th Street
(1896/QA; Martens & Coffey, A)

### 53. 1014 Shotwell Street
(c. 1885/SFS) The veranda on this home is unusual for San Francisco, but was common in warmer parts of the Bay Area.

### 54. 1016 Shotwell Street
(c. 1885/SFS)

### 55. 1020 Shotwell Street
(c. 1885/SFS)

### 56. 1070 Shotwell Street
(c. 1885/SFS) Notice that the old house number can still be seen in the transom over the entry door.

### 57. 3166 25th Street
(1889/SFS; John C. Weir, D)

### 58. 1200 Treat Avenue
(1890/SFS; John McCarthy, OB)

### 59. 1204 Treat Avenue
(1885/SFS; John McCarthy, OB)

### 60. 1232 Treat Avenue
(1885/IB; John McCarthy, OB) It is startling to find this home in San Francisco, for it is a brick and granite Italianate that looks as if it has been plucked out of an East Coast Victorian-era neighborhood.

### 61. 2906-08, 2976 Folsom Boulevard
(c. 1875/IB) These three resemble houses built by The Real Estate Associates.

### 62. 2914-34 Folsom Boulevard
(c. 1875/IF) Five houses; house 2928 is the most intact, while house 2924 has been completely covered with Permastone.

**63. 1164 Shotwell Street**
(1886/O; Robert Trost, OB) Trost supposedly built this Tudor Revival house because he was homesick for his native Germany.

**64. 1150 Shotwell Street**
(c. 1875/IF)

**65. 1112 Shotwell Street**
(c. 1885/SFS)

**66. 1100, 1106 Shotwell Street**
(c. 1890/QA) Both houses have unusually proportioned bargeboards.

**67. 1381 South Van Ness Avenue**
(1884/SFS; Charles I. Havens, A) The sagging stable behind is a reminder of horse and carriage days in the Inner Mission neighborhood.

**68. 1380 South Van Ness Avenue**
(1890/SFS; John Marquis, A)

**69. 1348 South Van Ness Avenue**
(1886/QT; Seth Babson, A) This house, with a tower sporting an eagle wind vane, is official San Francisco Landmark Number 74.

**70. 884-94 Capp Street**
(1888/SFS; John Coop, D) All four have Coop's signature details.

**71. 3261 23rd Street**
(1891/O; Percy & Hamilton, A) Now the Mission United Presbyterian Church.

**72. 703-09, 731-65 Capp Street**
(1889/SFS; T. J. Welsh, A) Fifteen homes, ten of which are intact. Part of the block developed by the Baroness Mary E. von Schroeder (see entry 46).

**73. 762 Capp Street**
(c. 1875/IF)

**74. 2700 Mission Street**
(1893/QT; Henry Geilfuss, A) Old photographs show that this corner building once had a witch's cap and a row of iron cresting.

**75. 3326 23rd Street**
(1877/IB; John Hinkel, OB)

**76. 3330 23rd Street**
(1886/SFS)

**77. 3336 23rd Street**
(1882/IB)

*Signature details of developer John Coop: cornice bracket, frieze panel swag and sawn shields, 884 Capp Street (entry 70)*

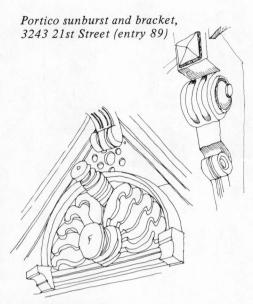

*Portico sunburst and bracket, 3243 21st Street (entry 89)*

### 78. 3339 23rd Street
(1877/IB)

### 79. 203 Bartlett Street
(1876/IF) Originally built for four families; probably one of the neighborhood's oldest apartment buildings.

### 80. 255 Bartlett Street
(1871/IF)

### 81. 259 Bartlett Street
(1877/IB)

### 82. 279 Bartlett Street
(1894/SFS)

### 83. 3350 23rd Street
(1877/IB) A large corner home that has had several additions.

### 84. 3356-64 23rd Street
(c. 1875/IB) One of these three is intact; the other two have been covered with stucco.

### 85. 3370 23rd Street
(c. 1875/IF) This Victorian has been so well disguised with aluminum siding and Permastone that only its high false front remains as a clue to its origin.

### 86. 145 Bartlett Street
(c. 1880/C) The rectangular bays of this early home appear to have been added sometime after the turn of the century.

### 87. 117 Bartlett Street
(1893/SFS; M. Linn, C) This double Stick-style building was converted into four units in 1932.

### 88. 113 Bartlett Street
(1890/SFS; J. McCloskey, B) Note the art glass transoms with the original house numbers.

### 89. 3243 21st Street
(1883/SFS) Originally built for George F. Pattison, this home is covered with a profusion of machine-made redwood embellishment.

### 90. 3239 21st Street
(1885/SFS)

### 91. 3233 21st Street
(1895/SFS)

### 92. 320-24, 354-76, 317-51 San Carlos Street
(1876/IB, IF; The Real Estate Associates, D) A cluster of seventeen Italianate homes that were inexpensive versions of the fancier houses the developers placed on the outer edges of this block.

### 93. 317-67, 330-80 Lexington Street
(1876/IB, IF; The Real Estate Associates, D) Thirteen houses, part of the same development as the San Carlos Street cluster.

# INNER MISSION WEST MAP

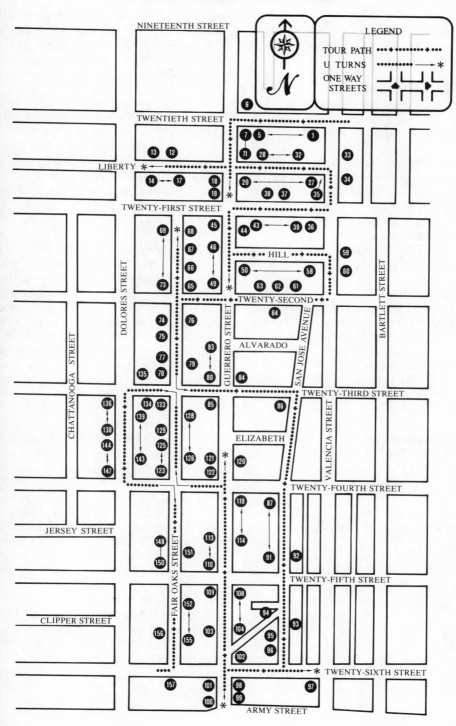

## INNER MISSION WEST

**1. 3625 20th Street**
(c. 1875/IB) Built for attorney Abraham W. Thompson.

**2. 3635 20th Street**
(c. 1885/SFS) Note the stairs, which have long cutwork ovals instead of the usual turned balusters.

**3. 3643 20th Street**
(1891/IB) Built for John C. Fischer, this home has a French cap covered with metal flashing.

**4. 3647 20th Street**
(c. 1875/IB) Decorated with segmented arches in the entry and over the windows.

**5. 3651 20th Street**
(c. 1895/QA) Massive newel post caps and an arched entry with egg and dart molding and floral panels in the gable.

**6. 3672 20th Street**
(c. 1875/IB) Its front has been stuccoed, but check the north side to see its intact embellishment.

**7. 801 Guerrero Street**
(1871/IB) The home is edged with quoins, and the slanted bay has an unusual 1-2-1 windowpane ratio.

**8. 811 Guerrero Street**
(1877/IB; The Real Estate Associates)

**9. 821 Guerrero Street**
(c. 1875/IB) Built originally for two families, with a bracketed entry on either side and the bay in the middle.

**10. 827 Guerrero Street**
(1881, 1890/QT; Samuel Newsom, A) Much smaller when it was originally built in 1881. In 1890, owner M. C. McMullen hired Newsom to make "additions,"

which included the tower and the clipped gables. Note the horseshoe arch in the portico, where three small faces and a daisy were revealed when a recent owner spent days with a dental pick carefully chipping away years of grime and old paint.

**11. 845 Guerrero Street**
(1871/IF) Built for Marsden Kershaw, a partner in the Kershaw and Ting Coal Yard. The present owner has added a garage on the south side of the house, a sensitive remodeling that adapts the house to modern needs, yet retains its architectural integrity.

**12. 176 Liberty Street**
(c. 1885/SFS) This home was well disguised by misguided improvements. Its redwood adornments were stripped and its French cap shorn, then the home was smothered with wood shingles and a garage was tacked onto the front. It was restored to its original exuberance in 1976 by San Francisco Victoriana, whose designer blended the garage sympathetically with the older structure.

**13. 180 Liberty Street**
(c. 1871/IB) This home was supposedly built originally as a one-story, then reconstructed into two stories in 1895.

**14. 159 Liberty Street**
(1878/IB) Built for Judge D. J. Murphy. Susan B. Anthony is said to have visited here when she helped launch the campaign for women's suffrage in San Francisco.

**15. 123 Liberty Street**
(1895/QT; Martens and Coffey, A) This house, which was built for W. J. Patterson, has had its entire lower floor remodeled. But look up at what remains: the round tower and the band of plaster garlands.

*Bay-windowed Italianate, 811 Guerrero Street (entry 8)*

*827 Guerrero Street (entry 10)*

### 16. 121 Liberty Street
(1889/QA) Built for Maggie Cook, according to a sign on the garage.

### 17. 109 Liberty Street
(1870/IF) A double lot with a mysterious, mossy garden. The house has an etched glass transom underneath a massive bracketed portico.

### 18. 860 Guerrero Street
(c. 1885/SFS) The ultimate dream of an aluminum products salesman, with that material used in the siding, the front stair rail, the window sash and the fire escape. Look at the main cornice on either side, where many of the original brackets remain.

### 19. 862 Guerrero Street
(1883/T) This house is a good example of the transition between two decades of building. It has the Italianate five-sided bay, combined with the exuberant, non-Classical wood motifs of the 1880 s. The cherubs on the portico are a later addition.

### 20. 79 Liberty Street
(c. 1875/IB) An unusual Italianate. The main cornice is flat, but the bay protrudes. It does not continue all the way up to the main cornice, but stops at the second story.

### 21. 70 Liberty Street
(1870/IB) Offers a good comparison to 79 Liberty Street. Notice how its bay is incorporated into the main cornice.

### 22. 58 Liberty Street
(1876/IB) Built as a single-family home, it has been converted into apartments. The bay windows are only two stories high; where they meet the main cornice, the top of the bay window forms an unusual balcony, which is reached through an arched window.

### 23. 53 Liberty Street
(c. 1900/QA) This home exhibits many of the restrained details associated with the later "Edwardian" era: small plaster brackets, a half-round bay, dentils and egg and dart molding.

### 24. 45 Liberty Street
(c. 1875/IB)

### 25. 37 Liberty Street
(c. 1875/IB) Original stairs and landing newel posts.

### 26. 50 Liberty Street
(1889/C; A. J. Barnett, A) A peculiar assemblage of details, with a clipped false gable, waffle pattern and sunbursts.

### 27. 44 Liberty Street
(c. 1885/SFS) A floral panel and a shield decorate the lower part of the rectangular bay.

### 28. 31 Liberty Street
(1892/T; J. E. Krafft, A)

### 29. 27 Liberty Street
(1894/QA; R. H. White, A) This home, with its massive arched entry, cost $5,000 to build for the original owner, G. B. Clifford.

### 30. 20-24 Liberty Street
(c. 1875/IB) Mirror twins, linked by a common belt cornice.

### 31. 19-23 Liberty Street
(1877/IB)

### 32. 15 Liberty Street
(1893/SFS) An uncommon spindled arch.

### 33. 929-45 Valencia Street
(1876/IB; The Real Estate Associates, D) A cluster of four. House 945 is the most intact, with its columned portico and urn-shaped finials. House 937 has had its entire main cornice amputated.

### 34. 953-59 Valencia Street
(1876/IB; The Real Estate Associates, D) Two examples of a less expensive product of The Real Estate Associates. House 959 has been almost obliterated by asbestos shingles.

### 35. 958 Valencia Street
(1893/SFS; A. J. Barnett, A) A commercial-residential building that cost $20,000 to construct. Although some of the commercial ground floor has been altered, the apartment entrances are intact, with brass hardware, paneling, buttons and spindled archways.

### 36. 3325 21st Street
(1885/SFS; Townsend & Wyneken, A) The front door of this cottage is a "$5 fancy" model used by many builders during the era.

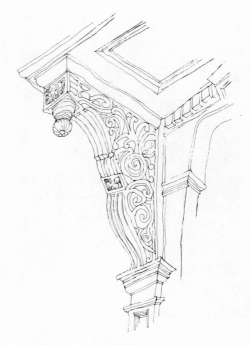

*Portico bracket and window hood over consoles, 109 Liberty Street (entry 17)*

*"$5 fancy" door,*
*3324 21st Street (entry 36)*

### 37. 3320-24 21st Street
(1877/IB; The Real Estate Associates, D) Note the iron fence that still graces the front of 3320: A five-pointed star is incorporated into its design.

### 38. 3364 21st Street
(1873/IF) All the windows on this facade have segmented hoods.

### 39. 3329 21st Street
(1883/IB)

### 40. 3333 21st Street
(1890/SFS, Charles I. Havens, A) Built for Amandus F. Schumacher, with a brace under the lower bay, a false gable and swags in the upper bay.

### 41. 3339 21st Street
(1890/SFS; James Kavanagh, OB)

### 42. 3345 21st Street
(c. 1885/SFS) Shield decoratives in several sizes, with smaller ones on the columns and pilasters and larger ones as bay window trim.

### 43. 3367-75 21st Street
(1885/SFS; Pissis and Moore, A) A cluster of three built for S. W. Fuller at a total cost of $11,000.

### 44. 915 Guerrero Street
(1879/C) The Italianate home was built in 1879; the Queen Anne Islamic arch was added sometime later. Perhaps at the same time, the Chinese dragon handrail was added to the stairway, where it still bares its fangs at passersby.

### 45. 900 Guerrero Street
(1895/QT; Daly and Coldwell, C) An enormous arched art glass window lights the main stairwell on the north side of the home. Cherub faces peek out from the second story of the bay. Supposedly the top story was added after the original roof burned.

### 46. 948 Guerrero Street
(1878/IB) This home makes a poignant contrast with the new as it snuggles up against its 1950 s stucco neighbor.

### 47. 966 Guerrero Street
(1890/SFS) This double-bayed house has three different kinds of dentil molding marching across its facade.

### 48. 986 Guerrero Street
(1883/SFS; Charles Geddes, A) Geddes's home. He also designed several Victorian churches in the City as well as the Spreckels mansion, a $70,000 extravaganza that used to stand at 21st and South Van Ness Avenue, now a parking lot.

### 49. 988 Guerrero Street
(1895/C; McDougall & Son, A) The exuberant wooden detail of the 1880 s mixes with the arched entry and witch cap of the 1890 s.

## 50. 83-91 Hill Street

(1884/SFS; T. J. Welsh, A) The middle of the three homes has a bay window that is three panes wide and extends all the way across the front, looking out of proportion.

## 51. 77 Hill Street

(1883/SFS) Look around to the side for a good view of the false front of this home, which was built for J. H. Lillian.

## 52. 69 Hill Street

(1887/SFS) This house was the victim of a peculiar remodeling effort: The original entry was made into a window and a larger entrance was added on the side.

## 53. 30 Hill Street

(1878/IB; The Real Estate Associates, D) This Italianate had been stripped of detail and covered with asbestos shingles; in 1975 it was completely restored by San Francisco Victoriana.

## 54. 14-28 Hill Street

(1878/IB; The Real Estate Associates, D) A stately cluster of eight homes, typical medium-priced products of The Real Estate Associates.

## 55. 16-20, 34 Hill Street

(1878/IB) Three identical homes, with segmented windows, colonnettes and shields.

## 56. 49 Hill Street

(c. 1885/SFS) The portico sports a flat sawn balustrade with urn-shaped finials.

## 57. 25 Hill Street

(1883/SFS; Charles Geddes, A) Built for Victorian-era actor Walter Leman, author of *Memories of an Old Actor,* published in 1886 by A. Roman Company, San Francisco.

## 58. 25 Hill Street

(1885/SFS; J. F. Gaynor, OB)

## 59. 1049 Valencia Street

(c. 1880, 1900/C) Really two buildings. The northern one has a balcony inset on the third floor and a main cornice with two large plaster stop brackets. The other is an early two-story flat-front Italianate, with a turned cornice balustrade, a later addition.

## 60. 1057 Valencia Street

(1875/IB; The Real Estate Associates, D)

*Doorway topped by a bracketed portico with a segmented hood, 79 Liberty Street (entry 20)*

**61. 3322 22nd Street**
(1875/IB)

**62. 3342-46 22nd Street**
(c. 1895/QA) Two rowhouses with a common wall and unusual fanlight windows in the gables.

**63. 3350-54 22nd Street**
(1884/SFS; M. J. Welsh, C) These two cost a total of $3,500 to construct.

**64. 3327-47 22nd Street**
(c. 1885/SFS) A cluster of four homes.

**65. 3434-38 22nd Street**
(c. 1895/T) Although these two have some SFS characteristics, they also have three-sided slanted bay windows.

**66. 77 Fair Oaks Street**
(c. 1885/SFS) Still has its original notched landing newel posts with applied buttons.

**67. 31 Fair Oaks Street**
(1888/QT; George A. Bordwell, A) The second story has a skin of shingles; alternating square butts and fishscales give a varied texture. Built for bookkeeper C. J. Maurer.

**68. 11 Fair Oaks Street**
(1883/SFS; J. T. Ayer, C) Unusual brackets pierced with holes. The false gable has a sunburst and a finial.

**69. 8 Fair Oaks Street**
(1892/QT; Percy & Hamilton, A)

**70. 14 Fair Oaks Street**
(c. 1890/QT) A delicate incised design in the triangular entry pediment.

**71. 68 Fair Oaks Street**
(1888/SFS; A. R. Denke, A) An unusual veranda: The flat sawn balusters give this home, built for Fortunatus S. Traveler, the look of an Eastern seashore summer cottage.

**72. 72 Fair Oaks Street**
(c. 1875/IB) Adorned with unusual colonnettes with squared keystones. The entry was probably stripped of detail when the house was converted into two units.

**73. 90 Fair Oaks Street**
(1887/SFS; T. H. Lufkin, C) Built for C. W. Eckstein, who bought the property from actress Lotta Crabtree for $1,800 in gold coin.

*Rectangular bay with a detail that looks like a grapefruit, 116 Fair Oaks Street (entry 77)*

**74. 108-10 Fair Oaks Street**
(1888/SFS; John Coop, D) Note the Coop signature detail in the lower bay.

**75. 112 Fair Oaks Street**
(1875/IB)

**76. 119 Fair Oaks Street**
(c. 1885/SFS)

**77. 116 Fair Oaks Street**
(1883/SFS; Charles Geddes, A) Badly "misguided" on the ground floor when it was converted into apartments. Some of the original embellishment remains on the top story, however, a reminder of the way it looked when built for William B. Cleveland.

**78. 118 Fair Oaks Street**
(c. 1885/SFS) The portico hood looks like a shed roof; the elongated cornice brackets are shaped like braces.

**79. 175 Fair Oaks Street**
(c. 1885/SFS) Note the iron cresting on the top of the portico, an ornament that once graced many rooftops and entries.

**80. 1086 Guerrero Street**
(c. 1900/O) St. James Catholic Church was originally a riotous mixture of Victorian details, but it was stripped and stuccoed into a more subdued version of its former self in the 1950s.

**81. 1076 Guerrero Street**
(1887/IB)

**82. 1074 Guerrero Street**
(1895/O; Samuel Newsom, A) Originally built for $9,575 as the Second United Presbyterian Church. It was firebombed in 1974, and its fate is uncertain.

**83. 1056 Guerrero Street**
(1889/SFS; Henry Geilfuss, A) Note the braces on the entry, one of Geilfuss's favorite embellishments.

**84. 1035 Guerrero Street**
(c. 1890/QT) Built as a combination of stores and flats, it still retains the two beautifully carved entrances to the upstairs apartments. Originally each of its bay windows was topped by a witch's cap and an iron finial. Supposedly all were shorn in the late 1960 s when one developed a leak.

**85. 1126-48 Guerrero Street**
(1896/QA) Most in this cluster of six have been altered; 1130 was transformed into a "Swiss Chalet," with eight units instead of the original one.

**86. 3503-11 23rd Street**
(1894/QT, QA; Townsend & Wyneken, A) The corner house has a square tower; 3507 has an uncommon arched entry in the shape of an ellipse.

**87. 200 San Jose Avenue**
(1877/IB)

**88. 210 San Jose Avenue**
(1878/IB; John Greenwood, OB)

**89. 216 San Jose Avenue**
(1877/IB) Stripped and stuccoed sometime after the earthquake. Look up at the main cornice, where partial remains of the brackets remind us of the original house.

**90. 220 San Jose Avenue**
(1871/IF, IB) Originally this was a flat-front house; sometime during the Victorian era, the bay window was added. Then still later its proportions were changed; the window openings were made smaller and the redwood sash was replaced with aluminum.

*248 San Jose Avenue (entry 91)*

**91. 248-54 San Jose Avenue**
(1884/SFS; George Bordwell, A) Mirror twin buildings; original owner O. F. Von Rhein also had a stable built in the back.

**92. 271-75 San Jose Avenue**
(1876/IB)

**93. 325 San Jose Avenue**
(1885/SFS) This home was converted into two flats in 1900.

**94. 1A Juri Street**
(1894/SFS; John Kidd, A) An uncommon flatiron building, its shape conforms to the lot, which is next to the railroad right-of-way.

**95. 330 San Jose Avenue**
(1893/SFS; James Norris, C)

**96. 380 San Jose Avenue**
(1884/IF)

**97. 1500 Valencia Street**
(1888/O; Macy & Jordan, A) Built for the Salvation Army, which still uses it, this three-story brick structure cost a substantial $100,000 to construct.

**98. 1403 Guerrero Street**
(c. 1885/SFS) A cottage with a French cap and portico brackets with circular insets.

**99. 1413-17 Guerrero Street**
(1894/SFS; Fernando Nelson, D) A cluster of three with Nelson's signature details.

**100. 3728 Army Street**
(1896/O; Charles Koenig, C) A "Victorian Gothic" church with one steeple topped by a crocket. Built for the trustees of St. John's Church.

**101. 1400 Guerrero Street**
(1897/QT; Charles Rousseau, A) Designed as a store with flats upstairs. Much of its original plaster detail has been removed.

**102. Mid-block of Guerrero between 25th and 26th streets**
Look for the diagonal railroad right-of-way. This strip will soon become a neighborhood park called Juri Commons.

**103. 1355 Guerrero Street**
(c. 1890/QT) Handsome swags and a balcony hidden behind a layer of chicken wire.

**104. 1366 Guerrero Street**
(1883/IF; James Gosling, A) Built for Frank Edwards, a prominent San Francisco importer and merchant.

**105. 1335 Guerrero Street**
(1918/O) Built as a convalescent home, this large structure has a mansard roof and Classical detailing.

**106. 1327 Guerrero Street**
(c. 1890/QA) Spindlework over the entry and small panes of beveled glass in the entry doors.

**107. 1325 Guerrero Street**
(1886/SFS; Townsend & Wyneken, A)
The cut glass transom over the front door
still has the old house number, 1309,
used when the home was built for master
mariner Captain A. Dodd.

**108. 1317 Guerrero Street**
(1889/QA; George Houston, A) A massive overhanging gable, two latticed stop
brackets at the gable ends and a third at
the end of the belt cornice.

**109. 1320-26 Guerrero Street**
(1887/IB; W. Mitchell, C) Two homes,
one intact. The front of 1326 has been
stuccoed, but some traces of its former
embellishment remain on the sides.

**110. 1286 Guerrero Street**
(c. 1890/QT) Built for Christian Hellwig,
an Austrian immigrant who established a
tannery in the Mission District and quickly became wealthy. According to his
grandson, Hellwig chose the tower house
because its grandeur proved how well-to-
do he had become.

**111. 1274 Guerrero Street**
(c. 1895/QA)

**112. 1259-65 Guerrero Street**
(1889/SFS; B. E. Henriksen, A) Both
still have their false gables and iron fences
intact. House 1265 still has its original
entry with a cut glass transom and an
Ionic colonnette where the doors meet.

**113. 1256 Guerrero Street**
(c. 1890/QA) A latticed arch in the entry
and a deep floral decorative in the peak
of the gable.

**114. 1257 Guerrero Street**
(c. 1890/QA) Unusually proportioned:
The bay window is thrust out from the
ground floor, and the gable is recessed. In
the doorway is a built-in bench, with an
art glass "picture window" over it.

**115. 1253 Guerrero Street**
(c. 1888/SFS; John Coop, D) Note the
Coop signature detail in the lower bay.

**116. 1241 Guerrero Street**
(1887/SFS) A portico with a shed roof
and deeply carved floral panels in the
lower bay.

**117. 1233 Guerrero Street**
(1889/SFS; A. J. Barnett, A) The architect worked with contractor T. Sullivan
to construct this home for B. H. Schenholf.

**118. 1227 Guerrero Street**
(c. 1900/O) A charming detail can be
found if you look closely. Study the segmented arch in the portico to find a tiny
face peering out.

**119. 1201 Guerrero Street**
(c. 1880/IB) A handsome example of a
combined commercial-residential structure with a corner octagonal bay window.

**120. 1169-77 Guerrero Street**
(1882/IF) Two narrow flat-front cottages.

*1253 Guerrero Street (entry 115)*

63

*Segmented hood and spindled archway, 1035 Guerrero Street (entry 84)*

### 121. 1180 Guerrero Street
(1884/IB) Graceful teardrops still complete the bottoms of each bay.

### 122. 1188 Guerrero Street
(1894/QA; Martens & Coffey, A) Originally the building had much more detail; you can still find the shadows of the lavish plaster swags that used to ring the upper bays.

### 123. 270 Fair Oaks Street
(c. 1875/IB) A curious misguided improvement. The house was shorn of detail, then a stucco addition and a garage were added. Yet the handsome portico brackets were left intact.

### 124. 260 Fair Oaks Street
(1870/IB) Instead of the customary cornice brackets, this home is crowned with plain molding.

### 125. 258 Fair Oaks Street
(1885/SFS) A braced gable and pierced decorative work over the windows in the front plane of the rectangular bay.

### 126. 283 Fair Oaks Street
(c. 1885/SFS) A triple bay windowed home with portholes and cut glass transoms that still have the original house numbers.

### 127. 261 Fair Oaks Street
(c. 1880/IB) A cottage with a central entry and an unusually high false front.

### 128. 217 Fair Oaks Street
(1886/SFS)

### 129. 214 Fair Oaks Street
(c. 1885/SFS) Still has the original iron fence with three stately newel posts.

**130. 212 Fair Oaks Street**
(1873/IB) The original art glass transom and entry door window were reinstalled in 1976. This simple but elegant home was built for Seeley B. Lyon, of the Mechanic Mills Company.

**131. 210 Fair Oaks Street**
(1889/SFS; S. Hatfield, A)

**132. 204 Fair Oaks Street**
(1885/SFS) The facade of this home was restored by San Francisco Victoriana in 1974.

**133. 200 Fair Oaks Street**
(1886/SFS)

**134. 3679 23rd Street**
(c. 1875/IB) An inexpensive building originally designed as four units. The entry doors were replaced sometime after the 1906 earthquake.

**135. 979 Dolores Street**
(1889/SFS) One of the few Victorian homes in the City that are still covered with tarpaper brick, a misguided improvement whose perishability contributed to its scarcity. Peek around the side of the house to see the decorative keystones remaining over the segmented windows.

**136. 1000 Dolores Street**
(1889/SFS; Percy & Hamilton, A) This home cost $22,000 to construct and was originally built as six units. A later owner added the eagles and planted the garden of wildflowers.

**137. 1006 Dolores Street**
(1882/IF)

**138. 1010 Dolores Street**
(1883/IB) The gate of the scrolled iron fence has a handrail in the shape of an acanthus leaf, the decorative motif in the capital of a Corinthian column.

**139. 1001 Dolores Street**
(c. 1890/QT)

**140. 1027 Dolores Street**
(c. 1885/SFS) The front has been severely changed with Permastone and stucco. On the sides, however, are left intact two slanted bay windows with Corinthian colonnettes.

**141. 1037 Dolores Street**
(1887/SFS; S. & J. C. Newsom, A) The Newsom brothers designed this house. In the lower bay, the frieze panels form a sunburst, either rising or setting.

**142. 1041 Dolores Street**
(1904/QA) Narrow lap siding, dentils, octagonal shingles and a balcony in the gable.

**143. 1083 Dolores Street**
(c. 1890/QT) Reclaimed from its stucco disguise in 1974, when the owner received a Certificate of Merit from the San Francisco Landmarks Preservation Advisory Board.

**144. 1070 Dolores Street**
(1902/QA) This home and its two neighbors, 1076 and 1080 Dolores, illustrate the three major styles of Victorian San Francisco side by side.

**145. 1074 Dolores Street**
(1885/SFS; Schmidt & Havens, A) Finials and long vertical brackets. The portico has deeply carved floral panels.

**146. 1080 Dolores Street**
(c. 1880/IB) This Italianate still has its original iron fence and newel posts.

**147. 1090 Dolores Street**
(c. 1910/O) A version of the "Bonus House" built after the 1906 disaster under the auspices of a government program to stimulate home building by earthquake

*463 Fair Oaks Street (entry 155)*

refugees. Compare its Edwardian cornice to the bracketed cornices, French caps and gabled roofs of the three Victorians next door.

### 148. 332 Fair Oaks Street
(c. 1870/IF) Its two large palms and stately staircase speak of grander times for this home, which has been hidden by asbestos shingles.

### 149. 384 Fair Oaks Street
(1896/QT) Plaster swags form a frieze band around the upper story of the half-round bay window.

### 150. 394 Fair Oaks Street
(1893/QT; William Shaughnessy, OB)

### 151. 387 Fair Oaks Street
(1897/QA; Martens & Coffey, A) Built for Edward J. Smith, the City tax collector. The front door has three oval panes of beveled glass.

### 152. 433-47 Fair Oaks Street
(1888/SFS; John Coop, D) Five homes: 441 and 447 are well-disguised with stucco, but the other three are intact, even retaining the original ironwork cresting on top of the porticoes.

### 153. 451 Fair Oaks Street
(1891/SFS; M. J. Welsh, A) A bold false gable topped by a finial and covered with various floral decoratives.

### 154. 455 Fair Oaks Street
(1890/O; Ernest A. Coxhead, A) Easily dated by the "1890" on its front door pulls, this Shingle-style church was called "the Mission Chapel" when it was built for $4,100. It is now the Holy Innocents Episcopal Church.

### 155. 463 Fair Oaks Street
(1890/SFS; Salfield & Kohlberg) An uncommon window over the front door. The top half is segmented art glass, and the bottom half is a deeply carved wooden floral panel.

### 156. 446-64 Fair Oaks Street
(1888/SFS; John Coop, D) All were once identical to 464. Houses 446 and 450 were stuccoed, and 460 was redone in 1975, when the owner removed the asbestos shingles and added a salvaged portico with Corinthian columns.

### 157. 3729-43 26th Street
(1887/IF, SFS, IB; Joseph M. Comerford, D) A cluster of five cottages that cost $1,500 each to build.

# NOE VALLEY

In the days before the 1848 Gold Rush, the neighborhoods now called Eureka and Noe valleys were part of the San Miguel Rancho, granted to José Noe by Mexican governor Pio Pico. Their Victorian flavor was not evident until the 1880s: Before that decade, dairy cattle grazed among a few farmhouses.

In 1846, John M. Horner immigrated to the City, then still the small pueblo of Yerba Buena, on the ship *Brooklyn,* which was filled with Mormon immigrants. He settled in the south Bay near San Jose, where his produce business prospered. Within three years he and his brother Robert had accumulated half a million dollars by selling fruit and vegetables to hungry goldseekers. They purchased 4,300 acres of the San Miguel Rancho for $200,000, then laid out and named the streets of "Horner's Addition," as it is called on early maps. The 1854 gold panic found the Horners overextended, and they were forced to sell their large land holdings to several homestead associations, who subdivided them into lots for sale to prospective home builders.

Noe Valley, bounded by Diamond Heights, 22nd, Dolores and 30th streets, still contains more than two thousand Victorian buildings. More than half are Queen Anne rowhouses, a favorite product of the carpenters and contractors who built in the neighborhood. Remnants of the 1870s can still be found: There are about three hundred flat-front Italianates, and another one hundred with bay windows. About six hundred San Francisco Stick-style houses remain, along with twenty-one rare Queen Anne tower houses.

# NOE VALLEY MAP

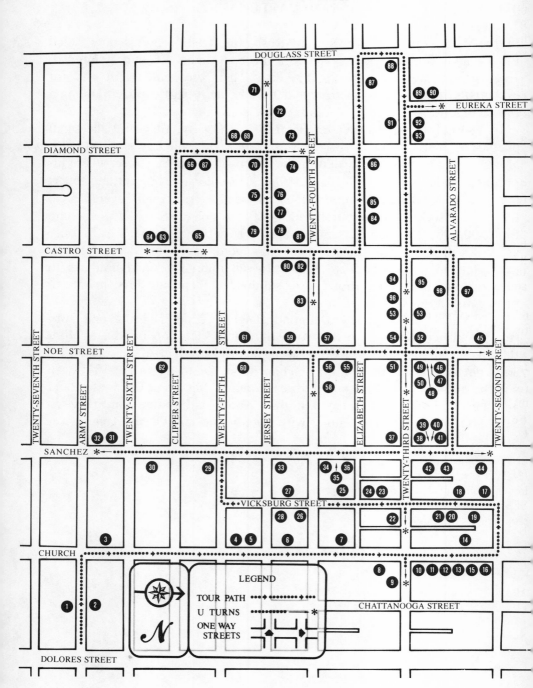

**1. 3831-45, 3853-67 Army Street**
(1888/SFS; John C. Weir, C) Two clusters, each with four homes. Originally all had false gables, French caps with finials and Weir's signature details.

**2. 3820-48 Army Street**
(c. 1885/SFS) Eight homes; only 3840 is still intact.

**3. 1408 Church Street**
(1886/IF)

**4. 1282 Church Street**
(c. 1880/IF)

**5. 1252 Church Street**
(c. 1880/IF) Well disguised in the 1930 s, when the front was enlarged with a picture window and a glass brick entry was added.

**6. 1236-38 Church Street**
(c. 1895/QA) Two homes with lap siding and plaster swags in the frieze band.

**7. 1164 Church Street**
(c. 1890/QA) Similar to "Cheap Dwelling" house plans prepared by architect John Pelton Jr. published in the *San Francisco Evening Bulletin,* 1880-1882.

**8. 1117 Church Street**
(1889/T; Schulze and Meeker, A) This home, built for Frank Girot, combines SFS and QA features. Note the massive stop brackets and the arched entry.

**9. 3767 23rd Street**
(1889/SFS; C.L. Sweeney, C)

**10. 1081-91 Church Street**
(1900/QA; McCullough Contracting Company, C) Three homes built for a Mrs. Sweeney. Note the faces on either end of the frieze band of 1091.

**11. 1069 Church Street**
(c. 1900/QA) Simple version of late QA, with egg and dart molding in the gable. Handsome original iron fence with fleurs-de-lis.

**12. 1055 Church Street**
(1896/QA; John T. Kidd, A) This home, which originally cost $2,800, has a large plaster scallop shell decorating the gable.

**13. 1037 Church Street**
(1890/QT) An unfortunately placed fire escape hides the graceful curved balcony in the gable.

**14. 1036 Church Street**
(1884/SFS; J.P. Shepard, C) This home, built for Mrs. T. Shields, is unusually wide, with floral buttons decorating the entry.

**15. 1027 Church Street**
(c. 1895/QA) The arched window in the front bay has art glass marginal panes. Delicate incised sunbursts have been carved in the gable and around the front window.

**16. 1023 Church Street**
(c. 1880/C) It is likely that this home was originally an IF, with the oversized Mission Revival cornice and brown shingles added after 1900.

**17. 2 Vicksburg Street**
(c. 1875/IB) On top of the five-sided slanted bay window is a shelf supported by two large stop brackets, which may have been added during the 1890s.

**18. 8-20 Vicksburg Street**
(1886/IB) Imagine how this row must have looked intact! All but one still have French caps. Note 16: Its false front and cornice have been amputated, revealing the peaked roof behind.

### 19. 27 Vicksburg Street
(1887/O) This unusual home has a clipped gable decorated with waffle pattern millwork.

### 20. 69 Vicksburg Street
(1892/QA; C. L. Sweeney, C) Art glass adorns the transom and the top of the front window. An unusual curved bay window on the south side.

### 21. 75 Vicksburg Street
(1891/SFS; W. W. Magary, B)

### 22. 3827-41 23rd Street
(c. 1895/QA) Two of these five homes have frieze bands and details similar to 1236 and 1238 Church Street.

### 23. 132 Vicksburg Street
(1891/QA; James T. McInnes, C) This twin-gabled home is identical to another McInnes building at 968 Sanchez Street.

### 24. 160 Vicksburg Street
(c. 1907/QA) Much plaster adorns this home: Note the four Ionic porch columns, two Ionic pilasters and the scallop shell in the gable.

### 25. 228 Vicksburg Street
(c. 1880/IF) Look carefully: This stuccoed home was originally an IF.

### 26. 3845 24th Street
(c. 1885/QT; Charles Rousseau, A)

### 27. 308 Vicksburg Street
(1888/SFS; D. Linden, OB) The false gable has a brace and a floral decorative that appears to be an inexpensive copy of a device used often by architect Henry Geilfuss.

### 28. 309 Vicksburg Street
(c. 1880/IF) This home, which also resembles one of Pelton's "Cheap Dwellings," has an uncommon L-shaped plan with the entrance on the side.

### 29. 1201-15 Sanchez Street
(1891/SFS) Only the corner house of this cluster of four is intact.

### 30. 1257-91 Sanchez Street
(1890/SFS; J. E. Loomer, A) When built for developer Louis Landler, these seven cottages cost a total of $9,450. Not one remains intact. Several of the original French caps have been replaced with "Spanish" red tiles.

### 31. 1306-20 Sanchez Street
(1892/SFS; James E. Schulz, A) A cluster of four homes with sewer grates that tell of their origins, from Dutton the plumber to the Rountree Brothers, developers.

### 32. 1328 Sanchez Street
(c. 1875/IB) Resembles the IB's built by The Real Estate Associates.

### 33. 1147 Sanchez Street
(c. 1895/QT) Unusual muntins are arranged to form a sunrise pattern repeated in windows on all three stories of this home, now clad in asbestos shingles.

### 34. 3896 24th Street
(1896/QT; Charles Rousseau, A) Textured coating blurs the handsome plaster detailing on this building, which was constructed for Mrs. Margaret Auctin.

### 35. 1067 Sanchez Street
(c. 1885/SFS) This relatively simple cottage sports an unusual turret.

### 36. 1021 Sanchez Street
(1888/O; Charles Geddes, A) This handsome Gothic church was called "Lebanon Presbyterian" because of the tower, supposedly built from Lebanon cedar.

### 37. 1004 Sanchez Street
(1891/SFS; Samuel T. Booth, A)

*1306-20 Sanchez Street (entry 31)*

**38. 3901 23rd Street**
(1893/SFS) Shops and flats were often combined in Victorian-era corner buildings such as this one.

**39. 968 Sanchez Street**
(1891/SFS; James T. McInnes, C)

**40. 974 Sanchez Street**
(1891/QA; William Curlett, A) Curlett designed an identical home for James T. McInnes at 608 Elizabeth Street.

**41. 952 Sanchez Street**
(c. 1895/QA) This simple home has a rear carriage house with a cupola and a wind vane.

**42. 971 Sanchez Street**
(c. 1885/SFS) This cottage was defaced with asbestos shingles, but still retains its art glass in the transom and the front bay.

**43. 963 Sanchez Street**
(c. 1895/QA) Note the deeply carved swags in the upper cornice.

**44. 919 Sanchez Street**
(1886/IB) The bay window of this home still has its handsome teardrop soffit. It is part of a cluster done by the developer of 8-20 Vicksburg Street.

**45. 906-42 Noe Street**
(1905-06/QA; John Anderson, C) A cluster of seven homes built by one of Noe Valley's most prolific developers. Note the misguided improvement of 930, in which the gable has been transformed into a false front. The finial on 912 has been replaced with a horse wind vane.

**46. 955 Noe Street**
(c. 1890/SFS) The bay window has unusual proportions and is topped by a bargeboard. The original front door has five buttons and a sunburst, a "$5 door" commonly used during the late 1880 s.

**47. 957 Noe Street**
(c. 1895/QA) This asbestos-clad home has the sewer grate of developer Fernando Nelson.

*1051 Noe Street (entry 55)*

### 48. 959 Noe Street
(c. 1895/QA) This simple house is decorated with buttons and shingles.

### 49. 3996 23rd Street
(1892/SFS; Edward Burns, A) Originally there was a store in the ground floor of this building constructed for Mrs. Mary Wulfing.

### 50. 3968 23rd Street
(1897/QT; William Plant, C)

### 51. 1001 Noe Street
(c. 1895/QT) This corner store with flats above still retains its ground floor dentils and Ionic columns and pilasters.

### 52. 4020-22 23rd Street
(c. 1885/SFS) These two homes were once identical in details, although different in size. The one-story building, 4020, is intact with stylized sunbursts over the entry and on the bay. House 4022 is stuccoed, but note that the east side of the structure was left untouched.

### 53. 4032-48, 4045-53 23rd Street
(1905/QA; John Anderson, C) Seven homes, another Anderson cluster.

### 54. 1002 Noe Street
(c. 1895/QT) Although the lower half of this house was stuccoed, you can still see many details if you look up at the tower.

### 55. 1051 Noe Street
(1891/QT; B. Pfarrer & Sons, OB)

### 56. 1071 Noe Street
(1891/SFS; B. Pfarrer & Sons, B) This home still has a trace of wooden cresting on the false gable.

### 57. 1082 Noe Street
(1892/SFS) Deep sunbursts and square floral applied decoratives, with some iron cresting left over the portico.

### 58. 3968 24th Street
(1888/IB) The fishscale shingles are an uncommon embellishment for an Italianate home.

### 59. 1104 Noe Street
(c. 1880/IF) The heavy Doric-columned portico was probably added when this home was converted to two units in 1909.

### 60. 1189 Noe Street
(1891/QA)

### 61. 1190 Noe Street
(c. 1885/C) On this corner are two houses joined together, an IF facing 25th Street and an SFS connected to it, facing Noe Street. The small barn has a bargeboard decorated with buttons; its hay hoist still dangles from the gable's peak.

**62. 1253-57 Noe Street**
(1892/SFS; Fernando Nelson, D) House 1257 has Nelson's signature details: donuts, button boards and bow ties. Its twin was stripped and stuccoed.

**63. 1604-06 Castro Street**
(1892/QA; Fernando Nelson, D) These two homes share signature details with the four to the south, but are of a different style.

**64. 1610-18 Castro Street**
(1892/SFS; Fernando Nelson, D) Five homes; originally all had the false gable which can still be seen on 1616.

**65. 1514-18 Castro Street**
(1890/QA; A. J. Barnett, A) A cluster of three built for Max Popper.

**66. 1015-19 Diamond Street**
(1892/QA; Fernando Nelson, D) Two QA's that share signature details with the two homes next door.

**67. 1001-07 Diamond Street**
(1892/SFS; Fernando Nelson, D)

**68. 940-46 Diamond Street**
(1895/QA; T. A. Born, OB) Although not identical, these two homes share spearpoint shingles and latticed stop and portico brackets.

**69. 918 Diamond Street**
(c. 1880/IF) This home was raised and a new ground floor was added. Note the two kinds of siding: channel rustic on the top story and lap on the lower. In front is a Vulcan Iron Works sewer vent with a handsome star in the center.

**70. 905 Diamond Street**
(c. 1895/QT) A graceful teardrop forms the bottom of the round bay.

**71. 583-97 Jersey Street**
(1895/QA; E. J. Plant, B) A cluster of four: three intact and one smothered with textured spray.

**72. 514 Jersey Street**
(1892/SFS; A. E. Davis, OB)

**73. 826-44 Diamond Street**
(1894/SFS) A cluster of four; only 838 is intact, although the others still have their false gables and French caps.

**74. 831 Diamond Street**
(c. 1885/SFS) This cottage has a rolling pin decorative over the entry. Notice the way the proportions of the windowpanes have been altered with aluminum sash.

*1001 Diamond Street (entry 67)*

*1019 Diamond Street (entry 66)*

## 75. 463 Jersey Street
(c. 1895/QA) Although this home has been sprayed with textured coating, in the gable the shingles and scallop shell are still recognizable.

## 76. 422-28 Jersey Street
(1891-92/SFS) Three delightful cottages; the transom of 428 was made by the 1976 owner, who searched the neighborhood to find an authentic pattern.

## 77. 416 Jersey Street
(c. 1890/SFS) Handsome wooden swags adorn the front of the rectangular bay.

## 78. 408-12 Jersey Street
(1892/QA; W. H. Meade, C) The California Investment Association was the original owner of these three cottages, which cost $1,400 each to build.

## 79. 409 Jersey Street
(c. 1880/IF) Look behind to see how the false front hides the peaked roof. This home was covered with textured coating and the front windows were replaced with smaller aluminum-sashed panes.

## 80. 1305-11 Castro Street
(c. 1885/SFS) This building was originally an SFS commercial-residential combination. Little is left of its former decorated self, but note the entry door and the art glass transom at 1311.

## 81. 1300 Castro Street
(c. 1885/SFS) The second story of this combined-use structure still retains its exuberant wooden embellishment.

## 82. 1301 Castro Street
(c. 1900/C) This corner commercial-residential structure combines the round corner bay and swags of the Queen Anne with the cornice of dentils and small brackets of the Edwardian style.

## 83. 4073-77 24th Street
(c. 1895/QT, QA) Two lavishly appointed Queen Annes, one with a tower and one without.

## 84. 608 Elizabeth Street
(1891/QA; William Curlett, A)

## 85. 610 Elizabeth Street
(c. 1895/QA) A simple version of the Queen Anne, with inexpensive buttons and spindles.

## 86. 649 Diamond Street
(c. 1880/IF) Look around at the rear of this corner store for a good view of the false front and side.

## 87. 780-88 Elizabeth Street
(1892-93/QA; O. W. Carlson, B) A cluster of four cottages.

**88. 4279-93 23rd Street**
(1892/SFS) Note the way that 4283 has been modernized. It is scarcely recognizable, but once it had the same French cap and delicate finials as its three neighbors.

**89. 4250 23rd Street**
(1893/QT; William Mooser, A) This towered cottage, which originally cost $3,000 to build for John Conley, still has its carriage house in back.

**90. 572 Eureka Street**
(1896/SFS) This cottage has handsome round windows in the front door and sports three finials.

**91. 4231-53 23rd Street**
(1906/QA; John Anderson, C) Five homes, the middle two intact. House 4235 has been "misguided" in an inventive way: Note how the peaked roofline has been altered into a flat cornice with shallow brackets.

**92. 4226 23rd Street**
(1892/SFS; Fernando Nelson, D)

**93. 4200 23rd Street**
(1892/SFS; Fernando Nelson, D)

**94. 4073-79 23rd Street**
(1891/SFS; A. S. Cook, A) Note the way these two homes tilt.

**95. 4078 23rd Street**
(c. 1885/SFS) This home had been sullied with stucco and was barely discernable as a Victorian. In 1975 its facade was restored by San Francisco Victoriana.

**96. 4069 23rd Street**
(1889/SFS; William H. Armitage, A) Peek into the garden east of this home for a glimpse of the "crystal room," designed and manufactured by Noe Valley craftsman Bruce Sherman, whose geometric glass crystal windows help brighten the kitchens of many Victorians in San Francisco.

**97. 518-68 Alvarado Street**
(1905-06/QA; John Anderson, C) Half of the dozen homes in this cluster are still intact.

**98. 559-73 Alvarado Street**
(c. 1895/QA) Three of the group of four are intact; note the oversize buttons and one-quarter sunburst on 565.

*1007 Diamond Street (entry 67)*

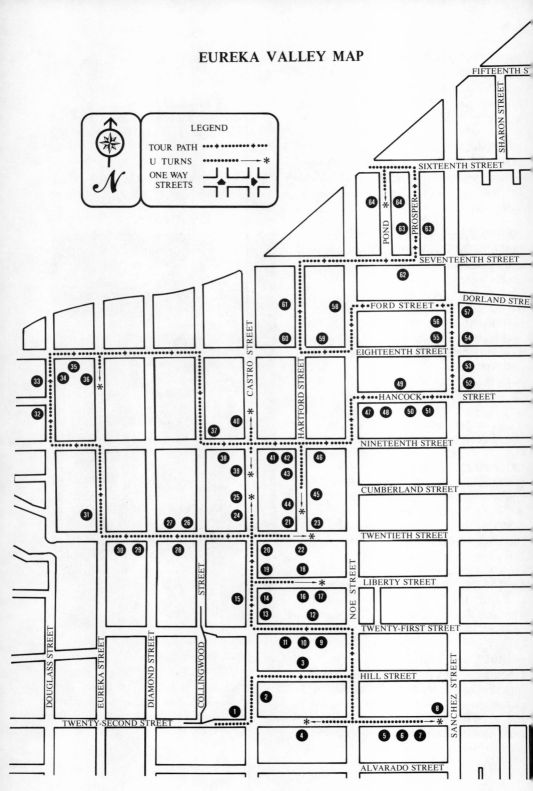

# EUREKA VALLEY MAP

**LEGEND**

TOUR PATH ••••••••••••
U TURNS •••••••••••→ *
ONE WAY STREETS

FIFTEENTH ST

SHARON STREET

SIXTEENTH STREET

POND

PROSPER

64 * 64 63 63

SEVENTEENTH STREET

62

FORD STREET

DORLAND STRE

61 58 57

56 54

60 59 55

EIGHTEENTH STREET

53

CASTRO STREET

HARTFORD STREET

49 52

HANCOCK STREET

47 48 50 51

37 40

NINETEENTH STREET

38 41 42 46

39 43

CUMBERLAND STREET

33 34 36 35 *

32

25 44 45

31 24 21 23

27 26

TWENTIETH STREET

30 29 28 20 22

19 18

NOE STREET

STREET

LIBERTY STREET

15 14 16 17

13 12

DOUGLASS STREET

EUREKA STREET

DIAMOND STREET

COLLINGWOOD STREET

SANCHEZ STREET

TWENTY-FIRST STREET

11 10 9

3

HILL STREET

2 8

TWENTY-SECOND STREET 1

* 4 5 6 7

ALVARADO STREET

# EUREKA VALLEY

Vivid examples of the tract builders' craft still line the hills and valleys of Eureka Valley, the neighborhood bounded by Dolores, Market, Upper Market and 22nd streets. The 1976 survey found almost fourteen hundred Victorian buildings in the neighborhood. More than half are Queen Annes, attesting to the decade when most of the area was developed. Clusters with signature details can be traced to Fernando Nelson, John Anderson and Louis Landler, builders who constructed rows of homes here in the eighties and nineties. Eureka Valley has many restored and repainted Victorians, a reclamation movement that signals a heartening revival of interest in nineteenth-century architecture.

**1. 3900-42 22nd Street**
(1909/QA; John Turner, B) This cluster of nine homes shows the modest embellishment that persisted in the Queen Anne rowhouse, even after the turn of the century.

**2. 865-85 Castro Street**
(1892/QA; M. J. Welsh, A) Compare Turner's houses with these two, designed by an architect seventeen years earlier.

**3. 510, 543, 544 Hill Street**
(1890/SFS; Isaac Anderson, A) These three are the only intact buildings left in what was originally a group of eight.

**4. 3817-71 22nd Street**
(1905-06/QA; John Anderson, C) Thirteen more homes by one of Eureka and Noe valleys' most prolific contractors.

**5. 3749-77 22nd Street**
(1908/QA; John Anderson, C) An almost intact row of seven; only house 3777 has been altered with aluminum siding. Anderson alternated decorations in the frieze bands: Some have egg and dart, others have banded laurel molding.

**6. 3733-45 22nd Street**
(1896/QA) Hans Petersen, C) House

3741 is the most intact of this cluster of four, with its petaled landing newel caps. The doors on these contractor-built houses are unusual, with three oval panes with beveled clear glass and side lights filled with art glass.

**7. 3711-15 22nd Street**
(c. 1895/QA) These two rowhouses look "Flemish" with their triple vents and diamond shingles in the gables.

**8. 3702-06 22nd Street**
(1892/QA; Daniel Einstein, C) Three exuberant rowhouses; only house 3702 has been disguised with asbestos shingles.

**9. 3833 21st Street**
(1892/QA; Charles Rousseau, A) Almost identical to another Rousseau home at 825 South Van Ness Avenue.

**10. 3845 21st Street**
(1896/QA; Hans Petersen, C)

**11. 3847-55 21st Street**
(c. 1890/C) These uncommonly proportioned homes still have their art glass transoms. Note how the house numbers have changed: This block used to be the 1600s.

*Landing newel post,*
*544 Hill Street (entry 3)*

**12. 3816-36 21st Street**
(1903-04/QA; John Anderson, C) Fourteen homes, another Anderson cluster.

**13. 787-89 Castro Street**
(1891/QA; Charles Hinkel, OB)

**14. 757 Castro Street**
(1897/QA; William Helbing, C)

**15. 740-48 Castro Street**
(1894/QA; Charles Hinkel, OB)

**16. 563-77 Liberty Street**
(1897/QA; John Anderson, C) All in this cluster of five were once identical, but the false front on 571 was added a few years after it was built, because the owner wanted his house to look different. Anderson also constructed the five at 513-33 Liberty Street, four years later.

**17. 541-59 Liberty Street**
(1897/QA; Carlson & Anderson, B) Five rowhouses; the owners of house 541 have begun an archeological expedition

by tearing away the asbestos shingles in the gable to discover how much decoration is left.

**18. 546-72 Liberty Street**
(1897/SFS; Fernando Nelson, D) Seven homes in a Nelson cluster of cottages and two-story buildings. Note the drips and donuts, two of Nelson's favorite signature details.

**19. 711-33 Castro Street**
(1897/SFS, QA; Fernando Nelson, D) A cluster of four Stick-style homes, with one Queen Anne rowhouse on the north end. All five homes were built in the same year, and both styles share some of the same signature details.

**20. 701 Castro Street**
(1897/QT; Fernando Nelson, OB) Nelson and his family lived here for ten years before moving to the Inner Richmond neighborhood, where he also built many homes. Bill, Nelson's retired firehorse who hauled lumber on the construction sites, used to live in the basement of this house. Originally it was built on the back of the lot, but a subsequent owner moved it forward and constructed the row of brick garages underneath.

**21. 4150 20th Street**
(1891/SFS; Louis Landler, B)

**22. 4119-41 20th Street**
(1898/QA; Fernando Nelson, D) According to Nelson's son, George, this cluster of six was built at a time when Nelson offered a choice of two home fronts, "A" or "B," from a card he carried in his pocket.

**23. 4100-38 20th Street**
(1899/QA, QT; Fernando Nelson, D) Ten houses. Nelson often combined rowhouses with a larger building on the corner, like a bookend.

**24. 668 Castro Street**
(1883/T; Henry Geilfuss, A) Geilfuss added the angular, geometric embellishment of the eighties to the flat-fronted shape of the home of the seventies.

**25. 642 Castro Street**
(1897/QA; W. H. Lillie, A) The original owner, Mr. E. W. Bennett, was the manufacturer of Brilliantshine Metal Polish.

**26. 284-90 Collingwood Street**
(1886/SFS; John A. Swenson, B) Slightly different variations in embellishment on these cottages, both of which have French caps and finials.

**27. 4324 20th Street**
(1896/QA; John A. McConnell, B) San Francisco Victoriana manufactured the millwork for this home, which had been covered with aluminum siding. The owner installed the redwood facade himself; the house is featured in the July 1975 issue of the *Old-House Journal*.

**28. 4327-31 20th Street**
(1890/SFS) Two furiously embellished examples of the rectangular-bayed homes that typified the buildings of the eighties.

**29. 4417 20th Street**
(c. 1895/QA) Delicate spoolwork around the entry and in the corner brackets.

**30. 4421 20th Street**
(1892/QA; John J. Clark, A) A rare elliptical arch makes a graceful frame for the front door.

**31. 282-86 Eureka Street**
(1893/SFS; Fernando Nelson, D) Almost identical to Nelson's cluster on the 700 block of Castro Street.

**32. 250 Douglass Street**
(1891/QT) Official San Francisco Landmark Number 80, this enormous home, which towers over the surrounding flats

and rowhouses in the rest of the neighborhood, was built for attorney Alfred "Nobby" Clarke. His wife refused to live in the then-unfashionable neighborhood, resulting in the building's Victorian-era nickname, "Nobby's Folly."

**33. 180 Douglass Street**
(1890/SFS; Cook & Wry, A)

**34. 109 Douglass Street**
(c. 1900/QA) Advertised for sale as "a ship captain's mansion" that supposedly had ground-floor servants' quarters.

**35. 4407-09 18th Street**
(1892/SFS; Louis Landler, B)

**36. 118-22 Eureka Street**
(1895/QT, QA; Daniel Einstein, C) Einstein's signature detail is obvious in these two homes, which are linked visually by a frieze band of decorative shingles.

**37. 197 Collingwood Street**
(1891/SFS; Gustav Pavel, A)

*725-33 Castro Street (entry 19)*

*3816-56 21st Street (entry 12)*

### 38. 4135 19th Street
(1891/SFS; George Eaton, A) Eaton listed himself as both architect and contractor when he built this $3,200 house for Elijah P. McKnew.

### 39. 602 Castro Street
(1883/SFS; John Coop, D) Unlike many of the houses in Coop's Inner Mission neighborhood clusters, this home retains its French cap.

### 40. 580-84 Castro Street
(1897/SFS; Fernando Nelson, D)

### 41. 4065 19th Street
(1888/SFS; William J. Peterson, C)

### 42. 4051 19th Street
(1891/SFS) This handsome Stick home is an apartment house that has another entry around the corner on Hartford Street.

### 43. 220 Hartford Street
(c. 1895/QA) This house had been stuc- coed in the 1930 s, then smothered with aluminum siding in the 1950 s. The facade was completely restored by San Francisco Victoriana in 1977.

### 44. 262-80 Hartford Street
(1891/SFS; Louis Landler, B) Landler built several different clusters in Eureka Valley, including these five cottages.

### 45. 255-59 Hartford Street
(1891/T; Louis Landler, B) These three Landler homes have the shape of the Queen Anne, but much of the embellishment of the eighties.

### 46. 4033 19th Street
(c. 1885/SFS) Few houses still have a small turret like the one sported by this building. Such a turret was advertised in the 1885 catalog of the Niehaus Brothers Planing Mill, West Berkeley, California.

### 47. 559 Noe Street
(c. 1870/O) This Greek Revival home was apparently built in the 1870 s, and it seems to be one of the oldest houses in the neighborhood. In 1887, the owner, Captain H. A. Dahler, commissioned contractor A. Miller to make "alterations and additions."

### 48. 177 Hancock Street
(1888/SFS)

### 49. 142 Hancock Street
(1880/IB; Paul B. Curtis, OB) Curtis was a shipwright; some of his skill is apparent in the house he built for himself.

### 50. 173 Hancock Street
(1898/QT)

### 51. 129 Hancock Street
(1877/IB)

### 52. 545 Sanchez Street
(1889/SFS; Thomas Elam, C)

**53. 517 Sanchez Street**
(1894/SFS; Thomas Elam, C) First built for Emery and Minnie La Vallie, who paid contractor Elam $3,780.

**54. 491 Sanchez Street**
(1889/SFS; Henry Geilfuss, A)

**55. 498 Sanchez Street**
(1897/SFS; A. J. Barnett, A)

**56. 462 Sanchez Street**
(1885/IF; Salfield & John, A) This simple home cost owner H. Echgelmeir $2,500.

**57. 443 Sanchez Street**
(c. 1885/SFS) This corner commercial-residential building had been stripped and covered with asbestos shingles. The owner took an old photograph to San Francisco Victoriana, who reproduced its embellishment authentically. The facade restoration was completed in 1975.

**58. 460-76 Noe Street**
(1901/QA; Fernando Nelson, D) A cluster of five.

**59. 4000-36 18th Street**
(1901/QA; Fernando Nelson, D) Nine houses.

**60. 4040, 4052 18th Street**
(1901/QA; Fernando Nelson, D) These were identical originally, but the western house had an attic fire, and the roof was shaved off.

**61. 20-68, 37-65 Hartford Street**
(1901-02/QA; Fernando Nelson, D) A cluster of nineteen homes on both sides of the street.

**62. 3863 17th Street**
(1886/SFS; Huerne & Everett, A)

**63. 35, 61, 59-75, 28-40, 52-56, 66-76 Prosper Street**
(c. 1885-95/SFS, QA) Fourteen Victorians line this quiet block and make up one of the most complete revivals in the City. Almost every house has been restored, repaired or repainted.

**64. 20-40, 52, 74, 27-33, 43-73 Pond Street**
(c. 1885-95/SFS, QA) Almost every Victorian on this block is "misguided" or neglected. Yet it has the same potential for revival as its neighboring street, Prosper, which is directly east.

*John Coop's anchor signature details over a sunburst, 602 Castro Street (entry 39)*

# MINT HILL-DUBOCE TRIANGLE

The Mint Hill and Duboce Triangle neighborhoods are part of the Western Addition, a vast section of the City west of Van Ness Avenue that was annexed in 1851. Much of it was sand dunes; in fact, the area was named "The Great Sand Waste" on early maps.

In the southern part of the Western Addition is Hayes Valley, recently renamed Mint Hill by residents eager to spotlight its revived Victorian homes. The neighborhood namesake is the Federal Mint, a large granite mass that dominates the view from the south.

Right next to Mint Hill is the Duboce Triangle, at the junction of Market, Castro and Duboce streets. The two neighborhoods join at Duboce Park, which early photographs show laid out in rows as a vegetable garden, before it was dedicated as public land in 1900.

The larger Western Addition, which includes the Alamo Square-Beideman Place area, still contains more than twenty-six hundred Victorians. The styles reflect accurately the development of the neighborhood: Almost half are the Stick style of the 1880s, and another third are the Italianates of the seventies.

The section of the Western Addition closest to downtown and more northerly along Geary Boulevard once contained the City's finest collection of Victorian mansions that had survived the 1906 earthquake, fire and dynamiting. They could not, however, survive the clearance plans of the San Francisco Redevelopment Agency, and some five thousand units were lost, replaced by new subsidized dwellings, privately financed apartments and the Japantown commercial complex. But perhaps they were a worthy sacrifice, as their loss helped to spur such actions as the adoption of the landmarks ordinance and the establishment of the Foundation for San Francisco's Architectural Heritage.

During World War II, parts of these neighborhoods housed war workers. The pressures of this influx of people created a wave of illegal conversions, as original flats and single-family homes were subdivided in a variety of ways by inventive property owners. This overcrowding caused much of the neighborhood to deteriorate quickly. The low-income tenant population may have actually aided later Victorian enthusiasts, however, as relatively few owners remodeled, stripped, or otherwise defaced their buildings. Only about forty percent of the Western Addition Victorians masquerade as something else, the smallest proportion in any of the surveyed neighborhoods.

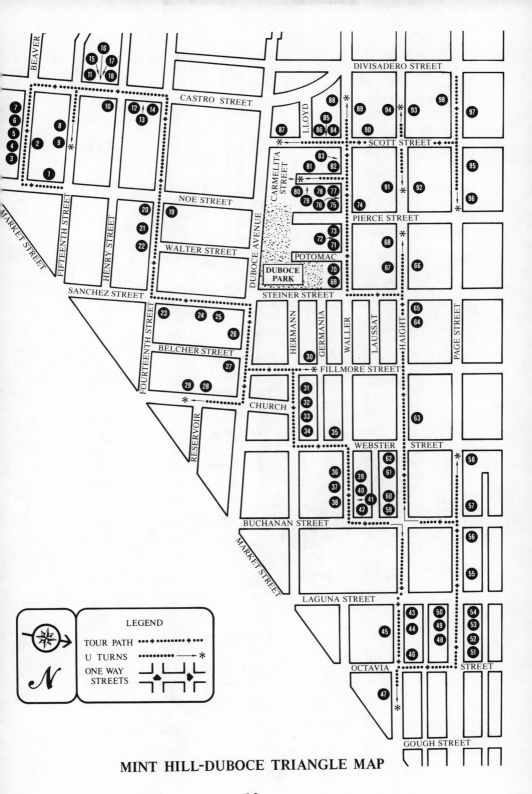

MINT HILL-DUBOCE TRIANGLE MAP

83

## 1. 226 Noe Street
(c. 1880/C) An unusual house, which combines the five-sided slanted bay window and bracketed cornice of the seventies with a Queen Anne-style spindled arch in the entryway.

## 2. 20 Beaver Street
(1882/IB) Peer through the trees and bushes in front of this home, said to have been built as a farmhouse for Jacob Benedict. It has a bay window on the side and a square witch's cap over the doorway.

*Rectangular bay window,*
*198 Castro Street (entry 11)*

## 3. 7 Beaver Street
(c. 1885/SFS) The upper story rectangular bay is supported by brackets with sunbursts.

## 4. 9 Beaver Street
(c. 1875/IB) Some early Italianate homes had this gabled roof with brackets.

## 5. 19 Beaver Street
(c. 1885/SFS)

## 6. 21 Beaver Street
(c. 1875/IF) A flat-front home, cleverly disguised by a misguided improvement.

## 7. 23 Beaver Street
(c. 1885/SFS)

## 8. 2235 15th Street
(c. 1895/QA) From the front, this house looks like an intact Queen Anne, but peek around behind. The gable, with its deeply cast floral decoration, is a false one!

## 9. 2229 15th Street
(c. 1895/QA) This building has lots of texture: The first floor is clad in lap siding, and the upper two stories have different kinds of shingles.

## 10. 191 Henry Street
(1892/SFS) This building was constructed for Charles F. MacDermott, a "capitalist" who lived in Oakland. Note the way the gables and witches' caps march down the hill.

## 11. 198 Castro Street
(c. 1885/SFS) This home, with uncommon cornice windows, might have been taken directly from a house plan presented in the *California Architect and Building News.*

## 12. 135 Castro Street
(c. 1875/IF)

**13. 129 Castro Street**
(c. 1885/SFS) This cottage still has its original wooden stairway.

**14. 125 Castro Street**
(c. 1895/QA) Another Queen Anne with a false front, much like entry 8.

**15. 166 Castro Street**
(c. 1880/T) This house combines the five-sided slanted bay window of the seventies with the non-Classical redwood millwork of the eighties.

**16. 160 Castro Street**
(c. 1875/IB) A stately Italianate with quoins and a Corinthian-columned portico.

**17. 158 Castro Street**
(c. 1885/SFS) The French cap is gone from this home.

**18. 150 Castro Street**
(c. 1885/SFS)

**19. 888 14th Street**
(c. 1885/SFS)

**20. 101 Noe Street**
(c. 1900/C) A handsome apartment house with both a Queen Anne tower with a finial and the simple main cornice associated with the Edwardian style.

**21. 879 14th Street**
(c. 1895/QT) A truncated tower makes this home look lopsided.

**22. 851-75 14th Street**
(c. 1895/QA; Fernando Nelson, D) A cluster of six houses much like Nelson's on Hartford Street in the Eureka Valley neighborhood. The two in the middle have been raised to accommodate a store beneath.

**23. 95 Sanchez Street**
(c. 1895/QT; Martens & Coffey, A)

*135 Castro Street (entry 12)*

**24. 77 Sanchez Street**
(c. 1875/IF) Note the vertical wood siding used to "misguide" the entrance.

**25. 43 Sanchez Street**
(c. 1885/SFS)

**26. 477 Duboce Street**
(c. 1890/C) A charming conglomeration, with massive landing newel posts, a rectangular bay window, a spindled arch and a peaked gable with fishscale shingles.

**27. 449 Duboce Street**
(c. 1890/SFS) Resembles "The Alameda" house plan in the Newsom brothers' *Picturesque California Homes No. 2,* a $2,500 home designated as "a cottage in the French Renaissance style."

**28. 120 Church Street**
(1893/QA; James Campbell, C)

*152 Church Street (entry 29)*

### 29. 152 Church Street
(1905/O) This brick "Gothic" church is San Francisco Landmark Number 39. Now the St. Francis Lutheran Church, it was originally the St. Ansgar Danish Lutheran Church.

### 30. 133 Fillmore Street
(c. 1895/QT)

### 31. 262 Hermann Street
(c. 1885/SFS) This cottage has a squeezed pediment in the cornice.

### 32. 256 Hermann Street
(1887/SFS; H. T. Bestor, A)

### 33. 232 Hermann Street
(1872/IB) This home has an unusual roofline: There is a segmented arch in the main cornice.

### 34. 222 Hermann Street
(c. 1885/SFS) The massive portico brackets almost fill the doorway.

### 35. 81-97 Webster Street
(c. 1885/SFS) A cluster of four, all with bracketed rectangular bay windows on the second story.

### 36. 269 Waller Street
(c. 1885/SFS)

### 37. 261 Waller Street
(c. 1880/IF) Note the small art glass window in the addition on the east side of the house.

### 38. 243 Waller Street
(c. 1885/SFS)

### 39. 252 Waller Street
(c. 1885/SFS) The vertical feeling of this house is enhanced by long bracket extensions and a fluted corner board.

### 40. 224, 234 Waller Street
(c. 1885/SFS) Two homes once identical. House 224 has been stripped of much of its architectural detail, while house 234 has had an awkward-looking fire escape tacked onto the upper bay window.

### 41. 210 Waller Street
(c. 1885/SFS)

### 42. 201 Buchanan Street
(1882/SFS; John Marquis, A) Official San Francisco Landmark Number 47, this home was built for developer John Nightingale. It was described quite dryly in the *California Architect and Building News* listing as a "one-story attic and basement cottage, $4,500."

### 43. 198 Haight Street
(1884/IB; T. J. Welsh, A) This home originally cost $12,000 when it was built for Farrell McMurry. It has a mansard roof with dormer windows; the original carriage house is around the corner on Laguna Street.

**44. 176 Haight Street**
(c. 1885/SFS) A massive false gable with a turned wooden finial. The metal prayer bells are a later addition.

**45. 185 Haight Street**
(1873/IF) This home is said to be the oldest one on the block.

**46. 100 Haight Street**
(c. 1885/SFS) An uncommon cornice with a rectangular corner bay window topped by a turret.

**47. 37-63 Haight Street**
(1883/IB; Schmidt & Havens, A) When all three sides of this triangular block were developed, there were eighteen identical homes. Only three remain.

**48. 249 Page Street**
(c. 1895/QA; John Anderson, C)

**49. 273 Page Street**
(c. 1875/IB) Look up to find the gaping gargoyle in the false gable.

**50. 287 Page Street**
(c. 1885/SFS)

**51. 256 Page Street**
(c. 1885/SFS)

**52. 276 Page Street**
(1883/SFS; Charles Geddes, A) This home cost $5,500 when built for the original owner, Mrs. Ellen E. Kennedy.

**53. 284 Page Street**
(c. 1885/SFS)

**54. 294 Page Street**
(1888/SFS; Henry Geilfuss, A) Notice that the original owner, bootmaker Charles Dietle, had his initials cut into the transom over the front door. Official San Francisco Landmark Number 48, this home has a small tower tacked onto the back, the interior of which was not finished.

**55. 308 Page Street**
(1889/SFS; John J. Clark, A)

**56. 390 Page Street**
(c. 1885/C)

**57. 434 Page Street**
(c. 1875/IB)

**58. 444, 450 Page Street**
(c. 1895/QA) Two Queen Anne homes; note the false front on house 444.

**59. 319 Haight Street**
(c. 1885/SFS) This house has an uncommon triangular bay window in the second story on the east side.

**60. 323 Haight Street**
(c. 1880/T) Lavish non-Classical decorations adorn this house, which has the slanted bay associated with an earlier decade.

**61. 391 Haight Street**
(c. 1885/SFS) The ground floor of this building is stuccoed, but look up! The top floors have colonnettes and pilasters with Corinthian capitals.

*294 Page Street (entry 54)*

**62. 395 Haight Street**
(c. 1885/SFS) This commercial-residential corner building has an unusual balcony on the second floor with "Egyptian" capitals.

**63. 414 Haight Street**
(c. 1885/SFS)

**64. 588 Haight Street**
(1884/SFS; S. & J. C. Newsom, A) A relatively inexpensive home designed by the Newsom brothers.

**65. 596 Haight Street**
(c. 1885/SFS)

**66. 606, 626 Haight Street**
(c. 1885/SFS) Apparently by the same builder, these two homes have similar cornices that combine false gables with unusually deep French caps.

**67. 605-09 Haight Street**
(c. 1885/SFS) Two homes with deeply carved wooden detail that casts playful shadow patterns.

**68. 673 Haight Street**
(c. 1885/SFS)

**69. 515-33 Waller Street**
(c. 1895/QA) Four homes by the same builder, but with different detailing. House 533 has two pregnant women in its plaster portico brackets; house 527 has a frieze of banded laurel leaf molding, and houses 515 and 521 have plaster frieze bands with a palmette pattern.

**70. 539 Waller Street**
(c. 1890/QT)

**71. 563 Waller Street**
(1899/QA; Fernando Nelson, D) These homes originally cost $5,000 each.

**72. 579 Waller Street**
(c. 1895/QA)

**73. 591 Waller Street**
(c. 1895/QA) Originally built as three flats, two of the original doors, with oval window panes of beveled glass, remain.

**74. 101 Pierce Street**
(c. 1895/QT) This tower house had deteriorated badly, but was rescued by the Preservation Group, who renovated it in 1976.

**75. 601 Waller Street**
(1899/QT; Fernando Nelson, D)

**76. 607-39 Waller Street**
(1899/QA; Fernando Nelson, D) A cluster of six houses.

**77. 643 Waller Street**
(1899/QT; Fernando Nelson, D)

**78. 78 Carmelita Street**
(1899/QT; Fernando Nelson, D) Almost identical to Nelson's own home, which still stands at 701 Castro Street in the Eureka Valley neighborhood.

**79. 58, 66-74 Carmelita Street**
(1899/QA; Fernando Nelson, D) Four Nelson homes; house 66 has an enormous sunburst in the peak of the gable.

**80. 50 Carmelita Street**
(c. 1900/A) This home looks like a Swiss mountain chalet; its gable is topped by a pointed metal finial.

**81. 49-77 Carmelita Street**
(1899/QA; Fernando Nelson, D) All of these eight homes have intact facades, although several have awkward-looking garage additions.

**82. 667 Waller Street**
(c. 1895/QA)

**83. 673-79 Waller Street**
(c. 1895/QA) Two homes with identical plaster swags.

**84. 95 Scott Street**
(1891/QT; John Foster, A)

**85. 93 Scott Street**
(1890/QT) Notice that the lower floor of the tower becomes an open balcony, or belvedere.

**86. 79 Scott Street**
(1888/SFS; Henry Geilfuss, A)

**87. 9-51 Scott Street**
(1888/SFS; William Hinkel, OB) A cluster of eight, three of which have been stuccoed. Look around at the sides of modernized house 51 for a glimpse of its former self.

**88. 771 Waller Street**
(c. 1885/SFS) This home is well hidden, perched above the street on its retaining wall.

**89. 708-22 Waller Street**
(1884/SFS; John Hinkel, OB) A cluster of eight cottages, only three of which are intact.

**90. 109-39 Scott Street**
(1884/SFS; John Hinkel, OB) Six homes by this prolific builder. House 127 is extremely well disguised by its stucco costume.

**91. 751 Haight Street**
(c. 1890/QA) This house has an oriel bay window, with a teardrop soffit, over the entryway.

**92. 758 Haight Street**
(c. 1890/QT; W. H. Lillie, A)

**93. 858 Haight Street**
(c. 1885/SFS) A massive false gable with a squat finial.

**94. 807-33, 847 Haight Street**
(1884/SFS; John Hinkel, OB) A cluster of six homes.

**95. 850-70 Page Street**
(c. 1885/SFS) Four different Stick-style homes.

**96. 824 Page Street**
(c. 1890/QA)

**97. 908-62 Page Street**
(1887/SFS; William Hinkel, OB) A cluster of seven; only four retain their false gables.

**98. 969 Page Street**
(1893/QA; Henry Geilfuss, A) A profusion of spindles on this double house.

*95 Scott Street (entry 84)*

# HAIGHT ASHBURY

The Haight Ashbury is at the eastern entrance to Golden Gate Park, and the Panhandle section of the park forms a tree-lined promenade through the center of the area. Both the park and the neighborhood were reclaimed from sand dunes, whose shifting topography slowed home-building efforts until the late 1880s.

Since most of the neighborhood was built up during the 1890s, gables, plasterwork and finialed towers dominate the architectural landscape. In 1976 about 1,160 Victorian structures remained in the Haight Ashbury, roughly three-quarters of them Queen Annes. Today many of these homes are being restored, as both the residential blocks and the Haight Street commercial strip are revived from some of the ravages of the "flower children."

The contracting firm of Cranston and Keenan built several clusters in the neighborhood, including the rare grouping of tower houses at 1214-56 Masonic Street. In a house that still stands on Buena Vista East, a recent owner found evidence of their work. When she had the interior stairway newel post taken apart to be stripped of paint, out fell a business card. On it was written: "Built and finished by R. D. Cranston for L. G. Lander, July 21, 1899."

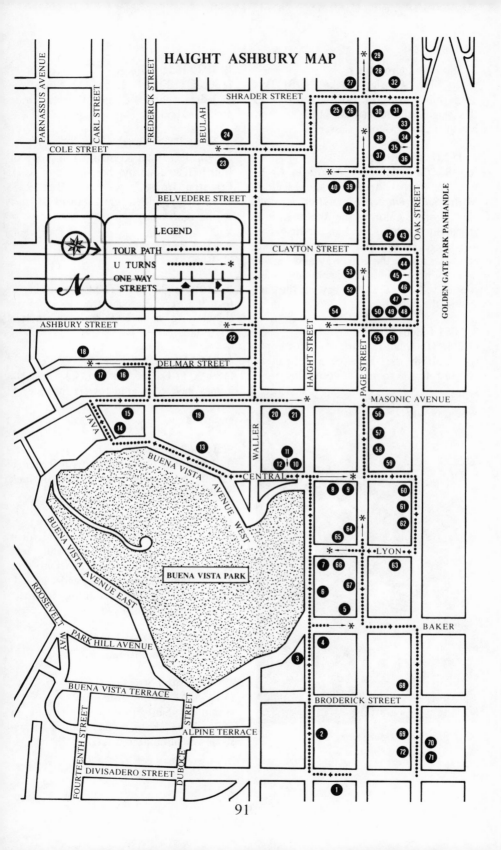

91

**1. 280 Divisadero Street**
(1885/SFS; Charles Hinkel, OB) This home has a mansard roof, uncommon in this neighborhood. It cost $17,000 when built for owner George Casser.

**2. 952 Haight Street**
(c. 1885/SFS; Miller & Armitage, A) Illustrated in the "Artistic Homes" section of the *San Francisco Newsletter,* a magazine published during the Victorian era. Originally the house had an ornate exterior: a French cap and iron cresting, and cameo faces in the entryway and on the belt cornice. For a tiny glimmer of its former self, peek at the bay on the east side of the building.

**3. 1081 Haight Street**
(1894/QT; John J. Clark, A) This home was built in the shape of a flatiron to conform to the triangular corner lot.

*1226 Masonic Street (entry 20)*

**4. 1080 Haight Street**
(1896/QT; Fred P. Rabin, A) Notice the Palladian window and the elaborate arched entryway.

**5. 15-21 Baker Street**
(1890/SFS; Hugh Keenan, C) A group of four homes done by the partner of R. D. Cranston. House 21 was restored in 1977, when its misguided improvement of stucco was removed.

**6. 1128 Haight Street**
(1891/QT)

**7. 1190 Haight Street (10 Lyon Street)**
(c. 1885/SFS) Rescued from its asbestos-shingle disguise in 1978 by San Francisco Victoriana.

**8. 142-52 Central Street**
(1899/QT; Daniel Einstein, C) These six homes have truncated towers that are almost lost in the bulge of the wide, round bay window.

**9. 156-60 Central Street**
(c. 1900/QA) Three houses with flattened "swell" bays with frieze bands of thick plaster embellishment.

**10. 91 Central Street**
(1904/O) This handsome Edwardian apartment house has many plaster faces decorating its facade. Particularly notable are the ladies upon whose heads the balconies rest, perhaps accounting for their anxious expressions.

**11. 79 Central Street**
(1896/QT; James Rountree, C)

**12. 67 Central Street**
(1898/QA) Before this house was restored by San Francisco Victoriana in 1975, it had been hidden behind Permastone and aluminum siding.

**13. 737 Buena Vista West**
(1897/O; Edward J. Vogel, A) A house in the uncommon Colonial Revival style, built originally for Richard Spreckles.

**14. 601 Buena Vista West**
(1895/QT; William H. Armitage, A)

**15. 1450 Masonic Street**
(1891/QT; A. J. Barnett, A)

**16. 124 Delmar Street**
(c. 1890/QA) A graceful arched window in the front of the bay window, with marginal panels of art glass.

**17. 130 Delmar Street**
(1890/QT; Eugene N. Fritz, B)

**18. 116, 151, 155-59, 168 Delmar Street**
(c. 1885-1905/SFS, QA, QT, O) A remarkable cluster of homes, all of which were completely restored by San Francisco Victoriana between 1974 and 1978. A tower was added to house 159 because the owner wanted to retain the floor space created by an earlier remodeling that added to the second story.

**19. 1322-42 Masonic Street**
(c. 1885/SFS) An old photograph of these six homes shows that originally they sported false gables and rooftop iron cresting. All the gables were removed, supposedly because they leaked.

**20. 1214-56 Masonic Street**
(1896-97/QT; Cranston & Keenan, C) An unusual cluster of eight Queen Annes with towers. Two are misguided.

**21. 1200 Masonic Street**
(1896/QT; Martens & Coffey, A)

**22. 704-14 Ashbury Street**
(c. 1890/QA) Several in this group of six homes retain their art glass transoms with house numbers. Although all were done by the same builder, the facades are quite varied.

**23. 708-22 Cole Street**
(1895/QT, QA; William Hinkel, OB) A cluster of eight by this prolific owner-builder, two with towers, six without.

**24. 705-43 Cole Street**
(1895/QT, QA; William Hinkel, OB) Ten more Hinkel houses, one with a tower.

**25. 524 Shrader Street**
(1889/SFS; John & Zimmerman, A) Stuccoed, but side decoration remains.

**26. 510 Shrader Street**
(1891/SFS) This cottage has a spindled arch that is usually associated with a later style.

*1214-56 Masonic Street (entry 20)*

*Plaster face between two*
*Ionic pilasters, 1247 Masonic Street*

### 27. 1901 Page Street
(1896/O; Edward J. Vogel, A) Another of Vogel's Colonial Revival homes. This house shares some details with 737 Buena Vista West.

### 28. 1910 Page Street
(1897/QT; Copeland & Pierce, A)

### 29. 1922 Page Street
(1892/QT; W. H. Lillie, A)

### 30. 1890 Page Street
(1890/QT; Samuel Newsom, A) Designed by one of the Newsom brothers, the architects of the Carson mansion in Eureka, California.

### 31. 414 Shrader Street
(1888/SFS; Hinkel Brothers, OB)

### 32. 411-15 Shrader Street
(1890/QT; Cornelius Murphy, OB) Three houses built for Mrs. Bridget Murphy.

### 33. 1979 Oak Street
(1894/QA)

### 34. 1949 Oak Street
(1888/SFS; R. Sinnott, C)

### 35. 1939 Oak Street
(1895/QA)

### 36. 1915 Oak Street
(1894/QA) Typical Queen Anne details: a foliated frieze band, a finial and an arched portico.

### 37. 1814 Page Street
(1893/QA; W. H. Lillie, A) A Palladian window in the gable's peak, a detail favored by Lillie, the architect who designed the landmark Coleman mansion at 1701 Franklin Street.

### 38. 1832 Page Street
(1890/SFS) The original owner was Rudolph Mohr, the secretary of the Germania, Humboldt and Monarch Mutual Building and Loan Association.

### 39. 500 Cole Street
(c. 1890/QT) This home has an unusual facade: The tower is in the middle, flanked by gables. The cloverleaf archway suggests the "Moorish" influence that was popular during the nineties.

### 40. 508-16 Cole Street
(1899/QA; Cranston & Keenan, C) Four more homes produced by these contractors, who built many homes along the Golden Gate Park panhandle.

### 41. 1777 Page Street
(c. 1890/QA; Cranston & Keenan, C) Robert D. Cranston built this home for himself; perhaps he chose the owl that winks out from below the gable.

### 42. 409-11 Clayton Street
(1893/QA; Soule & Hoadley, C)

### 43. 401-07 Clayton Street
(1894-95/QA; J. B. Hall, A) These four homes cost a total of $4,900 when built for original owner John English.

### 44. 1787 Oak Street
(1893/QA; William W. Rednall, C) Another product of the era's most prolific contractor.

**45. 1759 Oak Street**
(1891/QA; A. C. Soule, C) Note the "wrens' havens" in the gable, actually miniature versions of the birds' nests that English builders used to provide underneath the eaves of country homes.

**46. 1751 Oak Street**
(1896/QA; A. C. Lutgens, A)

**47. 1709 Oak Street**
(1896/QA; J. C. Newsom, A) This house was designed by the other Newsom brother.

**48. 1707 Oak Street**
(1891/SFS; William W. Rednall, C)

**49. 429 Ashbury Street**
(1891/QA; Shipman Brothers, B) The original owner was William H. Williams, who was a deputy superintendent of streets for San Francisco.

**50. 449-59 Ashbury Street**
(1893/QT; Cranston & Keenan, C) Two tower houses, originally with arched balconies.

**51. 440 Ashbury Street**
(1897/QA; Charles Rousseau, A) The triangular bay window and riot of "fancywork" signal the work of French immigrant architect Rousseau.

**52. 1617 Page Street**
(1899/QA; Daniel Einstein, C)

**53. 1649-67 Page Street**
(1901/QA; Lippert & Hahn, B) A cluster of three houses.

**54. 509-11 Ashbury Street**
(1900/QA; Daniel Einstein, C) Two houses, one intact, one stuccoed.

**55. 1542-50 Page Street**
(1891/QT, QA; Cranston & Keenan, C) Five homes in this cluster. The corner house has a special decoration that was a trademark of these contractors: Note the sun faces on the second story near the side gable.

**56. 1482 Page Street**
(1899/O; Newsom & Meyer, A) Originally built for Mr. and Mrs. Isaac Magnin of I. Magnin and Company, clothing and dry goods.

**57. 1478-80 Page Street**
(1899/O; Newsom & Meyer, A) Two Colonial Revival homes built by the same architects as house 1482.

**58. 1458 Page Street**
(1894/QT; Edward Burns, A)

**59. 209-33 Central Street**
(1891/SFS, QR; George Hinkel, OB) Five houses, three with false gables and two with real gables. Look behind the houses to tell the difference.

*1152 Oak Street (entry 70)*

95

*Plaster face under egg and dart and bead molding, 1341 Masonic Street*

**60. 1477 Oak Street**
(1891/QA)

**61. 1465 Oak Street**
(1893/QA; Louis Landler, B) Another gable decorated with "wrens' havens."

**62. 1439 Oak Street**
(1899/QA; Wilson & Lang, C)

**63. 108-24 Lyon Street**
(1891/QA; W. H. Lillie, A) Lillie designed these seven houses for the Rountree Brothers, Victorian-era builders and developers.

**64. 1303 Page Street**
(1890/QA; A. J. Barnett, A) Another house designed by an architect for the Rountree Brothers.

**65. 27 Lyon Street**
(1895/QT; J. F. Kenna, A)

**66. 26 Lyon Street**
(c. 1885/SFS) The French cap was replaced when this home was restored by San Francisco Victoriana in 1977.

**67. 1293 Page Street**
(1896/QT; Edward J. Vogel, A)

**68. 1200 Oak Street**
(1896/O; Percy & Hamilton, A) Originally the Howard Presbyterian Church, this Romanesque structure was designed by an architectural firm that specialized in churches.

**69. 1177-85 Oak Street**
(c. 1890/T) Three homes that combine Stick and QA details. House 1185 is covered with asbestos shingles, but the other two have huge sunbursts in the middle of their bay windows.

**70. 1152 Oak Street**
(1893/SFS; Henriksen & Mahoney, A) Note the square hose-drying tower on this Victorian-era firehouse, whose architects designed one almost identical at 3022 Washington Street. This is San Francisco Landmark Number 89.

**71. 1140 Oak Street**
(c. 1890/QT) An iron finial tops the witch's cap of the tower house.

**72. 1153 Oak Street**
(1885/SFS; McDougall & Son, A) San Francisco Landmark Number 62, this house was built for Mrs. Sarah Mish, a dressmaker. Originally it faced Divisadero Street, but it was moved around the corner September 1897 at a cost of $1,700. It was renovated in 1976 by the Preservation Group, which also has moved and refurbished several other homes on the block to create the "Phelps Place Historic District." The name comes from Official Landmark Number 32, the Abner Phelps home, which was landlocked at 329 Divisadero, in the center of the block behind the Mish house.

## ALAMO SQUARE-BEIDEMAN PLACE

Alamo Square is one of the three large public parks dedicated in the Western Addition in 1858, seven years after that area was annexed by the City. Surrounding the square are some magnificent examples of Victorian design. Henry Geilfuss, Charles I. Havens, W. H. Lillie, A. J. Barnett, and the firms of Martens and Coffey, Pissis and Moore, Laver and Mullany and the Newsom brothers were some of the finest of the City's architects. Each is represented by at least one building on this walk.

On the northern edge of this walking tour is Beideman Place, bounded by Divisadero, O'Farrell, Scott, and Eddy streets. Jacob C. Beideman was a produce and commission merchant who came to San Francisco in 1852. During the early 1860s, he was involved in a land dispute centering on the title to the Beideman Tract, a section of land near today's Civic Center. A one-block street named for him is in the middle of the Beideman Place area. These blocks are the focus of a house-moving and rehabilitation project sponsored jointly by the Foundation for San Francisco's Architectural Heritage, and the San Francisco Redevelopment Agency.

*1493 McAllister Street (entry 41)*

97

# ALAMO SQUARE-BEIDEMAN PLACE MAP

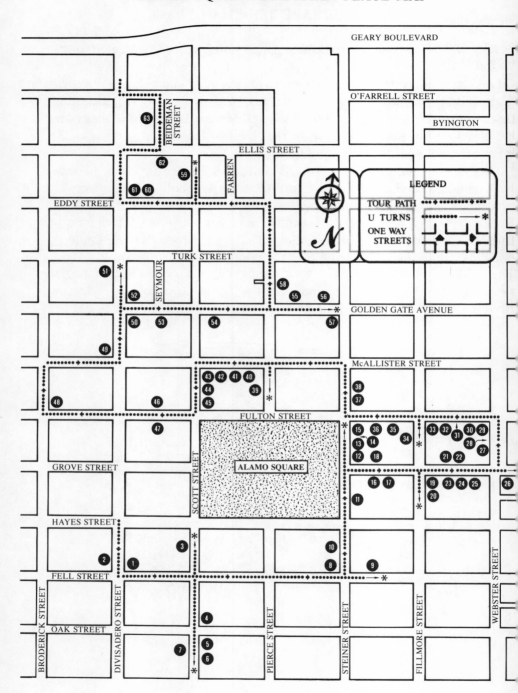

**1. 500 Divisadero Street**
(1889/QA; S. & J. C. Newsom, A) This house, designed by the Newsom brothers, is a study in curves. Note the many rounded openings, the rounded embellishment and the unusual pass-through oval on the corner.

**2. 501-07 Divisadero Street**
(1889/SFS) None of these four homes is intact; yet look at the lavishness of the decorations that do remain. All once had French caps and art glass windows in the bays. Deeply carved floral applique still lingers in some of the entries.

**3. 513 Scott Street**
(c. 1895/QA) Cove and fishscale shingles combine to decorate the gable.

**4. 988 Oak Street**
(c. 1885/SFS) This building has both rectangular and triangular bay windows and a false clipped gable.

**5. 999 Oak Street**
(c. 1905/O) Look up at the small tower adorning the corner of this Edwardian building. Inside the cartouche, or window frame, is an oval art glass pane.

**6. 348 Scott Street**
(1890/SFS) A cameo face peeks out of the false gable.

**7. 301-63 Scott Street**
(1886/SFS; Charles Hinkel, OB) When Hinkel built this cluster, the original eleven homes cost a total of $48,000. All remain, and five are still intact with alternating roofline designs, some having French caps, others false gables.

**8. 601 Steiner Street**
(1891/QT; Charles I. Havens, A) According to a local building magazine, before James Scobie had this home built he paid

$1,500 to "remove house known as the Irvine residence."

**9. 870 Fell Street**
(1893/QA; W. H. Lillie, A)

**10. 635-39 Steiner Street**
(c. 1895/QA) The round bays on the ground floors of these two houses support open lookouts, or belvederes, on the second stories.

**11. 710-20 Steiner Street**
(1894-95/QA; Matthew Kavanagh, D) When Kavanagh commissioned this row, the houses cost $3,500 each.

**12. 940 Grove Street**
(1895/QA; Pissis & Moore, A) Note the sensitively designed modern addition to this home, which now houses the French American Bilingual School.

**13. 814 Steiner Street**
(c. 1895/QA) A riot of plaster detail, including daisies and swags.

**14. 818 Steiner Street**
(c. 1895/QT)

**15. 850 Steiner Street**
(1899/QT; Tom Patterson Ross, A) The portico supports a large balcony, which offers a good view of Alamo Square.

**16. 975 Grove Street**
(c. 1895/QT) The California state animal, the grizzly bear, decorates the chimney of this large house.

**17. 957 Grove Street**
(1886/T; S. & J. C. Newsom, A) The Newsom brothers designed this home for widow Louise Amos for $5,000.

**18. 926 Grove Street**
(1897/O; Martens & Coffey, A) This Classical Revival home was built for John

L. Koster, president of the California Barrel Company and proprietor of the Mount Hamilton Vineyard.

**19. 730 Fillmore Street**
(c. 1895/QT; Martens & Coffey, A)

**20. 722 Fillmore Street**
(c. 1885/SFS) Faces peer out at you from above the belt cornice in the bay window.

**21. 834 Grove Street**
(1875/IB)

**22. 824 Grove Street**
(1886/T; Henry Geilfuss, A) Geilfuss often combined major details associated with different styles: This home has the five-sided slanted bay window of the 1870 s, but is covered with the exuberant redwood embellishment of the 1880 s.

**23. 825 Grove Street**
(c. 1875/IB) This home, with a French cap and arched windows, was the home of owner-builder John Hinkel from 1878 until 1887.

**24. 815 Grove Street**
(1882/IB)

**25. 813, 817-21 Grove Street**
(1877/IB; John Hinkel, OB)

*Landing newel post
and balustrade,
1451 McAllister Street
(entry 40)*

**26. 745-77 Grove Street**
(c. 1875/IB; The Real Estate Associates, D) Five of the six in this cluster are still intact. Compare them to the new housing across the street, part of the Western Addition Area-2 urban renewal project.

**27. 709 Webster Street**
(c. 1885/SFS) This house has two rectangular bays. One is in the conventional position near the entryway, the other is on an angle in the corner of the building. This configuration is unusual for a home not on a corner lot.

**28. 717 Webster Street**
(1890/SFS)

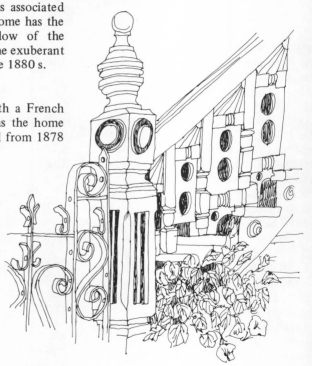

**29. 735-55 Webster Street**
(1876-77/IB; John Hinkel, OB)  Six more John Hinkel homes.

**30. 821-31 Fulton Street**
(c. 1895/QA)  Although different in size, these two homes share many details.

**31. 841 Fulton Street**
(c. 1895/C)  A funny conglomeration with both a half-round and a rectangular bay. Note the art glass transom, which shows that the house used to be number 815.

**32. 859 Fulton Street**
(c. 1885/SFS)  The same immense portico brackets can be seen at 1469-87 McAllister Street.

**33. 881-93 Fulton Street**
(1884/IB; Henry Geilfuss, A)

**34. 833-35 Fillmore Street**
(1895/QT, QA; Martens & Coffey, A) Two Queen Anne homes designed by Martens and Coffey, who produced many towered buildings throughout Victorian San Francisco.

**35. 915 Fulton Street**
(c. 1895/QT)  A spectacular bay of art glass.

**36. 921 Fulton Street**
(c. 1895/QT; Martens & Coffey, A)

*Bracketed portico,*
*859 Fulton Street (entry 32)*

*700 Broderick Street (entry 48)*

### 37. 908 Steiner Street
(1888/SFS) One of San Francisco's first multihued paint jobs, done around 1967. Originally the paint colors were much brighter, and above the portico was a ten-foot-long green papier-mâché alligator, which soon fell victim to the weather. More recently, the Sesame Street "Big Bird" head was added in the pediment of the entryway.

### 38. 910 Steiner Street
(c. 1895/QA) The gable has its own small round bay window.

### 39. 809 Pierce Street
(1894/QT; A. J. Barnett, A)

### 40. 1443-51 McAllister Street
(c. 1885/SFS) Three houses, two with their original false gables still intact.

### 41. 1463 McAllister Street
(1880/SFS) Another slanted bay window. Plaster cameo faces adorn the bay and the entryway.

### 42. 1469-87 McAllister Street
(c. 1885/SFS) Three of the original four are intact, with porticoes supported by huge brackets.

### 43. 1493 McAllister Street
(c. 1885/SFS) Double rectangular bay windows, with faces in the lower frieze panels.

### 44. 814-18 Scott Street
(c. 1885/SFS) The original ironwork fences remain.

### 45. 1198 Fulton Street
(1889/SFS; Henry Geilfuss, A) A visual landmark throughout the neighborhood, with its massive square lookout tower. One of the favorite "San Francisco Victorians" of tourists and residents alike.

### 46. 1214-60 Fulton Street
(1883/IB; Henry Geilfuss, A) Of the four, none is truly intact. A hint of Geilfuss detail can still be found on house 1216, which has an incised corner board.

### 47. 1255 Fulton Street
(c. 1895/QT)

### 48. 700-18, 701-11 Broderick Street
(1895/QT, QA; Cranston & Keenan, C) Fourteen houses in the most impressive cluster of Queen Anne homes left in the City. The sun face in the gable of house 707 looks like a later addition, but Cranston and Keenan used the same detail at 1550 Page Street in the Haight Ashbury neighborhood.

### 49. 905 Divisadero Street
(c. 1895/QT)

### 50. 924 Divisadero Street
(c. 1900/O) Look over the entryway to find a chubby demon face enmeshed in the plaster balcony of this Edwardian building.

**51. 1045 Divisadero Street**
(1901/0) This unusual home looks much like a Swiss chalet.

**52. 1690 Golden Gate Avenue**
(c. 1895/QT) The witch's cap on this towered home has been removed. Note the deeply carved floral decorative panels.

**53. 1671 Golden Gate Avenue**
(1894/O; Laver & Mullany, A) A unique house that illustrates the "Moorish" influence at work in the 1890 s.

**54. 1513-31 Golden Gate Avenue**
(1875/IB; The Real Estate Associates) A fine row of homes; only three of the ten have been stuccoed. Imagine how the neighborhood must have looked when these rows of false fronts and bay windows were a common sight.

**55. 1482 Golden Gate Avenue**
(1876/IB)

**56. 1400-12 Golden Gate Avenue**
(1884/SFS; John P. Gaynor, A) Owner William Sharon had all seven homes built for a total cost of $30,000.

**57. 1057 Steiner Street**
(1890/QT) Original owner D. B. Jackson is said to have built this structure as a boarding house.

**58. 1016 Pierce Street**
(1886/SFS; John W. Dooley, C)

**59. 1201 block of Scott Street**
Watch this block in years to come. It is part of the Beideman Place Historic Area. Many of the homes were moved here in 1974; they will all be renovated as a San Francisco Redevelopment Agency project, with the assistance of the Foundation for San Francisco's Architectural Heritage.

**60. 1830-34 Eddy Street**
(c. 1875/IB; The Real Estate Associates) A cluster of three, also part of the Beideman Place project.

**61. 1840 Eddy Street**
(c. 1885/SFS) This house was moved here in 1974 and renovated in 1977.

**62. 1900 block of Ellis Street**
(c. 1885/SFS) Enjoy the myriad redwood details as you look at these nine homes; the four clusters are the products of several different builders.

**63. 33-45 Beideman Place**
(c. 1875/IF)

*714 Broderick Street (entry 48)*

# PACIFIC HEIGHTS

In 1893, architectural critic Ernest Peixotto described the homes in Pacific Heights as "nightmares of an architect's brain . . . piled up without rhyme or reason—restless, turreted, loaded with meaningless detail, defaced with fantastic windows and hideous chimneys." Luckily the critics had as little influence then as now, for architects, contractors and builders continued to decorate the hills of Pacific Heights with mansions, flats and cottages.

For the purposes of this book, the Pacific Heights area is bounded by Geary Boulevard, Presidio Avenue, Broadway and Green Street, and Franklin Street. Pacific Heights has so many hundreds of Victorian-era houses that it has been divided into two walks, each organized around a public square, Alta Plaza and Lafayette Park. With so many homes to choose from, only those with new information about origin were included on the walks. Be sure to notice the many other fine examples of the era that abound in among the few that could be mentioned here.

## PACIFIC HEIGHTS WEST

**1. 1703-19 Broderick Street**
(1883/SFS, T; Charles Hinkel, OB) A transitional group. Seven houses have the five-sided slanted bay window associated with the Italianate style of the seventies, while two have the Stick rectangular bay of the eighties. All were built at the same time, however, and all have the exuberant, non-Classical embellishment associated with the 1880s. House 1707 was the first complete facade restoration done by San Francisco Victoriana. It was completed in 1973.

**2. 1609 Baker Street**
(1889/SFS; Michael J. Welsh, A)

**3. 2832 Bush Street**
(1895/QA; J. V. Hall, A)

**4. 2838-44 Bush Street**
(1884/IB; D. F. McGraw, OB) A cluster of two.

**5. 2850 Bush Street**
(c. 1885/SFS) San Francisco Victoriana restored the facade of this home in 1976. Originally its surface was covered with stucco.

**6. 2862 Bush Street**
(1886/SFS; D. F. McGraw, OB)

**7. 2891 Bush Street**
(c. 1896/QA) Note the "wrens' havens," the small holes that are part of the decorative treatment in the gable.

**8. 1652 Lyon Street**
(1885/IB; Michael J. Welsh, A)

**9. 2900-06 Bush Street**
(1892/QA; Soule & Hoadley, A) A cluster of four homes by this architectural firm.

**10. 2913 Bush Street**
(1878/IB)

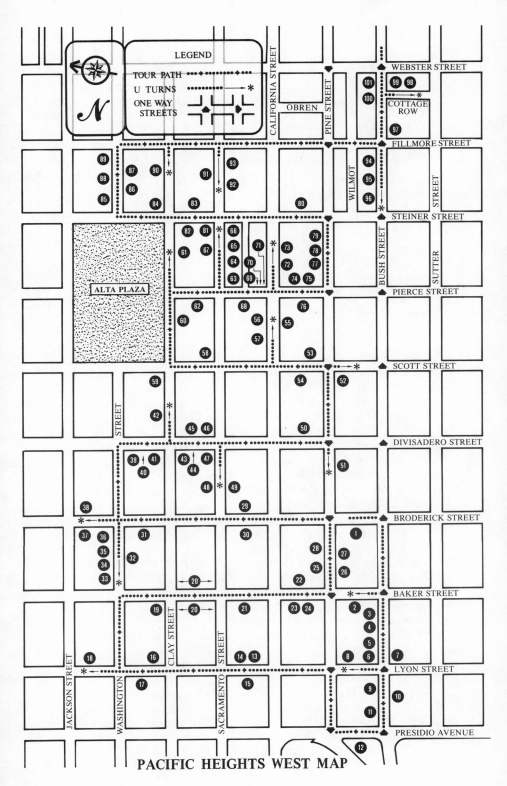

PACIFIC HEIGHTS WEST MAP

*Window with window shields
and a keystone,
1707 Broderick Street
(entry 1)*

### 11. 2908 Bush Street
(c. 1870/IF) The veranda on this home is unusual, as few City home builders offered them as an option to buyers. Perhaps this home was originally a farmhouse.

### 12. 655 Presidio Avenue
This building houses the San Francisco Fire Department Museum, which is operated by the department and the St. Francis Hook and Ladder Society. It contains a splendid collection of memorabilia and fire-fighting equipment from the Victorian era, including a display about Lillie Hitchcock Coit, who was made an honorary member of Volunteer Knickerbocker Company Number 5. Open to the public Wednesday through Sunday, 1 to 5 pm. For information about the tour schedule, call (415) 558-3949, Tuesday through Saturday, 9 am to 6 pm.

### 13. 1810-14 Lyon Street
(1882/T; George and Henry Hinkel, OB) A cluster of three transitional cottages combining slanted bays and the redwood detailing associated with the Stick style.

### 14. 1816 Lyon Street
(1882/T; George and Henry Hinkel, OB) A two-story version of the Hinkel cottages found in several Pacific Heights clusters.

### 15. 1817-19 Lyon Street
(c. 1885/SFS) Quite a startling misguided improvement was performed on these two homes, which have had their fronts completely stripped and modernized. Tiny clues to their origin can still be found on the sides, however.

### 16. 2006-10 Lyon Street
(1901/C; Daniel Einstein, C) These three homes are a combination of styles, with elements of Queen Anne, Colonial Revival and Shingle.

### 17. 2041 Lyon Street
(1889/SFS; Pissis & Moore, A) This square-towered villa was built for Charles W. Grant, who was listed as a clerk for the London and Liverpool Globe Insurance Company.

### 18. 2116 Lyon Street
(1893/C; Pissis & Moore, A) Another "combination" home, part Shingle style and part Colonial Revival.

### 19. 3100 Clay Street
(1897/QT; McDougall & Son, A)

### 20. 1905-13, 1902-06 Baker Street
(1882/SFS; William Hinkel, OB) Six cottages and two larger homes are in this cluster.

### 21. 1805-19 Baker Street
(1882/SFS; George and William Hinkel, OB) A cluster of six.

### 22. 1716 Baker Street
(1889/SFS; John Coop, D) Although this house looks unlike those in his clusters in

the Inner Mission, Coop's signature details can be found on the lower bay window.

**23. 1709 Baker Street**
(c. 1885/SFS; John Hinkel, OB)

**24. 1705-07 Baker Street**
(1885/SFS; Henry Geilfuss, A) A cluster of two.

**25. 2860 Pine Street**
(1887/SFS; D. F. McGraw, OB) Punctuated with several jaunty finials.

**26. 2823 Pine Street**
(1887/SFS) A huge flat bandsawn sunburst is in the middle of the bay window of this home.

**27. 2807-19 Pine Street**
(1883/SFS, T; Charles Hinkel, OB) Another cluster, part of the development around the corner in the 1700 block of Broderick Street. In this cluster of seven, Hinkel alternated rectangular and slanted bay windows, but used the same lavish wooden detailing on all the homes.

**28. 2832 Pine Street**
(1886/SFS; Charles Havens, A)

**29. 1916 Broderick Street**
(c. 1890/QT) A tent-shaped "pop-up" dormer window was added to the gable of this house. It is swagged with plaster embellishment like frosting on a child's birthday cake.

**30. 1919 Broderick Street**
(c. 1885/SFS)

**31. 2111-13 Broderick Street**
(1889/SFS; D. F. McGraw, OB) A cluster of two.

**32. 3021 Washington Street**
(1890/SFS; Huerne & Everett, A)

**33. 3074 Washington Street**
(1890/SFS) A riot of details: stars, circles, shingles and quoins.

**34. 3024-26 Washington Street**
(1886/SFS; George & Henry Hinkel, OB) A cluster of two.

**35. 3022 Washington Street**
(1893/SFS; Henriksen & Mahoney, A) Almost identical to the firehouse at 1152 Oak Street by the same architects. The building date in the pediment is encircled by a redwood firehose complete with coupling and nozzle. Official San Francisco Landmark Number 93. There are two good possibilities in front of this building for making rubbings: a large round star-studded "Enterprise Foundary" plate, and another one installed by the "S.F. Bowser and Co. Oil Storage System."

*1705-07 Baker Street (entry 24)*

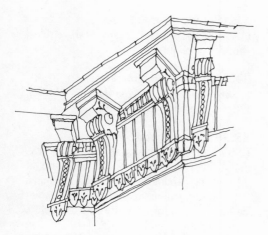

*Cornice brackets and a frieze band,*
*1805 Baker Street (entry 21)*

### 36. 3020 Washington Street
(1886/QT; W. Pluns, B) Although the *California Architect and Building News* attributes this house to Pluns, it is almost identical to a house designed by architect Henry Geilfuss at 2648 Bryant Street in the Inner Mission neighborhood.

### 37. 2203-07 Broderick Street
(1885/SFS) The middle house in this cluster of three has been altered almost beyond recognition as a Victorian building.

### 38. 2240 Broderick Street
(1885/SFS) Look up in the false gable to find the sunburst.

### 39. 2229-31 Divisadero Street
(1877/IB) Note how house 2229 has been altered, supposedly by architect Julia Morgan, who is said to have had its top floor chopped off to provide more light for her studio next door.

### 40. 2201, 2221 Divisadero Street
(1877/IB) These two were originally part of a cluster of four. Now they are separated by an apartment building.

### 41. 2900 Clay Street
(1880/SFS; E. Swain, A) From the side you can see the four three-dimensional colored glass windows in the renovated kitchen, which were designed and constructed by San Francisco artist-craftsman Bruce Sherman.

### 42. 2822-24 Clay Street
(1886/SFS) Note the sensitive remodeling of the lower floor of house 2822. It was converted into a garage, but the original opening proportions and much detail were left.

### 43. 2197 Divisadero Street
(1877/IB)

### 44. 2131 Divisadero Street
(1883/C) Perhaps the tower on this basically Stick-style house was added later, not unusual during the nineties.

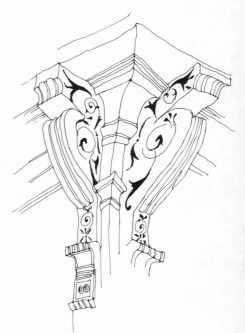

*Pierced-work cornice brackets,*
*2615 California Street (entry 5)*

*Queen Anne gables with finials, 2608 California Street (entry 56)*

**45. 2110-14 Divisadero Street**
(1891/C; W. H. Lillie, A) These two whimsical houses do not really fit into any style category, but seem almost like playful piecings together of odds and ends of detail.

**46. 2100 Divisadero Street**
(c. 1896/QT) Although the victim of a streamlining in the 1950s, this tower house retains its arched art glass windows in the entryway. Watch how the beveled glass catches the afternoon sun to splash the portico with color.

**47. 2101 Divisadero Street**
(1877/IB) The flagpole is a happy addition to the roof of this home.

**48. 2914 Sacramento Street**
(c. 1875/IB) San Francisco Victoriana rescued this house from its shingle covering in 1975.

**49. 2943-61 Sacramento Street**
(c. 1875/IB) A cluster of four cottages, two of which are intact and two "misguided."

**50. 1924 Divisadero Street**
(c. 1875/IB) Another facade restoration by San Francisco Victoriana, completed in 1975.

**51. 2719 Pine Street**
(c. 1885/SFS) This facade was remodeled by San Francisco Victoriana in 1974.

**52. 1806-10 Scott Street**
(1883/IB; Henry Geilfuss, A) A cluster of two.

**53. 2590 Pine Street**
(1885/SFS; John H. Littlefield, A)

**54. 1901 Scott Street**
(1870/IB) The Ortman-Shumate house is San Francisco Landmark Number 98.

**55. 2615 California Street**
(1889/QA; Schultze & Meeker, A)

**56. 2608-10 California Street**
(1881/SFS; S. & J. C. Newsom, A) The Queen Anne gables are said to have been a later addition to these two homes.

**57. 2660, 2664, 2678 California Street**
(c. 1885/SFS) Three different homes of the eighties, illustrating different gable treatments. Note especially the deep brooding quality of the gray gable of house 2660.

**58. 2100 Scott Street**
(1897/O) This Colonial Revival home was originally built for Frank W. Marvin.

**59. 2203, 2207 Scott Street**
(1885/SFS; George and William Hinkel, OB) Only two are left of a cluster of eight Hinkel homes.

**60. 2773-87 Clay Street**
(1890/SFS; D. F. McGraw, OB) These four exhibit some of the inventive variety possible using different combinations of millwork, "fancywork" and art glass.

**61. 2637-73 Clay Street**
(1875/IB, IF; The Real Estate Associates, D) A cluster of seven Italianate homes. The columned portico on house 2673 may be a later addition.

**62. 2123 Pierce Street**
(1888/T; Schmidt & Shea, A) This home combines some details of the Stick style with some of the Queen Anne.

**63. 2695 Sacramento Street**
(1894/QT; J. J. Manseau, A) Originally built for Gaston Bacon, the president of the California College of Pharmacy.

**64. 2687-91 Sacramento Street**
(c. 1895/QR) A cluster of two.

**65. 2625 Sacramento Street**
(1889/IB; John A. Shepard, A)

**66. 2601 Sacramento Street**
(c. 1885/SFS) This triple bay windowed home still has some wooden cresting on its porticoes.

**67. 2616 Sacramento Street**
(1874/IB)

**68. 2031-41 Pierce Street**
(1892/QA; Henry A. Schultze, A) Only four homes are left of Schultze's original cluster of nine.

**69. 2029-32 Pierce Street**
(1894/QA) A cluster of two.

**70. 2006-10 Pierce Street**
(c. 1875/IF) Compare these two somewhat plain flat-fronted houses with their more embellished neighbor next door.

**71. 2002 Pierce Street**
(1882/IF) Although the same basic house shape as its earlier neighbors, houses 2006 and 2110, this building carries some of the redwood "fancywork" that became popular during the 1880s.

**72. 2591 California Street**
(1877/IB)

**73. 2557-77 California Street**
(1878/IB) A cluster of four. House 2557 has a one-story lower bay of the five-sided slanted variety, topped by a pierced-work balustrade.

**74. 1918-32 Pierce Street**
(1877/IB; The Real Estate Associates, D) Four houses.

**75. 1900 Pierce Street**
(1886/QA; W. F. Smith, A)

**76. 1905-23 Pierce Street**
(c. 1880/IB) A cluster of five. House 1915 was restored by San Francisco Victoriana in 1973.

**77. 2428-34 Pine Street**
(1878/IB; The Real Estate Associates) Three of the four homes in this cluster are still intact.

**78. 2426 Pine Street**
(c. 1895/QA) Look closely at the plaster detail on the frieze band of this home; part of the band consists of cattails on their sides, stretching around the bay.

**79. 2424 Pine Street**
(1889/IB) The original owner of this building was Joseph Rhine, a salesman at Baker and Hamilton, importers and jobbers of agricultural implements.

*San Francisco Stick,*
*2773 Clay Street*

**80. 2030 Steiner Street**
(1884/SFS; Henry Geilfuss, A)

**81. 2231 Steiner Street**
(1874/IF)

**82. 2251 Steiner Street**
(c. 1885/SFS)

**83. 2204-08, 2242-44 Steiner Street**
(1873/IB) Five homes are left in this cluster, partially separated by an apartment building. House 2204 is another San Francisco Victoriana facade reconstruction, done in 1974.

**84. 2302 Steiner Street**
(1896/O; W. H. Lillie, A) This Colonial Revival home has the same plaster torch and wreath pattern that Lillie used when he designed the Queen Anne at 1701 Franklin Street.

**85. 2560 Washington Street**
(1879/IB) This Italianate has a mansard roof.

**86. 2561 Washington Street**
(1885/QT; Charles Geddes, A)

**87. 2527 Washington Street**
(1887/SFS; Huerne & Everett, A)

**88. 2548 Washington Street**
(1881/SFS; W. F. Smith, A) This home cost $4,500 when it was built for the first owner, Dr. O. V. Thayer.

**89. 2502-06 Washington Street**
(1879/IB; Henry Hinkel, OB) A cluster of two.

**90. 2524-36 Clay Street**
(1874/IB; Henry Hinkel, OB) A cluster of three. House 2524 was restored in 1977 by San Francisco Victoriana.

**91. 2530-38 Sacramento Street**
(1871/IB) Two houses of the same style and year, but with different details.

**92. 2519-21 Sacramento Street**
(1875/IB; The Real Estate Associates, D)

**93. 2509 Sacramento Street**
(1886/SFS; McDougall & Son, A)

**94. 2238 Bush Street**
(c. 1895/QA) This house front was reclaimed from its asbestos-shingle disguise by San Francisco Victoriana in 1975.

**95. 2250 Bush Street**
(c. 1880/IB) As was its neighbor, this home was covered with asbestos shingles until restored by Victoriana in 1975.

**96. 2256 Bush Street**
(1890/QA; William Curlett, A)

**97. 2115-25 Bush Street**
(1874/IF; The Real Estate Associates, D) Six houses; one of the nicest remaining clusters in the neighborhood. Peek around behind; these homes even have false fronts in the back.

**98. 1-6 Cottage Row**
(1882/O; John Nash, C) These simple cottages cost a total of $5,000 for all six, built for shipping merchant Charles L. Taylor.

**99. 2103-07 Bush Street**
(1874/IB) Three homes restored under the auspices of the San Francisco Redevelopment Agency.

**100. 2104 Bush Street**
(1884/SFS; Wolfe & Son, A)

**101. 2100-02 Bush Street**
(1883/SFS; S. & J. C. Newsom, A) A pair by the Newsom brothers, whose homes are sprinkled throughout Pacific Heights.

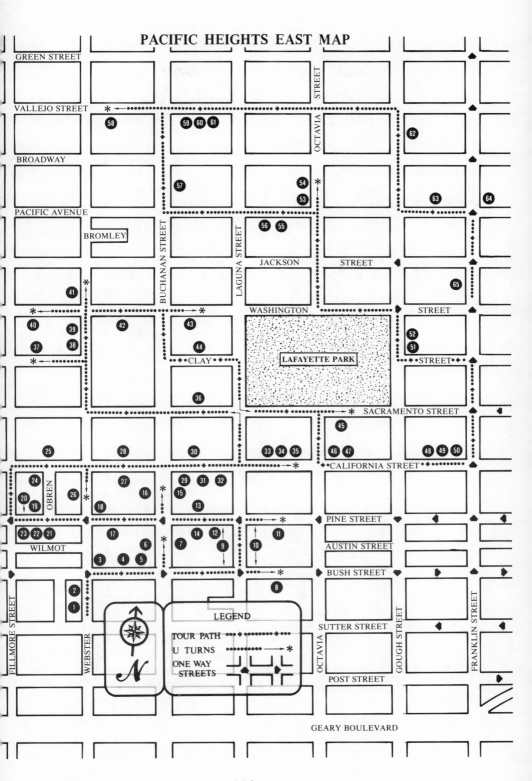

# PACIFIC HEIGHTS EAST MAP

GREEN STREET

VALLEJO STREET

BROADWAY

PACIFIC AVENUE

BROMLEY

BUCHANAN STREET

LAGUNA STREET

OCTAVIA STREET

JACKSON STREET

WASHINGTON STREET

CLAY

LAFAYETTE PARK

STREET

SACRAMENTO STREET

CALIFORNIA STREET

OBREN

PINE STREET

AUSTIN STREET

WILMOT

BUSH STREET

FILLMORE STREET

WEBSTER

SUTTER STREET

OCTAVIA

GOUGH STREET

FRANKLIN STREET

POST STREET

LEGEND

TOUR PATH ••••
U TURNS ••••••• *
ONE WAY
STREETS

N

GEARY BOULEVARD

*Portico detail and floral
decorative detail,
1737 Webster Street
(entry 1)*

## PACIFIC HEIGHTS EAST

### 1. 1737 Webster Street
(1885/SFS; S. & J. C. Newsom, A) This is one of the Western Addition homes restored under the auspices of the San Francisco Redevelopment Agency and the Foundation for San Francisco's Architectural Heritage. It was moved from 773 Turk Street in 1975.

### 2. 1717 Webster Street
(c. 1875/IF) The stately ornamentation on this Italianate home makes a good contrast to the riotous Stick-style decoration of the Newsom brothers' house next door at 1737 Webster Street.

### 3. 2070-76, 2088-94 Bush Street
(1877/IB; The Real Estate Associates, D) Two clusters, each with two homes.

### 4. 2018 Bush Street
(1878/IB) Rescued from a coating of stucco in 1977, when San Francisco Victoriana supplied a complete new facade.

### 5. 2006 Bush Street
(1852/O) This simple home is one of the oldest left in the City. It was owned by the family of San Francisco supervisor Charles Stanyan. Official City Landmark Number 66.

### 6. 1931 Buchanan Street
(1888/SFS; T. J. Welsh, A)

### 7. 1932 Buchanan Street
(1901/QA)

### 8. 1881 Bush Street
(1895/O; Moses J. Lyon, A) Originally this monumental structure was the home of Congregation Ohabai Shalome. It is scheduled for restoration in 1978-79 as Pacific Hall, a community performing arts center.

**9. 1801-65 Laguna Street**
(1889/SFS; William Hinkel, OB) One of the most intact clusters in San Francisco, which covers the entire length of the block, including the combined shop and residence at 1865. This row of eleven houses shows how Hinkel alternated rooflines, but built virtually the same house over and over with slightly different detailing. Especially dramatic are the two homes that are topped by small turrets.

**10. 1800-32 Laguna Street**
(1877/IB; The Real Estate Associates, D) Four of the houses in this group are intact, and two have been "misguided."

**11. 1911 Pine Street**
(1880/SFS; Wolfe & Son, A) The home of Captain Taylor, which was used on page 22 as an illustration of the research process in identifying Victorian homes.

**12. 2003-11 Pine Street**
(1889/SFS; William Hinkel, OB) Three homes similar to the row Hinkel built on the 1800 block of Laguna Street.

**13. 2018-66 Pine Street**
(1874/IB; The Real Estate Associates, D) These four homes show the irrationality of the numbering system used in some areas after the 1906 earthquake. Although the houses are adjacent, the numbers skip suddenly from the twenties to the sixties.

**14. 2017 Pine Street**
(1890/T; William Armitage, A) A combination of the styles of the eighties and the nineties.

**15. 2016-18 Buchanan Street**
(1885/SFS; Charles Devlin, A) These two homes cost a total of $6,700 when built for original owner C. Wrede.

**16. 2011 Buchanan Street**
(1878/IB) This home is easy to miss unless you peer up at its concrete perch.

**17. 2139 Pine Street**
(1890/SFS; Caspar Zwierlein, A) This home towers over its surrounding neighbors. Zwierlein used a checkerboard pattern of redwood decoratives as frieze panels on the two rectangular bay windows.

**18. 1900 Webster Street**
(1884/SFS; B. E. Henriksen, A) To learn the story of this home, designed on linen for Pierre B. Berge, turn to page 27.

**19. 2208, 2212 Pine Street**
(1877/IB) A flat-front Italianate is in between these two of the bay-windowed variety.

**20. 2210 Pine Street**
(1875/IF)

**21. 2231 Pine Street**
(1872/IF) An Italianate cottage.

*2218 Clay Street (entry 44)*

115

*2226 California Street (entry 28)*

### 22. 2255 Pine Street
(1880/IB; S & J. C. Newsom, A) The Newsom brothers added some uncommon flat-sawn decoratives to this home, which has had its portico amputated. Some of the embellishment resembles the cross section of an artichoke.

### 23. 2273 Pine Street
(1881/IB; Henry Hinkel, OB)

### 24. 2338-44 California Street
(1875/IB) House 2338 in this pair was owned for a while by Dr. Edward R. Taylor, lawyer, poet, and mayor of San Francisco from 1907 to 1910. In the rotunda of City Hall is carved the poem he wrote to celebrate the City's rise from the ashes of 1906.

### 25. 2307-11 California Street
(1876/IB) All three in this cluster were originally built for B. G. Allen.

### 26. 1931 Webster Street
(1895/O; Shea & Shea, A) This Colonial Revival house was the home of another of the City's mayors, Levi Richard Ellert, who served from 1893 to 1895.

### 27. 2217 California Street
(1890/SFS; John J. Clark, A)

### 28. 2226 California Street
(1885/SFS; Pissis & Moore, A) This house has a true mansard roof with dormer windows.

### 29. 2175-87 California Street
(1879/IB) A cluster of two Italianates.

### 30. 2174 California Street
(c. 1875/IB, O) Note the top floor of this three-story building. It must have been added during the "Edwardian" era, sometime around the turn of the century. Note the differences in detail, height, and window size between this and the two other floors.

### 31. 2165 California Street
(1882/SFS; McDougall & Son, A)

### 32. 2129 California Street
(1882/O; S. & J. C. Newsom, A) This home, with its profusion of playful details, is difficult to classify. Perhaps the Newsom brothers had a checkerboard in mind!

### 33. 2026 California Street
(c. 1890/SFS) An Egyptian face presides over the portico to this house, which has an uncommon "swell" bay window topped by the corner brackets associated with the Queen Anne style.

### 34. 2022 California Street
(c. 1880/IB) San Francisco Victoriana restored the columned portico and entry stairs to this house in 1977.

### 35. 2018 California Street
(1886/SFS)

### 36. 2212 Sacramento Street
(1895/O; Arthur Page Brown, A) This stately house was built in the Classical Revival style, which attained mild popularity during the 1890s.

### 37. 2448-60, 2472 Clay Street
(1880/SFS; Henry Hinkel, OB) Only house 2472 is intact in this group of four. Judging from the identical scalloped brackets in its cornice, the nearby store on the northeast corner of Clay and Fillmore is also a Hinkel product.

### 38. 2209-35 Webster Street
(1878/IB; Henry Hinkel, OB) Five houses in this cluster.

### 39. 2239-53 Webster Street
(1879/IB; Henry Hinkel, OB) These three houses are unusual for San Francisco because they share common, or party, walls.

### 40. 2405-61 Washington Street
(1888/SFS; Charles Hinkel, OB) Originally this cluster had eight homes, constructed for a total cost of $50,000. Now only one, house 2405, is intact.

### 41. 2311, 2315-21 Webster Street
(c. 1875/IB, The Real Estate Associates, D) Architect John A. Remer designed these five homes for the developers.

### 42. 2355 Washington Street
(1886/IB; S. & J. C. Newsom, A) The bloated mansard roof on this home is an example of the playful distortion of detail often found in houses designed by the Newsom brothers.

### 43. 2269-95 Washington Street
(1892/QT, O; W. H. Lillie, A) A rendering of these four homes appears in the May 1892 issue of the *California Architect and Building News*. Lillie was commissioned to design this group of four houses, each quite distinct from the oth-

ers, by the Rountree Brothers, the contracting firm that built the Lillie cluster on the east side of the 100 block of Lyon Street in the Haight Ashbury. This cluster demonstrates the way home building ideas were changing during the nineties. Although built at the same time, the houses are of different styles and are completely detached from one another. The corner building, house 2295, is barely recognizable as a Queen Anne with a tower, so much detail has been amputated. Some of the decorative shingles still remain, however, in the back of the house.

*Floral corner board,*
*2018 California Street (entry 35)*

117

## 44. 2218 Clay Street

(1890/QT; Samuel Newsom, A) Sorry evidence of the newest technique in misguided improvements. This handsome home by one of the Newsom brothers has been sprayed with a fuzzy layer of textured coating. It has the same moon gate horseshoe arch as 827 Guerrero Street, which Newsom remodeled in 1891.

## 45. 2015 Sacramento Street

(1891/SFS; Caspar Zwierlein, A)

## 46. 1990 California Street

(1881/QT; Moore Brothers, Charles Tilden, C) Look in the cornice of the original house, around the corner facing Octavia Street, for evidence of the work of the Moore Brothers, contractors who often worked with the Newsom brothers. They thoughtfully dated that part of the house by adding "1881." The front part of the house, the broad tower, and the clipped gable were added later, perhaps in 1882, when the June issue of the *California Architect and Building News* listed that contractor Charles Tilden made $3,000 worth of "additions to dwelling" for "Mrs. Atherton" on the corner of California and Octavia streets (see page 24). This is San Francisco Landmark Number 70.

## 47. 1976 California Street

(1883/IB; Schmidt & Havens, A) A $19,000 home originally, it exhibits an accumulation of eighties wooden detail on the basic Italianate form.

## 48. 1834 California Street

(1876/C) This building was originally designed for merchant Isaac Wormser. When gold miner John Coleman bought it in 1895, he remodeled the house, paying the architectural firm of Percy and Hamilton $3,750 to add the tower. San Francisco Landmark Number 53.

## 49. 1818 California Street

(1876/IB) San Francisco Landmark Number 55, the Lilienthal-Orville Pratt house.

## 50. 1701 Franklin Street

(1895/QT; W. H. Lillie, A) Landmark Number 54 completes this trio of Victorian mansions. The wreath and torch pattern on the plaster frieze band must have been a favorite of the architect, as it appears on several of his homes.

## 51. 2000 Gough Street

(1885/QA)

## 52. 2004 Gough Street

(1889/QT; T. C. Matthews & Son, A) The face of a weary demon can be found in the panel beneath the balcony of this home.

## 53. 2000 Pacific Avenue

(1894/QT; Henry Burns, A) This house has a stunning art glass window on the side facing Octavia Street. It has an arched top and is placed between two fluted pilasters with Ionic capitals.

## 54. 2405-15 Octavia Street

(1892/QA, QT; William Hinkel, OB) A cluster of five by this versatile builder, who was also responsible for the San Francisco Stick cluster on the west side of the 1800 block of Laguna Street.

## 55. 2019-23 Pacific Avenue

(1890/QT) A rare cluster of three Queen Anne tower houses.

## 56. 2027 Pacific Avenue

(1890/SFS; W. H. Wickersham, C) The entry door has a round window of beveled glass.

## 57. 2614-20 Buchanan Street

(1888/QT, QA; Charles Hinkel, OB) A varied group of four, three with towers and one without.

*Haas-Lilienthal house,*
*2007 Franklin Street (entry 65)*

**58. 2121-27 Vallejo Street**
(1890/O) Thus far the architectural magazine listings have yielded nothing about the origin of these two marvels, which look absolutely unlike any others left in the City. The water connection was turned on on June 24, 1890 by a person who signed only his last name, Wilford.

**59. 2065 Vallejo Street**
(1892/QT; Townsend & Wyneken, A) Mrs. Bertha Cellarius, the original owner, paid $7,875 to have this house built.

**60. 2059 Vallejo Street**
(1894/QA; Henry Geilfuss, A)

**61. 2053 Vallejo Street**
(1895/QT; J. C. Newsom, A)

**62. 2414-24 Gough Street**
(1895/QA, QT; George Hinkel, OB) Five houses are still left in this cluster.

**63. 1812 Pacific Avenue**
(1891/QT; Pissis & Moore, A)

**64. 1782 Pacific Avenue**
(1875/IB) The Talbot-Dutton house, San Francisco Landmark Number 57.

**65. 2007 Franklin Street**
(1886/QT; Peter R. Schmidt, A) The Haas-Lilienthal house, San Francisco Landmark Number 69. Now the home of the Foundation for San Francisco's Architectural Heritage. Heritage docents conduct regular tours of the house; for information, call (415) 441-3000.

*1990 California Street (entry 46)*

# Tours of Bay Area Victorians

The areas outside of San Francisco, thought of as largely rural by the Victorians, have lost many of their Victorian houses through modern development. Some treasure-troves of houses remain, however, and areas with relatively few remaining houses still have some that are important to anyone interested in Victorian architecture.

These tours are designed as walking-driving tours, and maps of the tours should be supplemented by a California state road map.

# ALAMEDA

*This section was written in collaboration with George Gunn, curator of the Alameda Historical Society.*

The development of Alameda began in 1851 when lawyer William W. Chipman and groceryman Gideon Auginbaugh bought the Encinal de San Antonio peninsula from Antonio Peralta for seven thousand dollars. Soon after, they sold half of it to six other investors. All parties agreed to a road running east and west, which became Central Avenue (the first north-south throughway was not constructed until 1878). In spite of such promotional efforts as free boat rides and watermelon lunches for prospective real estate clients from San Francisco and elsewhere, there was little building in the 1850s and 1860s. Three villages developed: Woodstock in the west end; Encinal, bounded by Santa Clara Avenue, Grand and Chestnut streets and the estuary; and the town of Alameda in the east end.

With the coming of the railroad era and the arrival of early capitalists (as they were called in the directories) such as E. B. Mastick, Charles Minturn, J. G. Kellogg, J. W. Dwinelle and A. A. Cohen in the mid-1860s, Alameda began to attract a substantial citizenry. A regular rail and ferry service from San Francisco to Niles, which ran through Alameda on Railroad Avenue (now Lincoln), began the network of transportation that was strengthened by Cohen's sale of his line to the Central Pacific in 1869. Construction of the South Pacific Coast Railroad in 1878 completed a system that linked Alameda to the whole East Bay and south to Santa Cruz, in addition to San Francisco.

The entrepreneurs who had made Alameda so convenient were, however, loathe to have it urbanized, hoping to preserve the peninsula as an area of large, tax-free estates. But accelerated real estate activity in the late 1870s clearly indicated another future for Alameda. Incorporated in 1872, the city was supplied with electricity in 1885 and, with the purchase of the Jenney Electric Company in 1890, became one of the first Bay cities to have a municipal power company. The commercial districts along Webster and Park streets prospered, while smaller commercial areas grew up around the railroad station stops. Today, Alameda retains most of its early street system with the vagaries of early platting still evident in the narrowness of Oak, Walnut and Willow streets, and in the changes in lot size from one tract to the next.

In the eighties and nineties Alameda had several prominent architects who had been attracted by the career possibilities in such a booming place. The degree of formal training these men had is a matter for conjecture. Many of them doubtless promoted themselves from builders to architects as the profession gained status. Nor do we know, at this time, who were the real designers. The names of Charles S. Shaner and Charles H. Foster are consistently connected with the practice of architectural design. Shaner was associated with a builder, Brehaut, in several buildings. Joseph A. Leonard appears to have had a complete office for architectural and building services as well as the means to acquire and develop his own tracts. Many substantial homes bear the name of A. W. Pattiani, who took pride in calling himself an architect. The offices of A. R. Denke and Marcuse and Remmels were particularly active in the designing and building of "modest dwellings."

Stylistic terms in the Victorian era were not standardized and were not applied to houses in a consistent fashion. George Gunn, an authority on Alameda history, reports that houses were described by a variety of names in the Alameda newspaper, *The Encinal,* in the years from 1879 to 1895. The earliest use of the term "Queen Anne" was in 1885; it was described as a "unique novel" style. Through the eighties the term "Elizabethan" was frequently used, but the most popular appellation was "Eastlake."

There is much work for architectural detectives in Alameda, but there is also much to simply enjoy. In spite of the sad curtailment of the south shore by fill and development, the city has preserved its nineteenth-century suburban setting to an enviable degree, and it is truly possible here to commune with the past.

**West End Alameda: Tour 1**
In the 1852 division of the Encinal peninsula, William W. Chipman kept 557 acres of the west end. Part of this land became the industrial town of Woodstock, containing an oil refinery and the Royal Soap Works. Webster was a principal commercial street, with smaller commercial centers around the South Pacific Coast Railroad stations on Central at Webster and Fifth. Residential tracts such as the Haight Tract and Damon's West End were built in the 1880s and 1890s. The most active architect-builders here were Marcuse and Remmels and A. R. Denke, whose office was on Webster. The most common house type was the Queen Anne one-and-a-half-story cottage, usually with a raised basement.

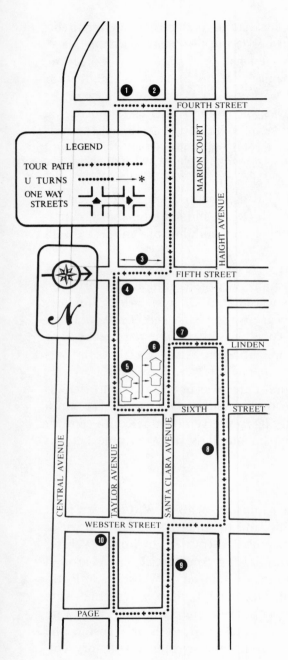

**1. 345 Taylor Street**
(c. 1890/QT) A Queen Anne house with tower in a relatively restrained style.

**2. 342 Santa Clara Avenue**
(c. 1895/QA; Marcuse & Remmels, AB) A richly detailed house. Note the lavish moon gate porch entrance.

**3. 5th Street between Santa Clara Avenue and Taylor Street, west side**
(c. 1888/QA) A varied row of Queen Anne cottages.

**4. 507 Taylor Street**
(c. 1895/QA; A. R. Denke, AB) Though the basement has been altered, the upper floor of this Queen Anne-"Eastlake" cottage has retained more of its decorative work than a similar cottage at 529 Santa Clara Avenue (entry 7). The gable composition with recessed window and rounded corners is typical of Denke's work.

**5. 545-47 Taylor Street**
(1893/QA; Marcuse & Remmels, AB) Back to back with similar cottages on Santa Clara, these two are good examples of the theme-and-variation styling of Marcuse and Remmels. One of the most active firms of the eighties and nineties, they specialized in one-and-a-half-story Queen Anne cottages whose facades resembled Victorian samplers in their rich decorative detail.

**6. 546-50 Santa Clara Avenue**
(c. 1895 /QA; Marcuse & Remmels, AB)

**ALAMEDA MAP TOUR 1**

**7. 529 Santa Clara Avenue**
(c. 1895/QA; A. R. Denke, AB) Denke's
designs featured a variety of shingle patterns and "Moorish" elements like the
corner composition here with keyhole
arches appliquéd with scrollwork.

**8. 614 Haight Avenue**
(c. 1895/QA) This type of Queen Anne
cottage with raised basement is found all
over the East Bay. Modest in cost, it may
very well have been a catalog design that
small builders used everywhere.

**9. 721 Santa Clara Avenue**
(c. 1895/QA; A. R. Denke, AB) Another
Denke design, similar to entries 4 and 7
but with a more generous porch.

**10. Webster and Taylor streets,
southeast corner**
(c. 1876/IB) Now a bar, this building formerly housed a well-known family resort,
Croll's, whose facilities included baseball,
boxing and rental cottages for the sports
fans. The remaining building, a bracketed
Italianate with a mansard roof, is a rare
example of a style that was common in
the seventies and eighties. Another example of the commercial buildings that
formerly lined Webster in the Victorian
era can be seen at Webster and Haight.

*548 Santa Clara Avenue (entry 6)*

**ALAMEDA MAP TOUR 2**

# North Side Alameda: Tours 2 and 3

The more industrial north side of Alameda, lacking a splendid bay view, developed a character different from the south shore. The majority of homes were relatively modest, though a few very large houses, evidently built on farm acreage, survive. The real treasure of the north side is found in the blocks of cottages, which are often embellished with as much ornament as the larger houses on the other side of town. Apparently the firm of Marcuse and Remmels was responsible for most of the cottages. Like most architects, however, they had imitators. Some designs that closely resemble theirs are not recorded under their name—a mystery that we leave to future detectives.

## ALAMEDA TOUR 2

**1. 1630 9th Street at Pacific Avenue**
(c. 1876/IB) A one-story cottage with a slanted bay and boldly scaled detail, particularly on the porch column capitals. Once the residence of a large farm, the house was one of several in this area with the same design.

**2. 930 Pacific Avenue**
(c. 1888/QT) A massive, shingled Queen Anne house. Notice the great front door with metal strap hinges.

**3. 934 Buena Vista Avenue**
(c. 1885/0) Although the Carpenter-Gothic styling of this cottage suggests an earlier building date, it is actually contemporary with the Queen Anne. The old-fashioned styling may have been used to create a "rustic farmhouse" look.

**4. Chapin Street and Pacific Avenue, northwest corner**
(c. 1876/IB) The density and character of the landscaping and the presence of some of the original outbuildings suggests that this house retains its original setting.

**5. 1500 block of Mozart Street**
(c. 1885-94/QA) A very interesting, well-preserved row of cottages. Houses 1549 and 1553 are by the same builder; house 1523 was designed by the Newsom

brothers for the builder Dennis Straub, and 1530-36 are by Marcuse and Remmels.

**6. 900 block of Santa Clara Avenue, south side**
(c. 1895/QA) House 924 is most notable for the elaborate two-story porch with latticework and elegant, curved porch entrance. The three cottages, 934-40, are by Marcuse and Remmels and have curved porch bracing.

**7. 1447 Ninth Street**
(c. 1876/IB) A good example of an Italianate cottage.

**8. 1430 St. Charles Street**
(c. 1885/0) A good example of a house style sometimes called "Galveston," with a second-story entrance and porch over a high basement. The style originated in frequently flooded areas.

**9. 1500 block of Verdi Street**
(c. 1895/QA) Houses 1548-56 constitute another stand of Marcuse and Remmels' extravaganzas. Across the street, house 1547 has elements that suggest the hand of A. R. Denke (see entries 4 and 9, Tour 1). House 1539 is unusual for its two-story veranda.

*1523 Mozart Street (entry 5, Tour 2)*

## 10. 1609-11 Bay Street
(1892/QA; Marcuse & Remmels, AB)

## 11. 1215-23 Pacific Avenue
(c. 1895/QA; Marcuse & Remmels, AB)
Three one-and-a-half-story cottages with lavish plaster foliate detail.

## 12. 1600 block of Sherman Street
(c. 1895/QA; Marcuse & Remmels, AB)
One of the most remarkable rows of cottages in Alameda.

## 13. Arbor Street and Pacific Avenue, northwest corner
(1889/QA; Joseph Leonard, AB) A unique cottage design by this famous Alameda architect and builder.

## 14. 1500 block of Benton Street, west side
(c. 1895/QA) A distinctive row of four miniature shingled "castles." At the other end of the block is a one-and-a-half-story cottage with a fine veranda.

## 15. 1430 Santa Clara Avenue
(c. 1895/QT)

## 16. 1402-10 Santa Clara Avenue
(c. 1885/O) A row of two-story, rectangular-bayed houses whose detail, particularly the gable brace, suggests a "Swiss Chalet." The gable brace also resembles "Eastlake" detail.

# ALAMEDA TOUR 3

## 1. 1724-34 Eagle Avenue
(c. 1895/QA) Though not recorded as such, these cottages resemble designs of Marcuse and Remmels.

## 2. 1908-12 Schiller Street
(c. 1895/QT) House 1908 is the same design, reversed, as 2125 Buena Vista. Both have fine plasterwork and tiny curving porches ending in peaked roofs so that the normally closed-in towers are abbreviated to elegant tokens. The spoolwork suggests lace curtains.

## 3. 1918-22 Lafayette Street
(c. 1895/QA; Marcuse & Remmels, AB) Decorative elements such as the sunbursts with ribboned rays and the "open fans" on these two cottages are used in a theme-and-variation manner all over Alameda.

## 4. 1917-19 Chestnut Street
(c. 1895/QA)

## 5. Chestnut Street and Pacific Avenue
(c. 1885/M) Around this intersection are a number of interesting buildings from the eighties and nineties. Houses 1916 and 1918 Pacific are well-restored Queen Anne residences; across the street on the corner, house 1919 is an Italianate that may have been built as a combined residence and store.

*1908 Schiller Street (entry 2, Tour 3)*

128

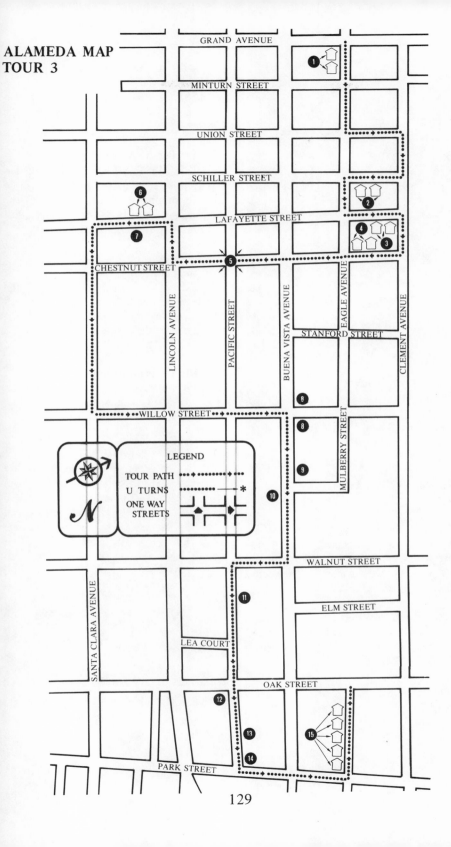

ALAMEDA MAP
TOUR 3

*2111 Buena Vista Avenue (entry 8)*

### 6. 1530-38 Lafayette Street
(c. 1895/QA) Two cottages, possibly by architect-builders Marcuse and Remmels.

### 7. 1525 Lafayette Street
(c. 1895/QA)

### 8. 2111, 2061 Buena Vista Avenue
(c. 1885/QA) Compare with 2149 and 2111 Central (entry 10, Tour 5).

### 9. 2125 Buena Vista Avenue
(c. 1895/QA) The twin of entry 2.

### 10. 2136-38 Buena Vista Avenue
(c. 1890/QA) An unusual Queen Anne cottage with a canted bay, perhaps copied from a published design by the Newsom brothers called an "Alameda."

### 11. 2225 Pacific Avenue
(1892/QT) A very large house with a grand veranda, possibly by architect-builder A. W. Pattiani.

### 12. Pacific Avenue and Oak Street, southeast corner
(c. 1885/C) An interesting house, perhaps an early Italianate remodeled in the 1880s.

### 13. 2325 Pacific Avenue
(c. 1885/QT) The former home of Dr. Ryen, this is an ample residence whose grounds originally included much of the surrounding land. It has been altered, but still preserves its "country villa" look.

### 14. Pacific Avenue and Park Street, northwest corner
(1885/IB) The J. C. Fossing store, the first brick store in Alameda. It has a residential scale and probably had living quarters for the owners on the second floor.

### 15. 2301-15 Eagle Avenue
(c. 1890/T) Five cottages moving from "Eastlake" to Queen Anne.

*2061 Buena Vista Avenue (entry 8)*

*Queen Anne gable with half sunburst,*
*1918 Lafayette Street (entry 3, Tour 3)*

*Queen Anne gable with full sunburst,*
*1922 Lafayette Street (entry 3, Tour 3)*

## South Shore Alameda: Tours 4 and 5

Alameda's shoreline has changed drastically since the Victorian era. When the south shore was developed, the bayside lots were the prime amenities. One of William W. Chipman's tracts, the Encinal Park Tract, was in the Weber Street area. Mrs. Caroline Chipman, later Mrs. Dwinelle, developed the tract after Chipman's death; Caroline Street commemorates her. An amateur pianist, she named streets for her favorite composers, Mozart, Weber and Verdi. Today the quiet streets ending on the south shoreline have few nineteenth-century houses, but pleasant lawns and street trees have created a parklike ambience that would have pleased the original residents. Franklin Park originally had several imposing mansions, which were destroyed when the park was expanded in the early twentieth century. Franklin School also replaced some fine homes. Still, the periphery of the park preserves its late nineteenth-century character.

## ALAMEDA TOUR 4

### 1. 1279, 1290 Weber Street
(c. 1895/QA) The first cottage is a potpourri of decorative detail salvaged from demolished houses by artist-owner Vince Perez. Note the roundel under the bay window. This ornament is normally used as a ceiling centerpiece. House 1290 was for many years the home of William F. Chipman, son of William W. Chipman, co-purchaser of Alameda. The house was built in 1893 for Peter Christensen. Modest in size, it has particularly elegant foliate ornament.

### 2. 1031 San Antonio Avenue
(1896/O; A. R. Denke, AB) For many years this was the home of one of Alameda's most prominent citizens, Major Tilden. The house was copied by Denke, at the owner's request, from one in San Francisco that was later destroyed in the 1906 fire. Its Classical Revival style was much more in tune with national fashions than most of the contemporary architecture in Alameda. Note, however, that the foliate frieze below the eaves is similar to those on Queen Anne houses.

### 3. 1100 block of Morton Street
(1890s/M) These four houses illustrate different levels of income. The towered Queen Anne at the corner of Encinal, and house 1124 across the street, were probably earlier and certainly were more costly than houses 1125 and 1120 on Morton, which are Queen Anne cottages with "Eastlake" detail. Perhaps land was sold off from earlier plots to build these cottages. House 1124 is by the architect-builder A. W. Pattiani, whose office designed many of Alameda's more expensive homes of the eighties and nineties.

### 4. 1117 Morton Street
(1891/QT; Charles S. Shaner, A/George Benseman, B) Shaner's designs show a sophisticated eye for the combination of architectural elements and detail. This house is notable for its visual unity and sparing use of ornament.

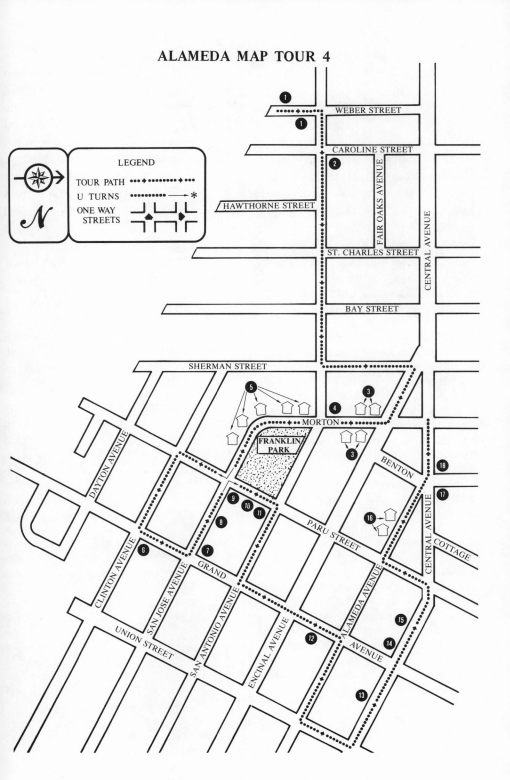

*1117 Morton Street (entry 4)*

### 5. 1000 block of Morton Street, west side
(c. 1890/QA) Houses 1023 and 1015 strongly resemble Pattiani's design at 1124 Morton with variations. House 1019 resembles designs by Marcuse and Remmels, but was built before 1890 when the firm was founded. Around the corner of San Jose and Morton are other notable houses with fine colored glass.

### 6. 900 Grand Street
(c. 1878-79/IB) One of Alameda's finest Italianate houses. The front porch and side bay are later stylistically and were added in the 1890s.

### 7. 1001 Grand Street
(1891/QA; Charles Shaner, A/Brehaut & Diamond, B) Shaner uses this bay-and-entrance composition on several of his Alameda houses, notably 2034 and 2103 San Jose. It borrows fake half-timbering and other detail from the Old English or Elizabethan style. Compare this house with 803 Grand.

### 8. 1615 San Jose Avenue
(c. 1895/QT) A large Queen Anne tower house using the same detail as the very large house at 1605 Clinton.

### 9. 1000 Paru Street
(c. 1890/QT) A very large Queen Anne tower house with boldly scaled detail.

### 10. 1018 Paru Street
(1890/QA) The "Moorish" corner suggests the hand of A. R. Denke.

### 11. 1602 San Antonio Avenue
(1889/SFS) A large house whose linear character, decorative elaboration of structural framing members and rectangular bays relate it to the San Francisco Stick style.

### 12. 1214 Grand Street
(c. 1885/QA) A miniature cottage with a graceful veranda and "Eastlake" detail.

### 13. 1724 Central Avenue
(1892-94/QT) Very probably the work of Ernest Coxhead, a famous Bay Area architect. The interior and exterior of the ground floor have been altered, but the entrance sequence is intact. Open to the public.

*1630 Central Avenue (entry 15)*

### 14. 1441 Grand Street
(c. 1897/QT) A towered Queen Anne open to the public.

### 15. 1630 Central Avenue
(1877/IB) Former home of railroad official John Anthony and one of the finest examples of the late Italianate style in the Bay Area.

### 16. 1524, 1532 Alameda Avenue
(c. 1885/SFS) Two good examples of the Stick style.

### 17. 1501 Central Avenue
(1894/QT; A. W. Pattiani, AB)

### 18. 1423 Benton Street
(1889/QT; Joseph C. Newsom, A) A large, rambling cottage by a prominent California architect. Some windows have been altered and some ornament removed.

*2103 San Jose Avenue (entry 22, Tour 5)*

## ALAMEDA TOUR 5

### 1. Union to Chestnut and Encinal to Clinton streets
(1890s/QA; Joseph A. Leonard, AB) This area was once known as Leonardsville after its developer, one of Alameda's most productive and well-known architect-builders. For the most part, Leonard designed in a massive Queen Anne mode with a very picturesque profile composed of complicated roof forms with gables and rounded towers, plus the usual balconies and verandas. A drive or walk around this area reveals numerous Leonard houses, some in groups like the splendid row of three at the end of Union in the 800 block, west side. The shingled house with tower at the end was Leonard's own home for a while. Note the rusticated stone basement. The roofline and tower have been sadly altered. Other fine houses are 1813, 1817 and 1832 Clinton, formerly the residence of Mr. Green Majors, and 1830 San Jose. Many

*2201-03 San Jose Avenue (entry 19, Tour 5)*

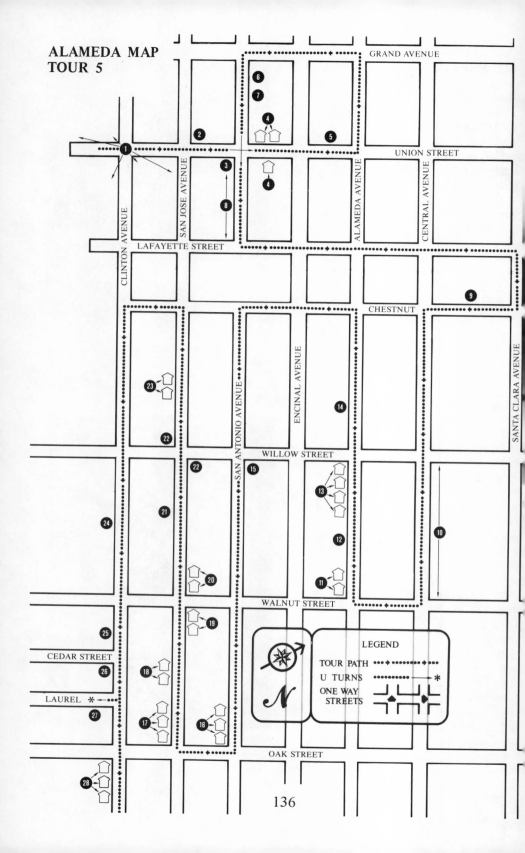

ALAMEDA MAP
TOUR 5

GRAND AVENUE

UNION STREET

LAFAYETTE STREET

CHESTNUT

WILLOW STREET

WALNUT STREET

CEDAR STREET

LAUREL *

OAK STREET

CLINTON AVENUE

SAN JOSE AVENUE

SAN ANTONIO AVENUE

ENCINAL AVENUE

ALAMEDA AVENUE

CENTRAL AVENUE

SANTA CLARA AVENUE

LEGEND

TOUR PATH ••••◆••••••••◆•••
U TURNS ••••••••••→ *
ONE WAY
STREETS

N

136

of Leonard's houses have been altered, stuccoed and otherwise disguised, but their silhouettes are nearly always recognizable. Like other architects, Leonard made use of elaborate decorative panels designed in triangular shapes for use in gables, and rectangular panels and friezes designed for other parts of the facade. A particular kind of scrollsawn strip, resembling a rippling ribbon and used in sunbursts and fan shapes, seems to have been a favorite, along with flat foliate patterns that fill gabled porch entrances and wind around towers.

### 2. 1021 Union Street
(c. 1893/QT) Compare this house with entry 5.

### 3. 1024 Union Street
(1890/QA; A. W. Pattiani, AB)

### 4. 1119-17, 1118 Union Street
(c. 1895/QA) The two cottages resemble the work of Marcuse and Remmels, but are not recorded as such. The cottage with the candle-snuffer tower is the same

*2165 San Jose Avenue (entry 20)*

design as 1908 Schiller and 2125 Buena Vista (entries 2 and 9, Tour 3). Across the street, 1118 may be by A. R. Denke.

### 5. 1209 Union Street
(1893/QT) A large towered villa very similar to 1021 Union and 2153 Central (entries 2 and 10) but with elements of the plans reversed. The three houses may have been designed by Charles Shaner working with the builder-contractor Brehaut, or by Charles Foster.

### 6. 1717 San Antonio Avenue
(1877/O) Designs with this kind of gable brace made of wood pieces turned like furniture legs were often described as "Swiss Chalets." Presumably the heavy framing was considered rustic or typical of alpine design.

### 7. 1721 San Antonio Avenue
(c. 1888/QA) A Queen Anne with "Eastlake" elements.

### 8. 1812-34 San Antonio Avenue
(c. 1895/QA) Eight houses, possibly by Joseph Leonard.

*876 Laurel Street (entry 27)*

**9. 1425 Chestnut Street**
(c. 1885/SFS) This house may have once been part of a row. In any case, it resembles the SFS rowhouses that were common in San Francisco in the 1880s.

**10. 2100 block of Central Avenue, northeast side**
(c. 1890/M) A block of fine houses, possibly by Charles Foster or Charles Shaner, or both. Houses 2105 and 2111 are in the Elizabethan or Old English mode, as is house 2149. Next door to 2149 is house 2145, which is in a deliberately rustic mode. House 2153 should be compared with entry 5.

**11. 2158-60 Alameda Avenue**
(c. 1895/QA) Two houses, possibly by Marcuse and Remmels.

**12. 2128 Alameda Avenue**
(c. 1895/QA) A substantial cottage with an ample front porch completely appliquéd with lacy ornament.

**13. 2102-08 Alameda Avenue**
(c. 1885/O) Four houses with "Eastlake" gable braces. These might have been called "Swiss Chalets."

**14. 2044 Alameda Avenue**
(c. 1870-80/SFS) Now converted to apartments, this house is the result of a succession of remodelings that expanded it from a small cottage. Mr. Siegfried, the original owner, was an Alameda tea merchant.

**15. 2105 San Antonio Avenue**
(1893/QA; Charles Foster, A) A remarkable house like the two in entry 22.

**16. 2250-58 San Antonio Avenue**
(c. 1895/QA) Three particularly elaborate designs that belong in the "can you top this?" category.

**17. 2250-54 San Jose Avenue**
(c. 1895/QA) These houses may be by architect-builder A. W. Pattiani.

**18. 2212-14 San Jose Avenue**
(c. 1888/QA) Two Queen Anne cottages with "Eastlake" detail.

**19. 2201-03 San Jose Avenue**
(c. 1895/QA)

**20. 2165-69 San Jose Avenue**
(c. 1895/QT, QA) A large Queen Anne tower house next to a cottage with "Eastlake" detail.

**21. 2122 San Jose Avenue**
(c. 1895/QA) This house may be by A. W. Pattiani or Joseph Leonard.

**22. 2103, 2070 San Jose Avenue**
(1891, 1893/QA; Charles Shaner, A) These two houses are among the finest Alameda has to offer. Their exuberant designs and display of ornament are unsurpassed. Just imagine whole streets of these fantasies and you will have an idea of what Victorian Alameda was like.

**23. 2034, 2020 San Jose Avenue**
(c. 1890/QA; Charles Shaner, A)

**24. 2104 Clinton Avenue**
(1885/QT; Nils Quist, B)

**25. 2162 Clinton Avenue**
(c. 1890/QA) Compare the bay window detailing of this house with entry 5.

**26. 2228 Clinton Avenue**
(c. 1895/QA) A particularly lacy cottage.

**27. 876 Laurel Street**
(c. 1895/QA) Elegant spoolwork in a fine two-story veranda with a moon gate. This house may be by Joseph Leonard.

**28. 2300-06 Clinton Avenue**
(c. 1895/QA)

*2070 San Jose Avenue (entry 22, Tour 5)*

# East End Alameda: Tour 6

The original town site of Alameda was in the east end of the peninsula. Remnants of its nineteenth-century past consist of a few commercial buildings and the former Masonic Temple at the corner of Park Street and Alameda Avenue, designed in the Romanesque style by C. F. Mau in 1891. As much of the interior is original, it would be a worthy restoration project. Just off Park Street on Santa Clara is the city hall, completed in 1896 according to the Romanesque design of Percy and Hamilton. The earthquake-damaged tower was removed in 1906. Fernside, the great estate of A. A. Cohen, bordered by High Street, Versailles Avenue, Santa Clara Avenue and the north shore, limited development in this area until the twentieth century.

**1. 1193 Park Avenue West**
(c. 1885/O) A large house in the Old English or Elizabethan style.

**2. 1206, 1240-44 Broadway**
(c. 1890, QA) House 1206 was designed by C. H. Foster; the other two may also be his work.

**3. 1412-16 Broadway**
(1887-90/O; C. S. Shaner, A) House 1412 was the architect's own home. Note the very elaborate ornamental plasterwork. In general, the design reflects the Old English or Elizabethan style.

**4. 2701 Santa Clara Avenue**
(c. 1895/QA)

**5. 1547 Versailles Avenue**
(c. 1880/T) A late Italianate house with "Eastlake" detail, perhaps a late farmhouse style. The house next door was moved here from Regent Street and San Jose Avenue in the 1880s.

**6. 2700 Central Avenue**
(c. 1889/QA) A larger-than-usual cottage with rustic detail.

**7. 1238 Versailles Avenue**
(c. 1855/O) One of the very rare examples of a once-prevalent cottage type. The central hall plan with front veranda and the high peaked roof with central gable and scrollsawn bargeboards are hallmarks of the Carpenter-Gothic style.

**8. 2900 block of Lincoln Avenue**
(1890s/QA) This block was part of Johnson Tract, which was developed by Alexander Johnson and other builders during the nineties. Houses 2904 and 2912 Lincoln Avenue were built by Alexander and William A. Johnson in 1889. The two Carpenter-Gothic farmhouses at 2905 and 2926 Lincoln Avenue, though in an earlier style, were actually built in the 1890s. Possibly this style was associated with rural living far from downtown. House 2929, which has particularly fine spoolwork on the porch, was built in 1891 by William Burges.

**9. 3200 block of Garfield Avenue**
(c. 1890/QA) A fine block of well-decorated one-and-a-half-story cottages.

**10. 3241 Encinal Avenue**
(c. 1890/QA) Note the porch.

**11. 3206-18 Encinal Avenue**
(c. 1890/QA) These cottages were built for conductors on the South Coast Pacific railway.

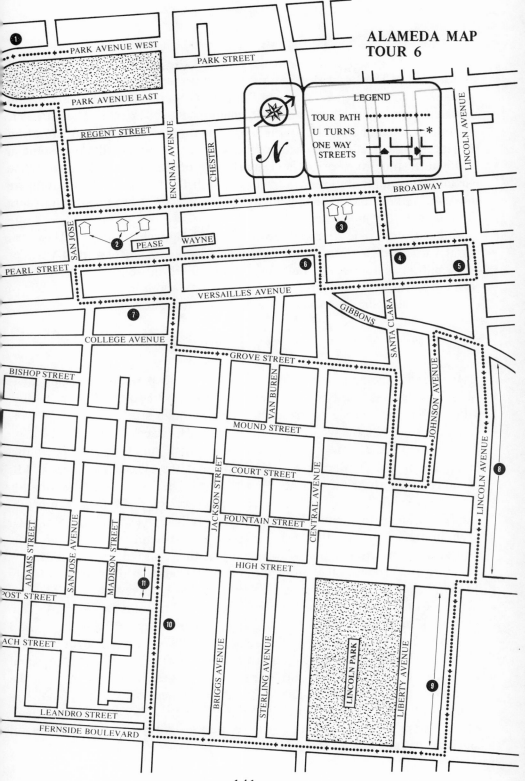

ALAMEDA MAP
TOUR 6

LEGEND

TOUR PATH ••••••••••••

U TURNS ••••••••••••*

ONE WAY
STREETS

141

# HAYWARD AREA

At the end of Hampton Road in Hayward is a municipal park that is all that remains of the once-great estate of William Meek, one of the pioneers of the fruit-packing industry in the West. Thompson and West's *Atlas* of 1878 shows the Italianate villa, built about ten years earlier, with a formal carriage drive, landscaping and outbuildings. Today the villa and some of the landscaping survives. The Department of Parks and Recreation has substantially altered the ground floor porch for its use, but what remains has great style, and a picnic on the grounds evokes images of what must have been a very gracious life.

On the other side of the freeway is the McConaghy home, on Hesperian Boulevard next to Kennedy Park between Bockman Road and A Street. This substantial Queen Anne farmhouse, built in 1886, has been refurbished by the Hayward Area Historical Society and is open to the public on Saturdays and Sundays from 1 to 4 pm, for a modest charge.

## OAKLAND

Before 1850 the area now called Oakland had no permanent settlers. The land had been granted by the Mexican government to the Peralta family, who grazed their herds of cattle in the grassy fields studded with venerable live oak trees. In the year 1850 three men—Horace W. Carpentier, Edson Adams and A. J. Moon—disturbed the rural quietude by becoming squatters on the Peralta land in the hope that the Mexican grant would be invalidated by the United States government. These men were described in Thompson and West's 1878 *New Historical Atlas of Alameda County* as "decisive, far-seeing men, who unquestionably had an especial care for their own interests, but in that particular were not distinguished above most Americans who sought their fortunes upon this coast in 1849 and 1850."

By 1852 Carpentier had enough political influence in the state legislature to bring about incorporation of the area, which he asked General Mariano Vallejo to name. Since "the Encinal" was the name already in use, Vallejo proposed its English translation, Oakland, which was accepted. In 1853 Oakland was platted by Julius Kellersberger, a Swiss-born surveyor and city planner. The new city extended from Lake Merritt to Market Street and from the Estuary to 14th Street. Broadway, then called Main, was the principal street. On either side of Broadway some blocks were planned as public squares. By 1868, when Dr. Samuel Merritt became mayor, these squares were planted and fenced in as parks. Today Lafayette, Jefferson and Madison squares remain.

*Moss Cottage, Mosswood Park, Oakland*

As the parks became community gathering places, palm trees, a great nineteenth-century favorite, were added to the original oaks. Later, Jack London came to Lafayette Park to lecture about socialism, and Isadora Duncan danced there. The decade of the 1860s witnessed the beginning of a boom that accelerated in the 1870s and 1880s. Daily service by railroad and ferry to San Francisco began to lure city dwellers to Oakland by the mid-sixties. Gas lamps were installed along Broadway, 8th Street and Telegraph Avenue in 1867. Horse car service began in 1873; a community water system began about 1876. The biggest event was the coming of the transcontinental railroad in 1869. The location of the terminal at Oakland appeared to settle the city's destiny as Queen of the West Coast. Population had increased from 1,543 to 10,000 in the 1860s; by 1880 the number reached 35,000.

As houses, churches and public buildings went up on all sides, the stands of oaks diminished. The wide streets of the original plat were tree-lined because of an 1852 shade tree ordinance requiring the planting of trees, but pepper and palm trees became as familiar as oaks. By 1860 Oakland was considered too urban for the College (later the University) of California, which relocated itself in the more "wholesome" setting of Berkeley. Increasingly the outskirts of town changed from rural landscape to formalized settings for estates of the prosperous. One of the few that survives was built in 1864 for J. Mora Moss, a San Francisco "capitalist." Designed by a San Francisco architect, S. H. Williams, it is the finest remaining example in northern California of the Gothic Revival cottage, popularized in the pre-Civil War period by the widely published writings of Alexander Jackson Downing of New York. Grand houses in this style were once prevalent around the Bay. Moss Cottage, as it is now called, is owned by the Department of Parks and Recreation and is located in Mosswood Park between Broadway and Telegraph Avenue at MacArthur Boulevard.

Farther out Broadway between the intersections of Pleasant Valley Road and College Avenue, on the campus of the California College of Arts and Crafts, is Treadwell Hall, formerly the Treadwell house of 1883, and one of the best remaining examples of an eighties house with a strong "Eastlake" character. It was designed by Clinton Day.

By the 1890s Oakland proper was solidly built. Italianate villas stood next to houses of the 1880s with their more intricate decoration. The 1890s brought the great towered Queen Anne villas, which were more spacious in Oakland than in San Francisco because of the generally larger lot sizes. Multiple dwellings began to appear as the city population increased although single-family cottages were still the mainstay of the real estate market.

*1125 12th Street (entry 7, Tour 1)*     *1034 10th Street (entry 10, Tour 1)*

Although Oakland has experienced an incalculable loss in its nineteenth-century heritage, enough remains today to astonish the beholder, as the following tours will reveal.

### Oak Center/De Fremery Park: Oakland Tour 1

The present De Fremery Park in Oak Center is what remains of the nine-acre De Fremery estate, which was known as The Grove because of its stand of coastal live oaks. Originally it extended from 14th Street to 22nd Street and from Adeline Street to Kirkham Street; today it is bounded by 18th and 16th streets and Adeline and Poplar streets. Around the park is the Oak Center Redevelopment area, a once-great nineteenth-century neighborhood urban-renewed almost out of existence in the 1960s. Pockets of old houses remain, many with misguided improvements such as aluminum frame windows and stucco finishes. But careful rehabilitation is also in evidence, and the next ten years may tell a different story.

145

# OAKLAND MAP TOUR 1

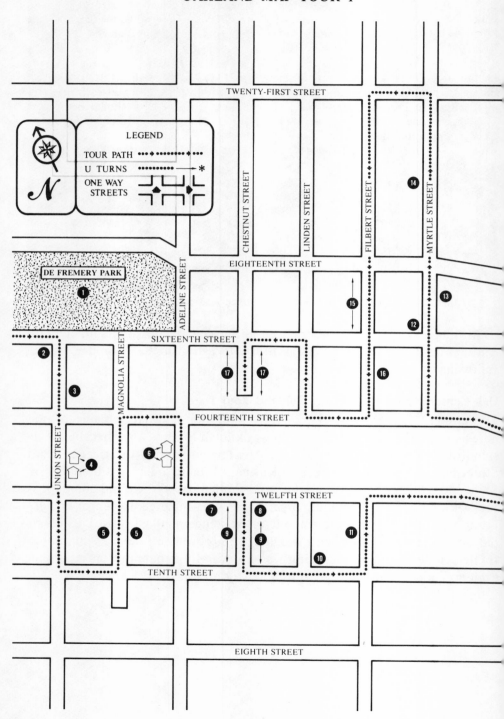

**1. The De Fremery House, De Fremery Park**

(1860 or 1867/T; James de Fremery, OB)
The De Fremery house was built in either 1860 or 1867 and was probably the first in the area. It is almost certainly the oldest surviving structure of its size in the city. James de Fremery, the owner and builder, was one of the founders of the Savings Union, the first legally organized bank in California, which opened in 1862. James, a Dutch immigrant, arrived for the Gold Rush in 1849. His brother, William Casparis Bastiaan de Fremery, arrived in 1854 and became the first man to pack California fruit for out-of-state shipment. He later engaged in the wine trade. In 1907 the family gave this house and grounds to the city.

The style is transitional, combining the high-peaked central gable, the front veranda and narrow clapboard siding of the Gothic Revival style with the paired brackets and Tuscan porch columns of the Italianate villa. The front two-story section is probably older than the rear wing. The interior has its original doors and doorframes, baseboards, plaster moldings and ceiling rosettes. The stairway and at least six marble, metal or carved wood fireplace mantels remain.

**2. 1527 Union Street**
(c. 1895/QA)

**3. 1430 Union Street**
(c. 1880/IB)

**4. 1228, 1222 Union Street**
(c. 1895/QT) Two very nice cottages with towers.

**5. 1022, 1103 Magnolia Street**
(c. 1895/QA)

**6. 1231, 1223 Adeline Street**
(c. 1890/QA)

**7. 1125 12th Street**
(c. 1895/QA) Very like the work of Marcuse and Remmels in Alameda.

**8. 1085 12th Street**
(c. 1880/IB) An unusual Italianate cottage with bay windows on each side of a central entrance. For similar houses see 1451 12th Street and 1141 11th Street.

**9. 1000 block of Chestnut Street**
(1885-95/M) A mixed block; notice houses 1022 and 1025 in particular. The cottages with front yards and fences on the even-numbered side of the street have the quiet country character for which Oakland was noted in the late nineteenth century.

**10. 1034 10th Street**
(c. 1880/IB) An Italianate cottage.

**11. 1101 Filbert Street**
(c. 1890/QA)

**12. 954 16th Street**
(c. 1875/IB) One of Oakland's finest remaining Italianate town houses, originally the Canning home. It should be compared to the Camron-Stanford house on Lake Merritt (see Oakland Tour 4).

**13. 1626 Myrtle Street**
(c. 1890/QA)

**14. 1901 Myrtle Street**
(c. 1890/QA)

**15. 1600-1700 block of Filbert Street**
(c. 1885-95/M)

**16. 1510 Filbert Street**
(c. 1890/QA)

**17. 1400-1500 block of Chestnut Street, west side**
(c. 1880-95/M) A mixed block of cottages and houses rehabilitated by Redevelopment Agency standards.

## Prescott: Oakland Tour 2

Point Oakland, as Prescott was originally called, was once Oakland's westernmost point. At that time it was an area of country residences for retired public servants from San Francisco. Bounded by the Bay and the Central Pacific Railway to the south and the Northern Railway to the northwest, the area had convenient transit to other parts of the Bay Area as well as to the East Bay centers served by the 7th Street Local, operated by the San Francisco and Oakland Railway. By the mid-1880s the area was fully developed, with thirty percent to forty percent of its residents employed by the Central Pacific.

Today, much of Prescott is badly deteriorated. The former railroad boundaries have been replaced by the United States Naval Supply Center and the Oakland Army Base, and State Highway 17 is a formidable eastern boundary completing the isolation of this precinct from the rest of town. Yet this area remains Oakland's oldest more or less intact Victorian neighborhood, with unique capabilities for rejuvenation. A drive around the district bounded by Wood, 8th, Center and 14th streets reveals many blocks of notable houses from the 1870s and 1890s, and a few houses that, stylistically, suggest the 1860s. The following houses and blocks are outstanding:

**1200 block of Wood Street** Queen Anne cottages, built around 1895.

**800 block of Wood Street, west side** A mixed block with good Italianate cottages.

**1700 block of 8th Street, south side** Italianates with flat fronts and bay windows, built around 1875.

**1026 Willow Street** A flat-front Italianate built around 1875.

**1100-02, and the 1200 block of Campbell Street** Queen Anne cottages, built around 1895.

**1000 block of Peralta Street, east side** The most stately section of Prescott, this is a mixed block with several fine bay-windowed Italianates from the 1870s.

**1000 block of Chester Street** A mixed block with a good row of 1890s houses toward the north end, east side.

**1000 block of Center Street** Houses 923 and 935 are unusual types whose simplicity suggests a date around 1870 or earlier; 1011, 1015 and 1019 are unusual Queen Anne cottages.

On the other side of 76th Street, in the area bounded roughly by Center, Peralta, and 1st streets, is a stand of cottages probably built by the Western Pacific Railroad for company employees (the Western Pacific succeeded the San Francisco and Oakland Railroad on the 7th Street corridor).

## Central Oakland: Tour 3

Much of central Oakland resembles a battlefield that nature has begun to reclaim. The sweeping areas of grassland are the product of the City Center Redevelopment Project. That other great destroyer, the Federal Highway Program, threatens many of the remaining structures that, unless moved, will be destroyed for the Grove-Shaftner Freeway. There is hope, however, that a remnant of this once-fine residential area will be preserved in Preservation Park, which is bounded by 14th, Grove, 11th and Castro streets. Several structures are already in the area; vacant lots could provide relocation sites for threatened buildings from surrounding blocks.

Other interesting houses are scattered throughout this area. Notable clusters are found near the intersection of 15th and Brush streets and on 17th Street between Castro and Grove streets. To the north the area becomes triangulated because of the intersections of Grove Street and San Pablo Avenue. Here too the persevering tourist will find pockets of the nineteenth century that are worth exploring.

*Pardee house, 672 11th Street (entry 10)*

149

# OAKLAND MAP TOUR 3

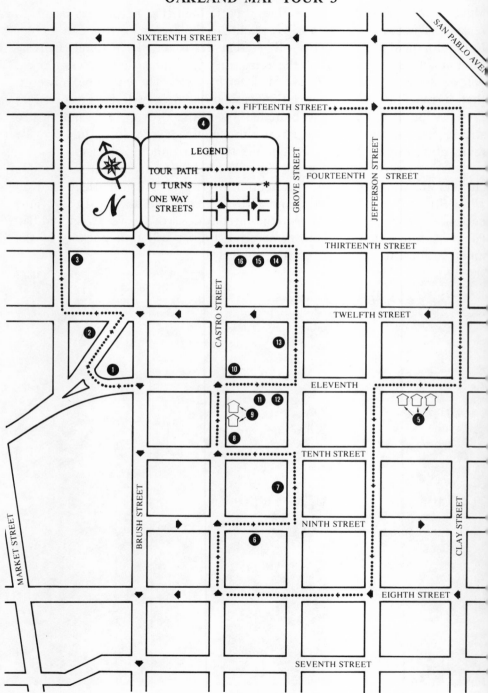

**1. 782-89 11th Street**
(c. 1880/IB)

**2. 782 12th Street**
(c. 1890/QA)

**3. 1228 West Street**
(c. 1895/QA) Notice also the cottage across the street.

**4. 1425 Castro Street**
(c. 1880/IB) The William H. Quinn home, which has been recommended for removal to Preservation Park.

**5. 571, 575, 583 11th Street**
(c. 1880/IB)

**6. 669 9th Street**
(c. 1865/O) A Carpenter-Gothic cottage that has clearly been raised a story—notice the difference in the siding—to accommodate garages. It is typical of the very early houses shown in lithographic views of Oakland.

**7. 905 Grove Street**
(c. 1890/QA)

**8. 696 10th Street**
(c. 1890/QA)

**9. 1014-16 Castro Street**
(c. 1890/QA)

**10. 672 11th Street**
(1868/I) One of the most intact of Oakland's much-diminished number of stately residences, this Italianate villa with a central hall plan, bracketed hip roof and central tower, is a very correct version of a house type that spread across the country in the mid-nineteenth century. Such features as the quoins, the paired, round-headed windows and the broken-pedimented gables were standardly found on this house design. Another hallmark is the scoring of the horizontal wooden siding to imitate courses of stone. This was the home of George Pardee, mayor of Oakland in 1893 and governor of California from 1902 to 1907.

**11. 663 11th Street**
(1885/QT)

**12. 653 11th Street**
(1885/IB)

**13. 1119 Grove Street**
(c. 1895/QA)

**14. 654 13th Street**
(1880/T) A transitional house whose rectilinear elements are more typical of the San Francisco Stick style of the 1880s than the Italianate style. The house was owned by Pierre Remillard, whose family began Oakland's first brick industry in the 1860s.

**15. 660 13th Street**
(1890/O; A. Page Brown, A) A rare house by the prominent San Francisco architect who designed the Ferry Building. The style reflects the English Arts and Crafts Movement associated with William Morris and others.

**16. 672 13th Street**
(c. 1895/QT )

**17. 682 13th Street**
(c. 1880/IB)

At 5th Street between Jefferson and Clay streets is the Bret Harte Boardwalk, an early Oakland preservation project. The Boardwalk consists of several Italianate houses owned by Jan and Paul Mills. Built in 1870, the houses were rehabilitated and opened for commercial use in 1962. For many years this bright yellow island in the gloomy shadow of the freeway has offered encouragement to others to preserve and restore the city's architectural heritage. Although Bret Harte did not actually live in this block, he did reside nearby for a time with his stepfather, Colonel Andrew Williams, and doubtless knew the area well as a substantial residential district, unscarred by a freeway wall.

*Bret Harte Boardwalk, Oakland*

**Lake Merritt and Madison Square: Oakland Tour 4**

On the corner of Lakeside Drive and 14th Street is the Camron-Stanford house, sometimes referred to as the "Lady of the Lake." Built in 1876, it is one of the finest examples of the Italianate villa in the Bay Area. If the past could be recreated, this fine house might seem relatively simple and restrained by comparison with the larger and grander estates that once occupied the lake shore. The house was built for the Camron family, who sold it after four years to David Hewes, the supplier of the solid gold spike that joined the transcontinental railroads. The next occupant was Josiah Stanford, brother of Leland. There was only one other private owner, Captain John T. Wright, before the city purchased the house for a public museum in 1907. When the present Oakland Museum was built in 1969, the Camron-Stanford house was vacated. For a time it seemed that its story would have an unhappy ending, but in the fall of 1976 a grant from the National Endowment for the Humanities bolstered the efforts of the Camron-Stanford House Preservation Association, which since 1971 had been working and raising funds for its restoration. When the restoration is completed, the house will serve as a resource center for the study of Oakland's history—a happy ending indeed.

South of Lake Merritt around Madison Square are more enclaves of nineteenth-century houses. On 7th Street, between Jackson and Oak streets, are several fine Queen Anne cottages all obviously built from the same design. In the 700 block of Oak Street is a row of exceptionally fine Queen Anne town houses. On the north side of Madison Square at 138 and 144 9th Street are two unusual houses with a strong "Eastlake" character.

*700 block of Oak Street*

## East Oakland: Tour 5

The present-day east Oakland area was once a number of small settlements stretching from Oakland to San Leandro: Brooklyn, Highland Park, Dimond, Allendale, Fruitvale, Melrose, Edendale, Fitchburg and Elmhurst. Before 1856, Brooklyn, the largest community, was divided into the towns of Lynn, Clinton and San Antonio. San Antonio Park commemorates the plaza of that early Spanish-speaking settlement. By the mid-1850s the area had been logged over to meet the urgent housing needs of San Francisco. A number of industries were thriving, and, in fact, Brooklyn was growing faster than Oakland. Brooklyn had the first steam ferry service to San Francisco, initiated in 1858 by James LaRue. By 1865 the San Francisco and Oakland Railway Company's 7th Street Local ran as far as LaRue's wharf at the foot of what is now 14th Avenue. A. A. Cohen of Alameda, who subsequently made the completion of the transcontinental railroad possible by buying this company and selling it to "the Big Four" and the Central Pacific, had used his influence to have the line extended into Brooklyn. In 1872 east Oakland was annexed by Oakland and became the Seventh Ward. Late nineteenth-century descriptions speak of the area as one of the most desirable suburbs of San Francisco, and as one favored in the summer by families from the city seeking "quiet and picturesque retreats."

Though it is by no means a solidly Victorian neighborhood, this area preserves enough of its early nineteenth-century housing stock to merit that general description. Contemporary development has left east Oakland behind so that today it is more or less as it was, a place of "quiet and picturesque retreats."

The hills above east Oakland are punctuated with large Queen Anne tower houses that must have been farmsteads. Hemmed in by much later

*1712 10th Avenue (entry 9)*

*Embarcadero Cove, Oakland*

development, they brood down over small bungalows and cottages. Two examples are 1047 Bella Vista Avenue and the corner of 17th Avenue and East 23rd Street; others may be spotted from the freeway or MacArthur Boulevard. Nearby, at 1807 and 1819 East 24th Street, are two houses, built in 1885, that epitomize the styling that was called "Eastlake." And one of Oakland's major landmarks, the A. E. Cohen residence, can be found at 1440 29th Avenue. A. E. Cohen was the brother of A. A. Cohen, the railroad magnate of Alameda. This transitional Queen Anne was built in 1884, supposedly without benefit of a specific architect, a testimony to the skill of the builders of the time.

Off the Embarcadero, about half a mile from the 16th Avenue-Embarcadero exit off Highway 17, is Embarcadero Cove. The Cove is a miscellaneous collection of old and new structures rescued from oblivion or demolition by Mr. and Mrs. Donald Durant and Mr. Pat Ryan, who now manage the Cove's various enterprises. These include 150 berths for sailboats and rental space for restaurants, offices and shops in a variety of buildings knit together by lush landscaping. Two houses from the late 1860s and 1870s are part of the collection. Both were moved here from east Oakland, where they stood at 1617 and 1635 16th Avenue. The square Italianate villa with a central hall plan and front porch was the home of a prominent local artist, Henry Raschen. Both houses have been restored.

155

# OAKLAND MAP TOUR 5

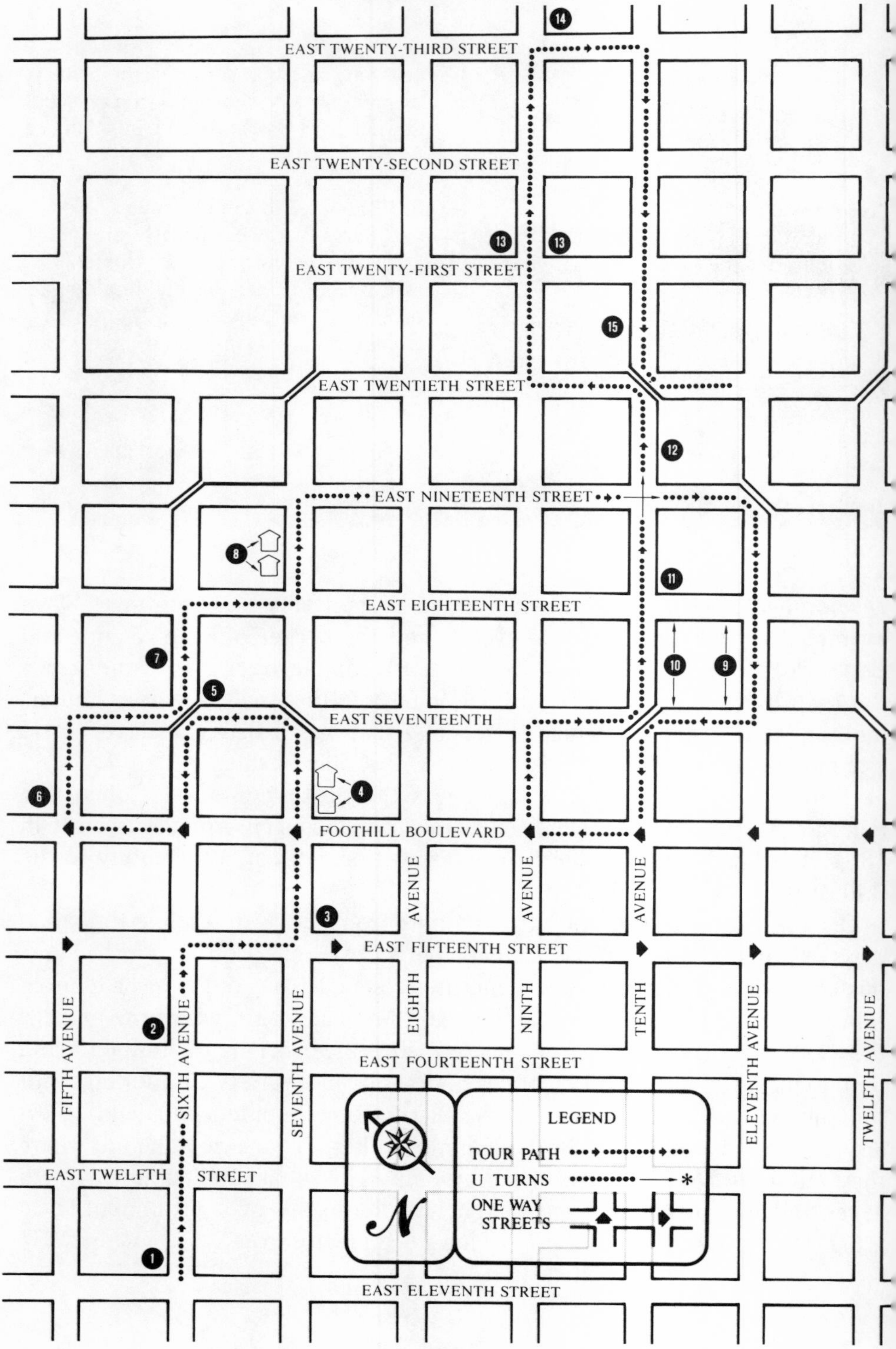

EAST TWENTY-THIRD STREET
EAST TWENTY-SECOND STREET
EAST TWENTY-FIRST STREET
EAST TWENTIETH STREET
EAST NINETEENTH STREET
EAST EIGHTEENTH STREET
EAST SEVENTEENTH
FOOTHILL BOULEVARD
EAST FIFTEENTH STREET
EAST FOURTEENTH STREET
EAST TWELFTH STREET
EAST ELEVENTH STREET
FIFTH AVENUE
SIXTH AVENUE
SEVENTH AVENUE
EIGHTH AVENUE
NINTH AVENUE
TENTH AVENUE
ELEVENTH AVENUE
TWELFTH AVENUE
1
2
3
4
5
6
7
8
9
10
11
12
13
13
14
15
N
LEGEND
TOUR PATH
U TURNS
ONE WAY STREETS

*1806 10th Avenue (entry 11)*

### 1. 546 East 11th Street
(c. 1885/QA)

### 2. 544 East 14th Street
(c. 1890/QA) A very large house with an unusual decorative detail: glass rounds that look like bottle bottoms embedded in the walls.

### 3. 704 East 15th Street
(c. 1895/QA)

### 4. 1630, 1634 7th Avenue
(c. 1880/IB) These two houses are good examples of the Italianate cottage.

### 5. 604 East 17th Street
(c. 1880/IB) A three-story house, elegantly detailed, that retains its wrought iron fence and has mature landscaping that could be original.

### 6. 1617 5th Avenue
(c. 1880/IB) An unusual Italianate.

### 7. 1725 6th Avenue
(c. 1880/IB)

### 8. 1931-37 8th Avenue
(c. 1890/QA)

### 9. 1700 block of 11th Avenue, northeast side
(c. 1895/QA) Four cottages of a somewhat unusual type with a canted bay at the corner. Very similar examples occur elsewhere in Oakland, and in Alameda and San Jose.

### 10. 1700 block of 10th Avenue
(c. 1885-95/M) A particularly nice block of cottages varying in style. House 1712 has a plaque listing the building date as 1887. The two cottages up the hill have canted corner bays like those in entry 9, but are different in general design.

### 11. 1806 10th Avenue
(1888/QT; Newsom & Newsom, A) One of the few examples of this famous firm's work remaining in Oakland.

### 12. 1930 10th Avenue
(c. 1890/QT)

### 13. 2101, 2106 9th Avenue
(c. 1890/QT)

### 14. 2304 9th Avenue
(1887/QA; Newsom & Newsom, A) A graceful cottage illustrated in the Newsoms' *Artistic Homes* series. It may have been the prototype for other similar cottages with canted corner bays.

### 15. 2035 10th Avenue
(c. 1890/QT)

*2304 9th Avenue (entry 14)*

# BERKELEY

In 1878, West Berkeley (also called Ocean View) and East Berkeley were incorporated into the city of Berkeley. Five years later the 1883 *History of Alameda County,* published by M. H. Wood of Oakland, observed: "This town has very little history beyond what is given to it by the presence of the University of California. It is a suburb of Oakland, and the day is not far distant when it will be absorbed by that rapidly extending and increasing city." The writer did not discount Berkeley entirely, however, going on to say that "a superior class of persons took up their residences there, have purchased property, erected houses, and have done much towards the establishment of a model town with systematically laid out streets, well-kept lawns, and handsome environs."

This "model town" of the 1880s has largely vanished by now. Ocean View is a spectral place "bombed out" by urban renewal. It is not clear at this writing if the forlorn but still serviceable cottages such as those at 1610 and 1614 6th Street, 1808 and 1824 5th Street, and along the 800 block of Delaware between 5th and 6th streets, will pass into private ownership or be destroyed to make way for an industrial park.

As for the many splendid and stately Victorian homes that once dotted the flatlands and the lower hills to the east, they are mostly a matter of photographic record. Fortunately, the smattering of nineteenth-century houses that remains has a sufficient range of style and scale to feed the imagination. Clusters of Victorian houses are scattered throughout the contemporary city. Maps are provided for the two areas with the most houses; the few isolated examples can easily be found using a standard road map.

## West Berkeley: Tour 1

A fine Queen Anne towered villa stands at 7th Street and Channing Way. It was built in 1889 by Edward F. Niehaus, the owner of the West Berkeley Planing Mills, which were purchased by Schuster and Niehaus in 1874. According to the 1883 record, the machinery comprised one planer, one sticker, four saws, one turning lathe, one band saw, one jig saw, one shaper, one tenanting machine and one boring machine. In that year they employed twenty-five men. Six years later business had no doubt increased substantially, as the eighties was a boom decade. Prosperity must have encouraged Mr. Niehaus to build this substantial home, which was also a fine advertisement for his business. The mills were the largest on the West Coast when they burned in 1899.

*Niehaus house, 7th Street and Channing Way, Berkeley*

# BERKELEY MAP TOUR 1

DANA STREET

ELLSWORTH STREET

WARD STREET

FULTON STREET

DURANT AVENUE

CHANNING WAY

HASTE STREET

DWIGHT WAY

BLAKE STREET

PARKER STREET

CARLETON STREET

DERBY STREET

WALKER

SHATTUCK AVENUE

MILVIA STREET

GROVE STREET

LEGEND

TOUR PATH ●●●●●●●●●●●●►●●●►

U TURNS ●●●●●●●●━━━━►＊

ONE WAY
STREETS

*N*

**1. Channing Way and Dana Street, southwest corner**
(c. 1895/QA)

**2. 2328 Channing Way**
(c. 1890/QT) A simple farmhouse that incorporates its tower in an unusual way.

**3. 1940 Channing Way**
(c. 1895/QA) A festive cottage with fine foliate detail, very probably by the Newsom brothers.

**4. 2012-22 Dwight Way**
(c. 1895/QA) A row of brightly refurbished cottages. The alterations are less noticeable because of harmonious and skillful painting.

**5. 2244 Dwight Way**
(c. 1890/O) The two-story porch and simplified detail of this house place it outside standard stylistic categories.

**6. 2336-38 Dwight Way**
(c. 1895/QA)

**7. 2205-11 Blake Street**
(c. 1895/QA)

**8. 2201 Blake Street**
(c. 1880/IB) A simple but substantial house with mature landscaping.

**9. 2198 Blake Street**
(1889/QA) A complicated house that may have been designed by Jay Volnay Laurence. It was built for John Withans, one of the many sea captains who once resided in Berkeley.

*1940 Channing Way (entry 3)*

**10. 2139-49 Ward Street**
(c. 1895/QA) A row of six cottages with canted bays and varying degrees of alteration, including one cottage embalmed in stucco. This is a house type that occurs in other parts of the East Bay; see entry 14, Oakland Tour 3.

**11. 2140 Ward Street**
(c. 1895/QT) A late Queen Anne design with an extensive use of fishscale shingles and ornamental plasterwork. Its tower has been pulled into the main block of the house and the roof is lower and not so dramatic in form as it generally was in earlier Queen Anne houses. Note the winged dragon finial on the tower.

161

## North Berkeley: Tour 2

On the periphery of Tour 2 are several interesting Victorian houses. In the hills west of town, on La Vereda Road, are two houses whose styles are unusual for this area. At 1631 is the Petersen house, built in 1895. Its simple form and near absence of decorative detail give it a rural farmhouse character. The Lezinsky house at 1730 La Vereda, built circa 1890, is clearly Colonial Revival due to its gambrel roof and expressed structural framing. Its hillside location was valued by another of Berkeley's sea captains because his wife could see his ship approaching on the Bay.

About two blocks north of entry 1, Tour 2, at 1301 Oxford Street, is "The Cedars," the oldest house of architectural significance in Berkeley. Built in 1868 for Napoleon Bonaparte Byrne, it has been much altered, yet the square form, simple but elegant Classical detail and the low bracketed hip roof exemplify the early Italianate villa style. The central tower is now missing.

### 1. 2163 Vine Street
(c. 1890/QA) Virtually all of the decorative detail on this house is new, carefully copied from the bits and pieces that remained before the house was restored in 1976.

### 2. 1505-10 Oxford Street
(c. 1890/QA) Two well-preserved houses that were probably built on speculation when this neighborhood was developed in the 1880s and 1890s.

### 3. 1536 Oxford Street
(1893/QT; Julius E. Krafft, A) A large and substantial home built for Captain Joseph Boudrow who, because of his endorsement of the advantages of Berkeley living, may well have been responsible for its large number of sea captains. Though the towers on many Queen Anne houses were non-functional, this one served the good captain as a watchtower for maritime activities on the Bay. The architect was a prominent professional in San Francisco; his skill in unifying the composition of porch, gables and tower raises this

house above the carpenter-builder or pattern book level.

### 4. 1608 Walnut Street
(c. 1895/QA) The facade resembles an embroidery sampler in the variety of its ornamental detail. Though not known to be by Marcuse and Remmels, the design is very like some of their cottages in Alameda.

### 5. 2026-28 Francisco Street
(c. 1895/QA) Two well-restored houses, one with an unusual canted two-story bay.

### 6. Milvia and Francisco streets, northeast corner
(1880/T; John Paul Moran, B) Built by a former ship's carpenter for Isaac Flagg, a professor of Greek at the University of California, the Flagg house is one of two designs known to be by Moran (see entry 10). Altered and added on to in the front around the turn of the century, this house is a transitional design moving toward the Queen Anne style but still

# BERKELEY MAP TOUR 2

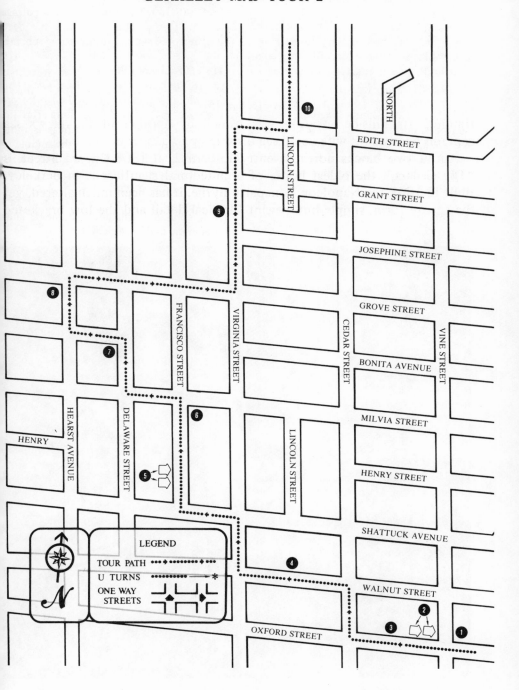

boxy in form like the Italianate villa. The rectangular tower with its high, pointed roof and peaked gables over the windows has a Gothic flavor. The house's rear gable has a roughly carved bargeboard that ends in a bracketed molding over a frieze panel with two carved anchors.

### 7. Delaware and Bonita streets, southeast corner
(c. 1875/I) A rare early Italianate villa recognizable by its square form and central cupola. The present porch is a later addition.

### 8. 1901 Bonita Street
(c. 1895/QA)

### 9. 1816 Virginia Street
(c. 1890/QA) This finely detailed cottage was built by a cabinetmaker. It has been well restored with a subtle color scheme.

### 10. 1708 Lincoln Street
(c. 1890/O; John Paul Moran, OB) This was Moran's home. Now walled off from the street by other houses built after the land was subdivided, the house is quite visible from the driveway in the middle of the block. It is a highly personal design with a square tower set diagonally in the center of the gabled roof. Here conventional decorative detail is mixed with fanciful column forms and ornaments such as anchors and cloverleaves.

*Flagg house, Milvia and Francisco streets (entry 164)*

*1608 Walnut Street (entry 4, Berkeley Tour 2)*

## VALLEJO

In 1848, General Mariano Vallejo offered his land on the Carquinez Straits to the fledgling state of California for its new capitol. Five years later the general's failure to build a capitol building and develop the town caused the legislature to move to Benicia instead. In 1854 the Mare Island Navy Yard, founded to build ships for the coastal defense, brought another kind of governmental employee to the town that had adopted the general's name. The heights northeast of the Mare Island Strait became a residential district for naval officers and other prominent citizens. Now an official historic district, the Heritage District, it preserves the relatively few nineteenth-century houses that remain in Vallejo. Among these are some of the oldest in the Bay Area.

Two other worthwhile houses in Vallejo are not on the tour map. At 1214 Sacramento Street is a flat-front Italianate built around 1875. At 110 Admiral Callahan Lane, on the east side of Highway 80, is a fine square Italianate farmhouse built around 1865—its shutters are later additions.

165

*738 York Street (entry 2)*

### 1. 626 York Street
(c. 1895/QA)

### 2. 738 York Street
(1894/QA) In 1956 this house was stripped of its ornament. The current owners have lovingly replaced it using old photographs of the house as a guide.

### 3. 740 York Street
(c. 1895/C) A good example of the Shingle style combined with the Queen Anne.

### 4. 912 Georgia Street
(c. 1870/IB) Erected by the same builder as 834 Georgia, this is a design found today only in Vallejo.

### 5. 915 Georgia Street
(1894/QA)

### 6. 705 Georgia Street
(c. 1890/QA) A large house reminiscent in form of several in Alameda.

### 7. 600, 610 Georgia Street
(c. 1895/QA)

### 8. 639 Virginia Street
(1868/I; Abbot, OB) The modern appearance of this fine early house is the result of its having been shingled in 1920. The landscaping and the barns behind testify to its original status as a farmhouse.

### 9. 626 Virginia Street
(1869/T) A late Greek Revival house on its way to Italianate.

### 10. 803 Capitol Street at Napa Street
(c. 1872/I) According to the records, this tiny house once commanded seven hundred acres.

### 11. 740 Capitol Street
(1860-62/O) A mysterious house that, although built sometime between 1860 and 1862, was either moved here from some other site or prefabricated on the East Coast, shipped around the Horn and erected here at a later date. In any case, it is a fine example of a Carpenter-Gothic cottage.

### 12. 1012 Sutter Street
(1869/O) The main floor of this house is the second story of an Italianate house moved here from 700 Capital Street in 1910. The remarkable front porch was added at that time.

### 13. 918 Sutter Street
(c. 1870/O) This is one of the most unusual nineteenth-century homes in the Bay Area. The verticality of the house, the narrow tower and the delicate scale of the "gingerbread" ornament are much more typical of eastern houses of the 1850s and 1860s than of any in this area. Its history is not yet known.

*740 Capitol Street (entry 11)*

## VALLEJO MAP

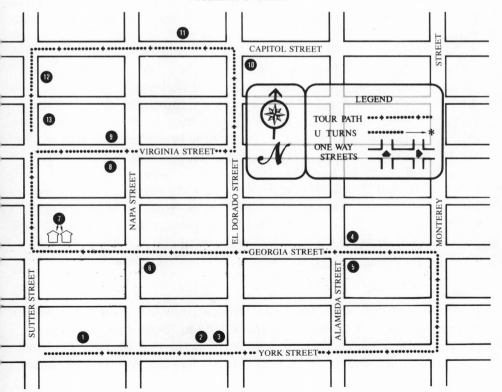

# MARIN COUNTY

## Sausalito

Marin was one of the original counties established in 1850 when California was admitted to the Union. In 1868 the Saucelito Land and Ferry Company purchased twelve hundred acres of the Rancho Saucelito, laid out lots and began a ferry service to San Francisco, thus initiating the commuter settlement of Marin. One of the company's clients was John Gardner, a former gold prospector who built the Carpenter-Gothic cottage at Cazneau Street and Girard Avenue in 1869. The design, with its high-peaked central gable, icicle bargeboards and front porch with split columns, was probably taken from an eastern pattern book. It should be compared with the simpler cottage at 740 Capitol Street in Vallejo (entry 11) and a fancier version at 1238 Versailles Avenue in Alameda (entry 7, Tour 6). The Gardner house has been maintained in its original state and is an official landmark.

In 1875, Peter Donahue, a San Francisco entrepreneur, began the North Pacific Coast Railroad, which took over the ferry service. Though the intention was to bring farm products from the rich Marin farms to needy San Francisco, the stations along the line to Tomales—Corte Madera, Kentfield, Ross, San Anselmo and San Rafael—gradually served more commuters than farmers.

The decade following the coming of the railroad brought the outside world to the former Portuguese fishing village of Saucelito in increasing numbers (the spelling of the name was later changed). Some fifteen hundred inhabitants and a half dozen hotels transformed the place into a pleasure resort. Sausalito has a number of homes from the closing decades of the nineteenth century, but nearly all have been altered. About the best the tourist can do is to explore the narrow streets and view the fragments of houses that can be seen through holes in the vegetation. An interesting house at 16 San Carlos Avenue is called the Villa Veneta. It was remodeled by the famous San Francisco architect, Willis Polk, in 1893, and gets its name from the Venetian-Gothic windows. Another quite eccentric house, built in 1899, is at 603 Main Street. Its owner-builder, Mr. Schuller, carved a most remarkable Gothic door for this otherwise Colonial Revival cottage.

## Tiburon

In 1884, Donahue's railway began service from San Rafael to Tiburon, completing the transportation network around Richardson Bay. Civil War physician Dr. Benjamin Lyford, who married Hilarita Reed and fell heir to a portion of her father's Rancho Corte Madera del Presidio, laid out the

*Marin Art and Garden Center, Ross*    *Schuller house, 603 Main Street, Sausalito*

first subdivision in the 1880s. The establishment of such conditions of purchase as celibacy and the prohibition of alcohol, however, resulted in few purchases and no building. One of the loveliest of Marin's nineteenth-century houses, the Lyford home, was moved from across the Richardson Bay to 376 Greenwood Beach Road, on the highway to Tiburon, in 1957. Built around 1876, the house is a miniature Italianate villa with a mansard roof and a central tower.

## Belvedere
Belvedere was first subdivided in 1890 by the Belvedere Land Company, which owned and developed the whole island as a summer colony and suburban community for San Francisco. Accessible by private boat and ferry, the island was favored by those who loved living near the water either in boats or in houses tucked into the steep hillsides. The Victorian houses on Belvedere are not easy to see because of the terrain and the vegetation. Many are brown-shingled summer houses that blend well with the landscape. A few have exuberant Queen Anne forms, such as 251 Beach Street with its fine veranda. But a drive around the peninsula (the island was connected to the mainland long ago) is still a pleasurable experience. The narrow roads and hillside walks remain from the early platting; the view of twentieth-century San Francisco is one of the best.

## Ross
Ross is a tiny township of three and a half square miles that incorporates the nineteenth-century ideals of suburban living. An ordinance protecting the trees that remained after the initial logging was passed by the first town

*Ira B. Cook house, Mission Avenue and B Street, San Rafael*

council. Albert Dibblee, whose mid-1870s Gothic Revival mansion was one of the first built, planted many of the replacement trees in the area around Fernhill Avenue, a street named for his estate. Nearby Shady Lane is a perfect example of how the early residents wanted their small town to look. This narrow lane, closely bordered by overhanging trees, has a banked roadbed without curbs or sidewalks. Below the grade level a gravel path, quite separate from the road traffic, accommodates pedestrians, bicyclists and horseback riders. House 34, one of the clearly visible houses on the lane, is a rustic Queen Anne with a tower and a sweeping veranda (now closed in). It dates from the 1880s.

At 2 Lagunitas Road is a house from the 1860s. The ground floor has been altered, but the gabled roof with lacy bargeboards, visible from the road, gives a good idea of how the Carpenter-Gothic style complemented the foliage of trees and shrubs.

Across the now-busy Sir Francis Drake Boulevard is the Marin Art and Garden Center, which preserves some of the original landscaping and the tank house, now a library, of the Worn estate. Note the mighty magnolia tree and other so-called "specimen" trees that, though not native to the area, have thrived in the benign climate.

## San Rafael

Both San Anselmo and San Rafael were major North Pacific Coast Railroad towns and, consequently, recreation and resort areas in the nineteenth century. Most of the large estates have been converted into subdivisions, but old photographs in the Marin County Historical Society in San Rafael show how large, complicated suburban villas once punctuated the hillsides. The business district of San Rafael grew up along the numbered and lettered streets near the original mission. Fragments of the Italianate business blocks remain. Alas, only the gateposts still stand at Belle Avenue and Rafael Drive to mark the site of the luxurious Hotel Rafael, a rambling structure with bristling gables that must have been one of the most picturesque sights in Marin.

The best-preserved building from these great days is the Ira B. Cook house, built in 1879 as the gatehouse of the Boyd estate, Maple Lawn. Located at Mission Avenue and B Street, the house is now the Marin County Historical Society Museum, open in the afternoons on weekends (times should be checked). This was considered Swiss Cottage design, but its intricate ornament and gable treatment were also called "Eastlake." The above-mentioned photograph collection is on the third floor. The original interiors and fireplaces are worth seeing, as is the collection of artifacts. West of the museum on Mission is what remains of Maple Lawn after drastic alterations, as well as the Dollar mansion, now owned by the city. No longer a mansion, the building does have some original interiors. As is typical of Marin, the chief legacy of the former estate is the landscaping. Those who are interested in this aspect of the Victorian era should explore the area around Grand Avenue and Coleman Drive, a major subdivision developed by San Francisco capitalist William T. Coleman in the 1870s. In 1887 he sold land to the Dominican Sisters, who built their still-existing convent at 1520 Grand Avenue in 1889. Two homes from the 1880s, now residence halls on the grounds of the Dominican College, are Meadowland, the country home of M. H. de Young, and Edgehill, home of William Babcock.

A last choice piece of Victorian Marin was built on the grounds of a large estate, Culloden Park, owned by Alexander Forbes. It is the charming cottage at 230 Forbes Avenue, built about 1889 and designed by Newsom and Newsom. The summer cottage quality is accentuated by the moon gate balcony with reclining beasts on either side of the railing.

*230 Forbes Avenue, San Rafael*

706 Cowper Street, Palo Alto      1184 Washington Street, Santa Clara

## THE PENINSULA

The nineteenth-century development of the San Francisco peninsula was accelerated, as was development in the rest of the Bay Area, by the coming of the railroads in the 1850s. Much of the area was the the province of very wealthy families from San Francisco. The grand estates proliferated and endured well past the turning of the century, only to be decimated in modern times. Areas such as Redwood City and Palo Alto also preserve little of their Victorian heritage.

Those who take the Victorian quest seriously will be rewarded by a visit to Ralston Hall in Belmont, built in 1865 but greatly enlarged from 1865 to 1875 by architect John P. Gaynor for William C. Ralston, founder of the Bank of California. In its most spacious days Ralston Hall accommodated 120 weekend guests and was illuminated by a private power supply. Today it is owned by the College of Notre Dame (Ralston Avenue at Notre Dame Avenue) and is open to the public. Although it does not retain its original splendor, the main rooms are well worth seeing.

Further south, in Redwood City, is the Benjamin G. Lathrop house at 627 Hamilton Street. One of the Bay Area's finest Gothic Revival cottages, it was built in 1860 and was moved here from another site in Redwood City.

Palo Alto's largest and most flamboyant nineteenth-century house is found at 706 Cowper Street. It belonged originally to T. B. Downing, an early city councilman. It should be compared with other large Queen Anne villas with towers and exuberant detail—notice the porch columns—such as

*981 Fremont Street, Santa Clara (entry 5)*

the Morse mansion in Santa Clara (see entry 5). At 1023 Forest Street is a large transitional house built in 1896. In style it is mostly Queen Anne but is moving toward Colonial Revival. At 1009 Forest Court is an elaborate former carriage house, built in 1895. It has an impressive central square cupola and unusual treatment in the gables. Nearly swallowed by the downtown area of Palo Alto is the 1894 Queen Anne home built for Dr. Charles Decker, a dentist, at 510 Waverly Street. Now an antique shop, the house is well preserved, with an interior worth seeing.

## SANTA CLARA

Like San Jose, Santa Clara was a center of an agricultural area that maintained its rural character well into the twentieth century. Although the city does not have an extensive nineteenth-century neighborhood, the blocks around the old Santa Clara Mission site, now the University, have some of the Bay Area's oldest houses. Few of them are unaltered. Most were so simple to begin with that it is difficult to point to any distinguishing features. The viewer is advised to look for plain facades and simple, often abbreviated, detail as signs of the earliest parts.

## 1. 1217 Santa Clara Street

(1875/O; Landrum, OB) A simple Gothic Revival cottage. Landrum was a carpenter who designed this house for himself.

## 2. 1191 Benton Street

(1895/T) The Robert Menzel home, a late Queen Anne villa moving into the Colonial Revival style with the delicate detail and narrow clapboard siding that became fashionable toward the turn of the century.

## 3. 1116 Washington Street at Benton Street

(c. 1895/QA) Though weatherbeaten, this exuberant cottage preserves all of its decorative detail.

## 4. 1184 Washington Street

(c. 1870/O) A beautifully restored Gothic Revival cottage.

## 5. 981 Fremont Street

(1891/QT) Santa Clara's grandest mansion, built for Charles Copeland Morse, whose company became the Ferry Morse Seed Company. The house is now a California historical landmark.

## 6. 1159 Main Street

(1851/O) Originally the Sam Johnson home, which was prefabricated and shipped around the Horn. This house has been added on to, making it difficult to discern its original parts. Across the street are other simple and probably early houses that suggest the rural farmhouse style of the 1860s. Notice also 1091 Fremont, built in 1865, whose original character is revealed by the first-story windows and doors and the porch details.

## 7. 1111 Harrison Street

(c. 1890/QA)

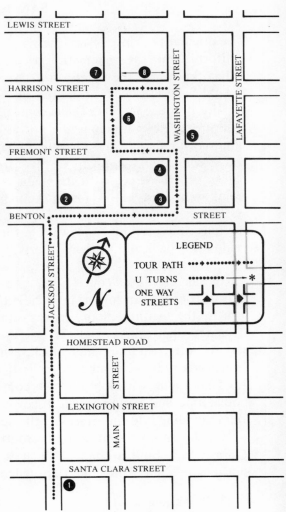

SANTA CLARA MAP

## 8. 1000 block of Harrison Street, north side

(c. 1890/M) A mixed block of houses in the Queen Anne and Colonial Revival styles. Houses 1077 and 1051 have been well restored.

175

# SAN JOSE

The original pueblo of San Jose was one of the first secular settlements in California. But the systematic agricultural development of the Santa Clara Valley, known in the nineteenth century as "The Garden Valley of Heart's Delight," did not occur until after the Gold Rush turned San Francisco into a major produce market. The accompanying residential development of San Jose proper grew up along the north-south streets east of downtown, and some acquired a "stately avenue" character because of generous lot sizes and street trees. A remnant of this garden city is found along the northern blocks of 4th Street with its median strip and rows of palms. The truly grand avenue was the Alameda, running from San Jose through Santa Clara and connecting with the El Camino Real. The Alameda today is still gracious and spacious, and waiting for the landscaping and re-zoning that could bring back all its original glory.

## North Side San Jose: Tour 1

This district was an important residential area from the 1860s through the turn of the century. Some blocks and some streets show signs of greater affluence than others, and the area is a mixture of houses from different periods, often in the same block, which may indicate the presence of farmsteads that were subdivided as the population increased. The houses listed here represent only the high points of the north side; the tourist with ample time and curiosity will discover more treasures in a block-by-block tour extending into the fringes of the mapped area.

Not shown on the map is 305 South 11th Street, at the corner of Santa Clara Street. Built around 1890, it is a well-restored Queen Anne tower house with a notable second-floor balcony and fine spoolwork.

**1. 284 Washington Street**
(c. 1890/QA) An uncommon example of the miniaturized Queen Anne villa.

**2. 300 block of North 6th Street, west side**
(c. 1890/M) A block with an interesting variety of houses and cottages in various stages of restoration.

**3. 193, 197 North 5th Street**
(c. 1880/IB)

**4. 489 North 4th Street**
(c. 1890/QA) A Queen Anne cottage with good "Eastlake" detail and original iron cresting.

**5. 200 block of North 3rd Street, west side**
(c. 1885-95/M)

**6. 330-36 North 3rd Street**
(c. 1875/IB)

# SAN JOSE MAP TOUR 1

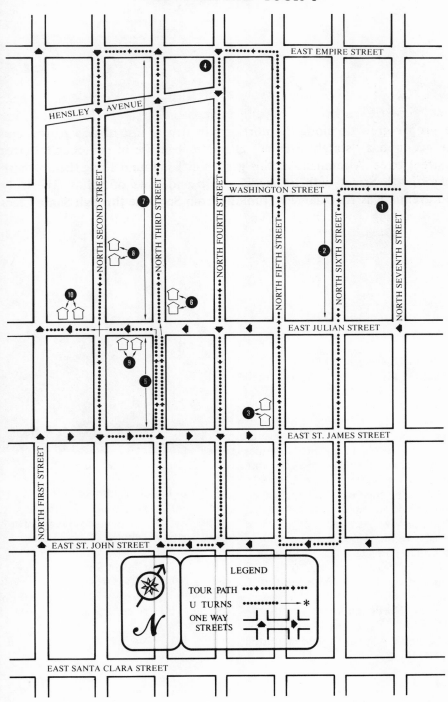

*Window detail,*
*800 block South 3rd Street*
*(entry 13, Tour 2)*

*467 North 3rd Street (entry 7, Tour 1)*

### 7. 400 block of North 3rd Street

(c. 1885-95/M) A variety of very interesting houses, particularly on the west side. Houses 411 and 429 are fine examples of the Queen Anne villa with towers and verandas. House 467 is a towered house from the eighties; identical houses are found in at least three other San Jose locations. This house still has its tower, balconies and much of its original detail. On either side are more rustic houses that might once have been described as "Swiss Chalets." House 499, at the corner of East Empire Street, is an example of a transitional design moving from the Queen Anne to the Colonial Revival style.

### 8. 428, 438 North 2nd Street

(c. 1885/SFS) Variations of the eighties cottage; house 428 has an unusual central hall plan.

*523 South 6th Street (entry 4, Tour 2)*

### 9. 70-76 East Julian Street

(c. 1890/QA) Two notable houses with fine "Eastlake" detail such as spoolwork and carved panels.

### 10. 35-37 East Julian Street

(c. 1890/QA) Two elaborate and well-restored Queen Anne houses, one of which is now an antique store.

*446-50 South 2nd Street (entry 9, Tour 2)*

*482-86 South 2nd Street (entry 10, Tour 2)*

## South Side San Jose: Tour 2

In 1870 the State Normal School, now San Jose State University, moved to this site to join an earlier college founded in 1857. The surrounding neighborhood developed as a genteel residential section related to this and other academic institutions that followed, including St. Mary's School at the corner of 3rd and Reed streets—look for its fine early brick hall. Expanding college needs in this century have sadly eroded the neighborhood, which suffered an additional blow when the freeway was built to the south. Still, there are hopeful signs that the absentee landlords will eventually come to care for this fine stand of nineteenth-century residences. The lover of old houses will be rewarded by a block-by-block exploration.

**1. 297 East Reed Street**
(c. 1885/O) A house in the Old English or Elizabethan style. Notice the fine detail, including the carved panel in the portico pediment.

**2. 593 South 6th Street**
(1885/IF) The original owner of this house, Mr. C. Cory, was the proprietor of the Lick House Saloon.

**3. 525 South 6th Street**
(c. 1890/QA) Once occupied by Mr. Belden, the first mayor of San Jose, this house has a wealth of ornamental detail.

**4. 523 South 6th Street**
(1895/QA) Built for a Judge Welch of the superior court, this is one of the most elaborate houses in San Jose. Note the "Oriental" garden gate adapted as a porch entrance, and the carriage house in back.

**5. 530 South 6th Street**
(c. 1885/O) One of the most unusual towered houses in the Bay Area, this design has the kind of flattened, machine-made ornament that is more commonly found on Victorian masonry houses on the East Coast. The porch roof has been altered but the rest of the house appears to be original. Note the tower finial and the cluster of windows at the peak of the hip roof.

**6. 483 South 6th Street**
(c. 1878/O) A rare example of the so-called Second Empire or Mansard style, which was derived from mid-nineteenth-century French architecture of the reign of Napoleon I. Classical detail and the high, concave roof called mansard are the hallmarks of the style. This house was supposedly built as a ranch house or farmhouse.

**7. 465 South 6th Street**
(c. 1885/QA)

**8. 425 South 2nd Street**
(1880/O) A house in the Old English or Elizabethan style.

**9. 446-50 South 2nd Street**
(1897/QA) Twin houses built for two members of the Kooser family. The barn-carriage house still stands in back.

**10. 482-86 South 2nd Street**
(1880/IB)

**11. 551 South 2nd Street**
(1865/IB) This house was built for Renaldo Carter in 1865 although stylistically it seems later; perhaps it was remodeled in the seventies.

**12. 693 South 2nd Street**
(c. 1880/IB)

**13. South 2nd and South 3rd streets between Martha and Margaret streets**
(1880s-90s/M) The three blocks south of Interstate 280 on South 2nd and South 3rd streets have a variety of houses that is typical of this historic core section of San Jose.

**14. 620 South 3rd Street**
(c. 1880/T) A late Italianate design whose rectangular rather than slanted bays and flat, incised detail show an "Eastlake" influence.

**15. 418 South 3rd Street**
(c. 1890/QT) One of the most gracious of the Bay Area's Queen Anne villas, with a tower, veranda, a satisfying range of patterned shingles and turned woodwork, and a good art glass window. The size and scale of the house, including the carriage house in back, testifies to the much larger lot size it once had. The original owner was Joseph H. Rucker.

# SAN JOSE MAP TOUR 2

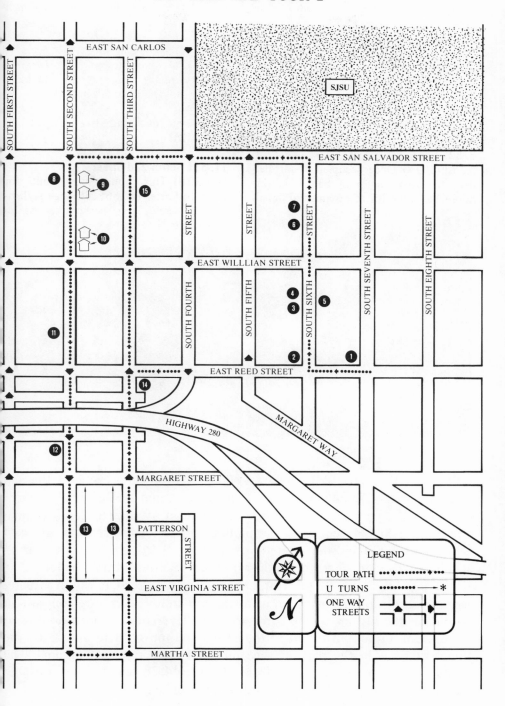

*418 South Third Street (entry 15)*

On the other side of Interstate 280 lies Kelley Park, home of the San Jose Historical Museum Complex, which is located in the southernmost section of the park near Senter Road and Phelan Avenue. Since its foundation in 1971, the Museum Association has worked to raise funds to move or reconstruct buildings that were once part of the downtown area, in an ongoing attempt to recreate a portion of nineteenth-century San Jose. One of the buildings, the Pacific Hotel, is a new structure that will eventually house a variety of resources for historical research. It currently contains an exhibit on the history of the Santa Clara Valley. The Umbarger house and the Chiechi house, both built in the 1870s and moved here intact, are the only structures in the park at this time that are completely original. The complex is open to the public from 10 am to 4:30 pm, Monday through Friday, and noon to 4:30 pm, Saturday and Sunday.

# The Victorian House

# INSIDE THE VICTORIAN HOUSE

Few aspects of the Victorian era were more commented upon by its chroniclers than the home. The post-Civil War city, which was controlled by industrial and commercial interests, developed in response to technological rather than social needs. Dramatic increases in urban population produced crowding, disease, and a new complexity widely perceived as unnatural and as a threat to traditional values. In response, the home was increasingly thought of as consecrated to preserving these values. Removing home life from urban contamination became a moral imperative.

The new technology, which had created the city, also made possible the construction of housing at prices within the reach of the common man. At the same time, the development of the electric tram made areas removed from the center of the city accessible for home building.

A faith in scientific progress and a widespread hyprocisy about the desire for material comfort marked the age. The home was at once a haven and the primary place of consumerism, and nowhere is the Victorian effort to veil simple acquisitive drives with morality more evident than in the field of home design, decorating and furnishing. Home decorating manuals read like religious tracts, exemplified here in the preface to a book titled *Household Elegancies, Suggestions in Household Art and Tasteful Decorations,* by Mrs. C. S. Jones and Henry T. Williams, published by the Ladies Floral Cabinet Company in New York in 1884:

> Home! Is there any sweeter word in any language than that of Home? What can bring brighter pictures of joy; what can give images to remain longer on the mind; what can we treasure more tenderly than memories of Home; and where, in all the earth, can happier hearts be gathered, but in the delightful precincts of Home? ... The beauties and attractions of Home can be none too pleasant or tasteful. Here gather the young to learn for all years to come. Here social life gains its lessons of utility and sense. And in these pages all may find a stimulus for new thoughts, more active work, with pretty fancies, and aesthetic beauty to gild the days for years to come—"Bright moments shall still brighter grow,/ While Home becomes our Heaven below."

## The Halls and Staircases

As the introduction to the moderate-sized house, the manual writers recommended that the entrance hall be quiet and undemonstrative and yet provide a keynote for the entire house. The furniture was to consume as little space as possible, consisting of a table and chair at the most and at the least a hatrack and umbrella stand. Warm tones were permissible, but no striking brilliancy of color.

In the affluent house, a "great hall" was considered indispensable. Here, in addition to the grand stairway of polished wood, was a fireplace alcove with seats, an inglenook, symbolizing the hospitality of the house as a whole. This hall space was part of the revival of medieval imagery and of the dimly understood grand hospitality of the baronial hall. It was also a place where richness of surface decoration and detail were important. "Putting up a good front" was not just confined to the facade of the house but extended to the front rooms. In the absence of a great hall, an inner and outer hall, separated by doors with etched and beveled glass patterns, provided insulation and a processional sequence of spaces. Tile floors in a range of browns, Indian red, yellows and greens, and in both complicated and simple patterns, were highly recommended for ease of cleaning and durability. The cheaper patterned linoleum was recommended for the modest budget.

Walls were sheathed with the new wallpapers that the importation of tough paper from Japan had made possible. Though the wall hanging named Lincrusta Walton, invented by Frederick Walton in England in 1877, has become a generic term, there were many such linoleum-based, flexible wall hangings produced in this country under other names. These frequently covered the upper part of the wall with an embossed, repeated design. Dados (the lower section of the walls) were painted dark or filled with "frieze papers" of intricate designs, either geometric, foliate, or imitating paneling and architectural molding. Flocked and gilded papers and damask papers with shiny and mat surfaces were also popular. Toward the end of the century most patterned design was concentrated on the upper part of the wall at the ceiling cornice where it took the place of three-dimensional detail such as a concave section with moldings or brackets, or was placed below as a figured frieze band. The underside of the staircase might also be covered with embossed metal or paper. In a substantial home the hall set the stage for the other rooms. As Robert W. Shoppell expressed it in 1883 in his book, *How to Build, Furnish and Decorate:*

> Your hall and staircase may present charming glimpses of classic or medieval
> periods, or we may find ourselves surrounded with imagery of tropical luxuri-

ance while the forms and fragrance of real plants will complete the delusion. Only, the [other] apartments must be sumptuous in proportion, or our expectations will be raised only to be disappointed later on.

## The Parlor or Drawing Room

The parlor of the modest house was the drawing room of the mansion. Here the most diverse furnishings could be used because they were for the "varied uses of social and intellectual recreation." Shoppell stated that, if possible, the whole room should not reveal itself at first glance. Alcoves or bays contributed variety and created the desired cozy corners. If an irregular space was not possible, there were other ways to create the "picturesque room with a variety of heights and a diversity of shadow." The versatile folding screen could interrupt the space while furniture was arranged so that the only route across the space was circuitous. Modernists like Sigfried Gideon were perplexed by what he termed "the devaluation of space," or the deliberate destruction of the spatial character of the room itself. But just as the Victorians delighted in the irregularities they found in nature, incorporating the principles of the "picturesque" in landscape and garden design, so the arrangement of furniture in a room became an analagous design problem: It was an even greater challenge to make the path across the room like a meander through the bosky dell.

In furnishing the room the periphery was considered first. Set pieces such as the piano, the cabinet and heavy couches lined the walls. Tea tables and chairs occupied the corners, making them cozy and, as Ella Rodman Church put it in her small book, *How to Furnish a Home,* published in 1881, "destroying the mathematical precision so fatal to poetry and grace." Lounging chairs alternated with light chairs, tables, stools, floor vases and tripods for ferns, to break up the "stiffness of the room." Most middle-class houses placed a round reading table in the center of the room. Over it was suspended a lamp, often with a rose-colored globe, which was shaded in a variety of ways, from fringed cloth to stained glass. Tables had felt or canvas covers though more costly cloths were also in use, particularly on the tea tables.

A cabinet was a necessary piece whose size varied with the amount of space and the budget. A standing cabinet had drawers or compartments with doors in its base and shelves above, either open or enclosed by glass doors or by ringed curtains, a fashion credited to Charles Eastlake by some. The top could be given a concave shape to create a shelf above for the display of the ubiquitous Delft plates or other treasures. Cabinet shelves were reserved for fragile treasures from travel or the family past. Other appointments for this room included wall sconces for candles, wall brackets for more china or statuary, perhaps a marble bust of a famous man, and shadow boxes for Japanese fans. If budget and space were small, a wall cabinet held the treasures.

The fireplace with mantel and mantelpiece, or over-mantel, was a counterpart of the cabinet. The hearth itself, edged with ceramic art tiles whose subjects ranged from swans to cherubs, provided the requisite cheery glow. The mantel above was often covered with a lambrequin, a curved and fringed hanging also used to cover up tops of drapes, or with felt or cotton cloth. The height of the over-mantel was also a matter of budget. The affluent drawing room generally had a paneled composition with a beveled mirror in the center, sconces for candles to either side, and a series of niches or shelves for more display. At the ceiling cornice the structure might be given a coved molding like the ceiling in the more affluent homes. More economic versions of this over-mantel had only one or two shelves or a paneled section with a mirror. For the modest home, a tiled hearth with a mantel shelf sufficed.

The piano, that most treasured symbol of culture, posed problems, particularly in the modest home. Its bulk, even in the upright form, was uncompromising though it could be softened with a paisley shawl. In larger homes an alcove for the piano was recommended. The ideal was a music room that could open off the parlor or, if very large, hold seats for the audience.

As for the parlor's decor, floor coverings, like everything else, ranged in costliness. Two choices were a basic matting or felting over which Oriental rugs were scattered, or one central rug bordered by matting.

Walls received a variety of treatments. The base part of the wall, the dado, was usually stopped by the chair rail, a molding about three feet above the floor. The dado might be expensively paneled or painted but was usually in a darker tone than the upper portion of the wall—in general, tones lightened toward the ceiling. Between the chair railing and the picture railing near the ceiling was a zone that might be frescoed by some talented hand, papered with landscape or floral compositions, or left blank as a background for oil paintings, steel engravings after the old masters, family portraits or photos and the chromo reproductions of the day. Above the picture rail was an area that, if concave, might be stenciled, or if flat, papered with frieze papers of ornamental design or simple bands of color. A plaster cornice with brackets or other architectural elements and an elaborate plaster foliated medallion composed the ceiling. Even in the modest cottage a plaster medallion was standard.

Color schemes varied and changed. Because the parlor and dining room in the typical middle-class house were related by use, many thought their color schemes should be complementary. For the parlor, Shoppell recommended dull red, dark olive or sage, dull peacock-blue, chocolate or fine browns; for the dining room: gray-blue, turquoise or pale sage-green, salmon-pink, pale apricot-yellow, Nile-blue, lemon-yellow or citrus, and pale blues. Oak, walnut and mahogony were recommended for the woodwork though redwood was most common locally.

Like the music room, the library existed as a room in its own right only in the larger houses. Shelves of books were its main feature, but a large table of sturdy design in oak or mahogany for the reading stand, inkwell, pen tray, lamp and other accouterments was needed, along with a library chair. A quality of sternness and dignity was best produced by rich, dark woods and solemn hues. Sometimes the space was labeled a study, an enigmatic word that communicated the idea of a place for general privacy or for instruction of the young, in any case a multipurpose space.

## The Dining Room

Depending on the scale of living, the dining room ranged from a simple eating room used three times a day and even doubling as a second living room, to a place for banqueting. Mrs. Church says that in many homes the greater part of the day was spent there. In this context she suggests that the room have an air of "sprightliness and yet repose, an absence of monotony." Unlike the parlor or the drawing room, the furniture arrangement was more regulated by use. The dining room over-mantel shelves were the best place for display of fine china plates. Mrs. Church adds:

> Good engravings and paintings of fruit and flowers are suitable for a dining room, but representations of dead game are not very agreeable subjects. Neither does one enjoy being stared out of countenance, while eating, by one's ancestors or those of other people, although the dining room is generally considered the proper place for family portraits. A judicious sprinkling of them in the library or hall is in better taste.

The chief qualities desired in a dining room table were dignity and solidity. Extendible tables were standard. High-backed chairs, padded and covered with a good horsehair fabric, completed this central ensemble.

The other major piece was the sideboard or buffet. Here again our writers of the 1880s emphasized straight lines for strength, criticizing the curvaceous, veneered, ornate mid-century pieces for weakness and sham. The sideboard's composition ranged from simple, with a cabinet below drawers and one or two shelves above for display, to complex, with a variety of storage and display spaces.

Floor coverings, according to Mrs. Church, were least noticed in the dining room. A central rug with a discreet, all-over pattern was the common solution in the middle-class house. Costly Orientals were of course available for upper-income homeowners, but Mrs. Church was not in favor of wall-to-wall carpet because of the difficulty of cleaning corners.

Finally, bracketed wall shelves and plant stands, along with whatever else suited the uses of the room, consumed the empty spaces. In the modest house the dining room was the favored place for colored glass windows since a view was not important. In the interests of light, however, a composition leaving some clear or white ground glass was preferable. Designs with alternating squares of colored glass—red seems to have been a must—around a central, clear panel were economical and effective. The home craft manuals had large sections on painting glass. Stencils were available for the untalented, who could also varnish lace or muslin onto glass for a frosted effect that did not entirely shut out the light.

While on the subject of window treatment we may note that while large windows in parlor bays standardly had colored glass sections through the 1880s and 1890s, the other common places for colored glass were stair landing windows and small windows in storage spaces and bathrooms. To insure privacy and still admit light, muslin or lace curtains were used at the windows. Heavy drapes were used to close off bays to minimize drafts or simply to veil the room, for while there was great advocacy of light and air, there was also a fashionable preference for creating an airless and artificial atmosphere.

### The Kitchen

Planning and furnishing the kitchen varied depending on whether the servants or the lady of the house and her family were the principal occupants. In any case the manual writers were full of humanitarian concerns for those who toiled there. The basement kitchen was standard in urban locations; the kitchen as a wing was used in the country or suburb. In the San Francisco Bay Area full basement excavation was rare and the kitchen was typically on the first floor.

Mrs. Church's discussion of this room begins: "Grace and color are not to be studied here, but convenience and practical results. A kitchen that thoroughly answers the purposes for which it is intended has a beauty of its own." For all the devotion of the Victorians to food, cooking odors were treated like poisonous gases. Hence the kitchen at the back of the house, accessible by a long hall, was practical in this respect. Another major concern was cleanliness: The floor covering was a subject of endless discussion with plain tiles recommended first and linoleum following, although Mrs. Church thought it was easily injured by grease. Washable rag rugs were considered to be homey.

The kitchen table was the most important piece of furniture. With or without storage spaces, it was sturdy and plain in most cases. Wall cabinets were in use, and combinations of sinks, cabinets, counters and storage spaces, arranged for efficient use, were part of kitchen planning. Naturally, these were more extensive, as was the range of cooking utensils, as the family's needs and budget increased. Shoppell featured an elaborate kitchen cabinet with numerous drawers and cupboards of all sizes plus a hinged leaf that could also serve as an ironing board. Stoves and gas ranges in a variety of sizes and styles were sold, but the manual writers did not devote much space to their qualities. A clock was a specified item. Some chairs, a "settle," and a rocker with footstool were recommended even for the servants.

A "cheerful" (along with "cozy" the most overworked adjective for any part of the house) atmosphere lifted the kitchen above the utilitarian level, but for most it was hardly a place to seriously decorate since it was not meant for entertaining. Ideal kitchens with colored wall tiles, monumental cabinets that approached the scale and elaboration of sideboards, and an array of gleaming pots were illustrated, but they were fantasies. It would be another fifty years before the kitchen really came into its own as a display area.

## The Bedrooms
Shoppell states that "the furniture of a bedroom presents no great difficulties in the way of selection, the different pieces being dictated by the requirements of rest and of the toilet." Still, the family chambers reflected the sex and status of their occupants quite clearly. The principal chamber might also be a sitting room or "office" for the lady of the house where she could sit mornings "in her wrapper with hair unbound" and contemplate the affairs of the day. A writing desk or table, which also held the all-important "work basket," would then be added to the requisite low easy chairs, lounges and sofa. These were grouped in the bay window alcove and around the fireplace. Another sign of the lady's domestic skills would be the embroidery frame where diligent hands had produced the crewelwork firescreen. A simple toilet table with narrow drawers for the gentleman was countered by the lady's dressing table with toilet trays and swinging mirror; its lower recesses were elaborately or simply curtained and ruffled. The indispensable folding screen provided privacy for the wash basin and the

dressing area if there was no separate alcove or room. Closet space was amplified by the wardrobe with its curtained or wooden doors and drawers for shoes below. Such an arrangement, like the dining room "china closet," was frequently built into the wall structure. Built-in storage space conserved floor space, as did shelves and tables supported by wall brackets. One of these, by the bed, held the Bible and prayer book.

The choice of the bed was affected by considerations of health as well as by fashion. Here Mrs. Church advised standing the expense of good springs and a thick hair mattress, invisible though they may be. If the budget was inadequate, springs attached to the bed slats and a cornhusk mattress would do. Metal bedsteads, particularly brass, were very fashionable and considered hygienic since their smooth surfaces shed dirt and vermin, unlike the wood bed. Also in vogue was the carved wood frame with high carved headboard possibly topped off with a half-canopy, draped and fringed, from which hung side curtains. Curtaining the whole bed was by now considered unhealthy, but, as in the case of window drapes, partial concealment was thought attractive. Dotted or plain Swiss and cambric were recommended materials because they were light and airy. Muslin or Bolton sheeting was used for sheets; colored silk was also well thought of. Pillow shams and bolsters, which gave the ladies a chance to demonstrate embroidery skills, were stock items. A puffy "comfortable," or "comforter," was added to the pile. Soft colors, such as pinks, pale green, buffs and gray-blues, were recommended in general, with flowered wallpapers and cretonne, a cotton fabric printed on both sides, advised for curtains.

Children's bedrooms and nurseries were treated in lighter and more whimsical ways. The "spare room" was neutral and respectable, perhaps doubling as an upstairs study or sewing room. Other rooms in the house—servant quarters, laundry rooms and bathrooms—are mentioned in the manuals but not in a prescriptive manner. They were not "public," front-stage areas like the parlor and dining room where the reputation of the homemaker was at stake. With the exceptions of the dwellings of the very rich and the very poor, the Victorian home registered the pressures of fashion in a descending scale from front to back. The modest working-class cottage of this period might well have a fancy front; the wealthy "capitalist's" mansion often had a utilitarian back.

## The Reform Movement

We tend to think that the reaction against Victorian ostentation did not take place until the twentieth century, and certainly in terms of the modern preference for uncluttered space this is true. Still, though we may see the interiors of the seventies, eighties and nineties as very similar, those

191

who were then attempting to influence fashion saw them differently. In 1881 Mrs. Church wrote this description, which reads like the indictments of Victorian taste written thirty to forty years later:

> City houses are painfully lacking in individuality. . . . There are the same monotonous suites of drawing-room furniture—red, blue green, yellow or brown . . . the same regulation number of mirrors in the same regulation places; the orthodox amount of gilding, cornicing, and curtaining; the rich carpets that offend by their very richness, and present dazzling surfaces of flowers to be walked over . . . the infinite and perplexing number of footstools, little tables, and huge china jars that cover so much of the floorspace, and render locomotion both difficult and dangerous, the lofty walls flashing with rich gilded paper. . . . One would gladly turn to a simple country house for a refreshing change. But great is the pity, country and simplicity are not always synonymous . . . if the country house is what the novelist calls "the abode of wealth," it is apt to be a literal imitation of the city mansion.

Still, Mrs. Church's simplicity is not synonymous with today's simplicity, as illustrations in her book reveal. Her words—fitness, appropriateness, proportion, simplicity, harmony and durability—are still current, but her taste stops well short of the later modern revolt in which ornament was resolutely banished. Her concern is rather that "ornament always be a part of a structure and never attached." She is offended by the kind of materialism that demanded that everything look costly.

> Art does not exact costly things . . . it accepts the plainest objects that are in good form and of honest material, but condemns veneered wood, ornaments glued on, or substances that, being one thing, pretend to be something else. . . . Ornament is to heighten the general effect, to give character and beauty, not simply to pile one substance upon another.

Statements like this reflect the platform of the Reform movement in architecture, which began in England under the auspices of A.W. Pugin and John Ruskin, and continued with the work of William Morris, Philip Webb, Richard Norman Shaw, Bruce Talbert, William Burges, and Charles Eastlake, most famous in the United States through his book *Hints on Household Taste* (London, 1868, and at least nine editions following the Boston publication of 1872).

The Reformers were dedicated to ending what Siegfried Gideon called "the age of the upholsterer," and all that the phrase implied. By mid-nineteenth century the metal coil spring, which dramatically changed the degree of comfort as well as the appearance of seating furniture, was universally used. Packed with inches of padding and punctuated with deep buttons to hold the padding in place, coil-spring upholstery created the hallmarks of the age: the over-stuffed armchair, settee and footstool. Other products of technological advance that utterly transformed the concept of furniture manufacture were the veneers, overlays of thin wood glued to a frame, which brought expensive and exotic woods within the middle-class price range, and the mechanical processes of laminating and bending wood into shapes scarcely to be found in nature. With typical lack of concern for "honesty," the style produced by the new technology was termed Naturalistic or, in more sophisticated circles, Neo-Rococo. With it went a consuming fascination with the machine's ability to imitate everything, and to provide imitations that were cheaper than the originals.

While the proliferation of meaningless ornament and plush horrified the educated and sensitive, it produced a prosperity for the new capitalist manufacturing interests that seemed to justify everything. Also, it could be argued that the charge of falsifying and cheapening products that was brought against the use of veneers ignored the fact that those goods were more democratically distributed as a consequence. The issue of honesty in materials and craftsmanship versus a beneficial leveling of standards embroiled the critics, designers and manufacturers in the century's closing decades. William Morris's famous advice, "Have nothing in your house that you do not know to be useful or believe to be beautiful," could only be taken seriously by members of his own upper class as his firm's products were beyond the reach of middle- and working-class incomes.

To facilitate the distribution of these new factory-made goods whose mass production contributed to their lower price, the new department store concept of retail trade rapidly took shape. Besides answering the basic need for a larger display space, the department store changed the style of shopping for clothes and home products. In the small specialty shop, the owner took charge of the sale of his goods, and bargaining decided the issue of price. In the larger department stores, where a number of employees sold all products, bargaining was unmanageable. Hence there was a fixed price, plainly marked on each item, and the customer was under no obligation to buy. Shopping with a single purpose changed to browsing and impulse buying.

Still, the public had to be induced to change its shopping habits, and, here the retail entrepreneurs used techniques that were current in the great exhibitions. These began in London with the Great Exhibition of 1851 in the Crystal Palace, and continued at almost yearly intervals in world capitals such as London, Paris, Vienna and New York. Here, with vast areas of space crowded with display sections of all sorts, exhibitors explored techniques of attracting the public's attention. Of course exhibitors' show-pieces were not on sale in department stores, but the concept of novelty was carried over in merchandising. Many products were "naturalized" so that their use was all but concealed by ornament. In addition to the creation of "novelties," merchandising techniques that today we take for granted were introduced at this time. Displays became theatrical. Instead of separating products into categories throughout the store, they were combined in seductive stage settings. For this purpose the display window on the street became an integral part of department store design. Passersby could pause, reflect and perhaps be convinced that through the purchase of this combination of things their home life would be transformed.

It is difficult to truly assess the impact of these new sales techniques on the average buyer. Newspaper advertising, which came into its own in the latter part of the nineteenth century, and the welter of home furnishing publications also contributed to making the home, though sequestered from the public arena, increasingly vulnerable to the enticements of retail entrepreneurs and the dictates of fashion. Karl Marx called it "commodity fetishism."

Again technological progess controlled the spread of fashion. In the secondary cities as well as in the metropolises it was possible to read current newspaper accounts of the dress of European royalty or the New York "400." The same newspapers would soon advertise locally available copies of these styles.

This brief sketch of the context in which Victorian "taste" developed should help explain why there is no one, clear Victorian style, but rather a broad array of loosely defined styles suited to industrial processes and merchandising techniques that were increasingly refined in the course of the period. Harriet Prescott Spofford writing for *Harper's Bazaar* in New York, 1878, in an article titled "Art Decoration Applied to Furniture," lists these as recent styles: Gothic, Renaissance, Elizabethan, Jacobean, Louis Quatorze, Louis Quinze, Louis Seize, Pompeian, First Empire, Moorish, Eastlake, Queen Anne and Oriental. Ms. Spofford believed that, "provided there is space enough to move about, without walking over furniture, there is hardly likely to be too much in the room."

All styles were more or less in vogue until the end of the century, but clearly the Reform aesthetic became dominant beginning in the late 1870s. The furniture offered by such designers as Bruce Talbert, Norman Shaw and Philip Webb had a Gothic appearance but was more practical and less scholarly than earlier such designs. Curves and naturalistic, glued-on carvings were discarded in favor of low relief forms or incised designs and panels inlaid with geometric forms derived from Gothic detail. Pieces had a strong linear quality because of an emphasis on the basic frame of construction. In many cases the designs were architectural, employing the same decorative detail in the interiors and on the exteriors of buildings. The similarity of detail on buildings and furnishings was most evident in what was called, in this country, the Eastlake style. This was based on the furniture designs and writings of the Englishman, Charles Eastlake, but in actual appearance the American Eastlake style was kin to the more elaborate work of Bruce Talbert, who designed for Holland and Sons.

The sequence of events that led to transposing Eastlake's name from his rustic designs to the richly decorated surfaces that covered a whole range of designed forms in the 1880s is still mysterious. It is sufficient here to note that the most aberrant development of the style occurred on the West Coast, particularly in San Francisco and its satellite communities. Here, the style was as distressing to most of the professional architectural community as the mid-century Naturalistic style had been to the Reform architects. San Francisco architects James E. and George H. Wolfe, who edited and produced the *California Architect and Building News,* begun in 1879, conducted a tireless campaign against the "Eastlake monstrosities" that tract developers and their architects were erecting block by block in the City. In February of 1882 they editorialized: "It is a great misfortune . . . that these ingenious gentlemen cannot all be skewered . . . upon one of their so-called Eastlake elevations and sent spinning down the illimitable reaches of eternal bosh. This class of character . . . who will build houses so flimsy the wonder is they don't fall down like a pile of gingerbread." (Note the contemporary use of the word "gingerbread" to describe elaborate ornament.) The redoubtable Wolfe brothers wrote to Eastlake, sending editorials and drawings of the local work that bore his name. In April 1882, they triumphantly published his reply which said, in part:

> I now find, to my amazement, that there exists . . . an "Eastlake" style of architecture, which, judging from the specimens I have seen illustrated may be said to burlesque such doctrines of art as I have ventured to maintain. . . . I feel greatly flattered by the popularity which my books have attained in America, but I regret that their author's name should be associated there with a phase of taste in architecture and industrial arts with which I can have no real sympathy and which by all accounts seems to be extravagant and bizarre.

Eastlake's disclaimer had little effect on popular attitudes. Newspapers in San Francisco, Alameda and Oakland continued to advertise houses as "Eastlakes," and in fact the style is so rarely defined further that one has to conclude that it triggered a familiar, if inaccurate, image.

*Flat-front Italianate*                    *Bay-windowed Italianate*

## ITALIANATE: Late 1860s to 1880

From the late sixties through the seventies, the Italianate style was predominant for both the inner suburban, or city neighborhood, residence and the country suburban villa. In San Francisco the typical Italianates of the period were of two types: the flat-front and the bay-windowed. The flat-front is a somewhat earlier type, and is usually fairly simple in design and ornamental detail. It is really a wooden version of the brownstone or brick rowhouse, produced in great numbers in eastern cities such as New York and Baltimore. The bay-windowed Italianates had the "five-sided" bay: a three-windowed slanted bay projected from the facade of the house by narrow side walls.

The country suburban villa in "the Italian manner," as it was usually described, was designed for a larger lot, which encouraged two plan types: an L-shaped plan with a porch and a high, flat-topped tower in the angle of the L, or a large square plan with a central hall, a veranda across the front, and a central tower or cupola. (More modest country Italianates did without a tower but usually had a porch.) Of the many such houses that were built around the Bay, only a few survive, among them the Pardee house in Oakland, the Meek house in Hayward and the Casebolt house in San Francisco. The style was derived from late eighteenth-century paintings of Italian landscapes, which inevitably depicted a villa or farmhouse whose towered form complemented the picturesque landscape. English and American pattern books helped popularize the style.

## Characteristics
- A vertical emphasis in overall form and detail.
- Rounded, Classical ornamental detail.
- The Italianate villa has a low-pitched, broadly projecting hip or gabled roof whose eaves are supported by single or paired brackets sometimes alternating with modillions.
- Enlarged dentil courses, panel moldings, and a molded architrave often complete the entablature, which can be quite plain in more rustic examples.
- Both the flat front and the bayed front of the inner suburban rowhouse have parapets above that disguise the gabled roof and, by creating this "false front," further the illusion of a larger, masonry structure.
- A cornice runs across the top of the fenestrated section of the bay, with a triangular or segmental form over the middle window. Pilasters and thin colonnettes flank the windows, whose bases are detailed with panel moldings and other ornament.
- Pilasters or quoins often reinforce the building's corners, the latter in imitation of the rusticated stone blocks that strengthen the corners of Italian pallazzos.

*Window topped with a keystone, window shields and a frieze band*

*Window hood with a squeezed pediment*

- Entrance porticos on inner suburban rowhouses have plain or fluted columns with Corinthian capitals, and a complete Classical entablature with a turned or flat sawn balustrade and corner posts with urn-shaped ornaments.
- Simpler versions of the portico consist of flat, segmental or triangular door hoods supported by consoles or brackets.

The exteriors of Italianate houses were generally painted in shades of gray or beige to recall their masonry prototypes. Some were even painted white and spattered with gray, brown and black to imitate stone. Interiors during this period were generally light in tone with white ceilings and much gilded detail. Gold mirrors and white or light gray marble fireplaces were common, and floral carpets and richly textured wallpapers in strong colors were popular.

## SAN FRANCISCO STICK STYLE: 1800s

The San Francisco Stick style is a variation of what architectural historian Vincent Scully defines as the American Stick style: a building whose skeletal structure is emphasized and whose decorative detail resembles "bundles of sticks." The great rustic villas built in the rural areas of the East Bay and Marin County, which better fit Scully's definition, have all vanished. The San Francisco Stick style survives in great numbers in San Francisco. These terms were not in use in the Victorian era; houses of this

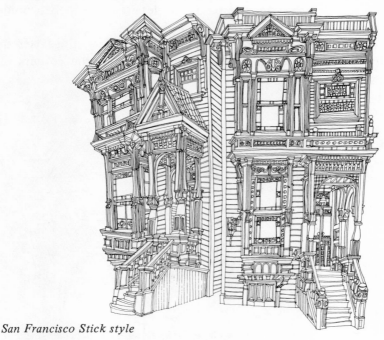

*San Francisco Stick style*

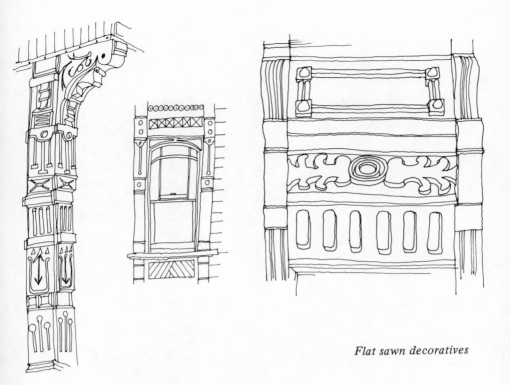

*Flat sawn decoratives*

style were known by a variety of names, one of them "Eastlake."

By the 1880s house facades had taken on a more cut-out or stamped-out look in response to the ever-expanding technology of tools and machinery. The Stick style is characterized by the thin, flat wood strips that articulate the structural frame of the house. These strips are used as decorative detail around windows and doors, and also to form vertical panels that are filled with channel rustic siding or shingles in a variety of patterns. Often these narrow pseudo-framing elements mimic the half-timbering of a medieval or Elizabethan house. Whether or not it has a historical origin, this style was clearly a reaction to the Italianate's more rounded, three-dimensional surface treatment.

### Characteristics
- Increasing verticality and rectangularity.
- Decorative detail consists of a whole new vocabulary of ornament made possible by the machine; most characteristic is the use of flat, thin wood strips. Classical ornament, when used, is treated in an inventive and often playful manner.
- Rectangular bays.
- Side or central hall plan like the Italianate house.

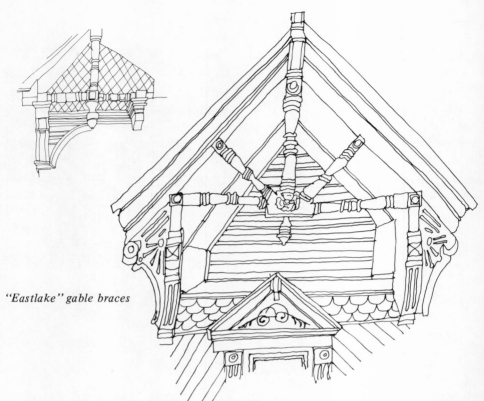

*"Eastlake" gable braces*

Exterior colors were generally more varied, with emphasis on the colors of nature (browns and greens) rather than the masonry tones of the previously fashionable Italianate houses. Bright accents in "lime green" or violet or Indian red were used, but these hues were dull compared to their twentieth-century counterparts because the chemicals used today to make colors so vivid were unknown at the time. Interior colors echoed those used on the exterior. Frieze papers and wallpapers with geometric patterns were fashionable, as was dark woodwork and paneled dados.

## The Eastlake Question

Ornamental detail applied to houses in the 1880s was often labeled "Eastlake" after Charles Eastlake, an English author and designer of furniture and interiors (see page 195). Eastlake's *Hints on Household Taste* went through many editions in this country. The book's high moral tone was directed toward abolishing the curvaceous, veneered furnishings of the 1850s and 1860s, and promoting an honest use of materials in rationally constructed designs. Eastlake's own work was simple and rustic. Square-framed pieces were doweled and pegged together; ornament was confined to a minimum of shallow-carved or incised geometric forms. American

200

furniture manufacturers, however, responding to the widespread popularity of the author's ideas, produced lines of inexpensive, rectilinear furniture with turned legs or supports, and a range of quite elaborately carved and incised decorative motifs on the framing elements and in-set panels. This work was in the general category of "art furniture," which had a free Gothic styling but was adapted to practical needs. Soon, the turned and chamfered supports used as braces for tables and chairs began to appear in the gables of houses along with chamfered balusters in galleries over windows and doors. Windows, doors and the wall areas under the eaves were treated with incised and shallow-carved ornament. Another motif used interchangeably on "Eastlake" furniture and houses consisted of a round hole ringed with smaller holes. These perforations occurred on the rounded brackets, or consoles, supporting hoods over windows and doors on houses, or the shelves and concave tops of sideboards and over-mantels.

The subject is further confused by the fact that some house designs that featured this kind of cabinet detail, particularly in the braces and brackets, were also called "Swiss," indicating a general rustic association that Eastlake had advocated.

Both the Stick style and the Queen Anne style employed "Eastlake" detail. By the 1890s, the "Eastlake" craze merged with the Queen Anne style to produce an all-over surface treatment of the house facade that resembled a Victorian embroidery sampler. This development was particularly characteristic of the houses built on speculation in the San Francisco Bay Area.

## QUEEN ANNE STYLE: 1890s

The American Queen Anne style was named for the wrong monarch. The source of the confusion is the work of Richard Norman Shaw, whose domestic architecture was indirectly influential here in the 1870s, 1880s and 1890s through widely circulated illustrated publications. Shaw's much-published English country house designs belonged to the English "domestic revival" movement, which took medieval or Elizabethan houses as models. Shaw himself went on to design commercial buildings in London that were derived from the more Classical architecture of the time of Queen Anne, who reigned from 1702 to 1714. Somehow the terms were transposed in this country so that houses in the Shavian manner were called Queen Anne rather than Elizabethan or Old English.

Despite Shaw's influence, the Queen Anne style was considered an American style. Henry Hudson Holly devotes a chapter to it in his 1878 pattern book, *Modern Dwellings*. Holly observes:

*Queen Anne tower house*          *Queen Anne rowhouse*

The Queen Anne revival shows the influence of the group of styles known as the Elizabethan, Jacobite, and the style of Francis I, which are now indeed to be arranged under the general style of "free classic." ... [It] has also been influenced by what is known as "cottage architecture" of that period. ... These cottages are partly timbered, partly covered with tile hangings, and have tall and spacious chimneys.... They have really nothing by which to fix their date. Their details partook strongly of the classic character, while the boldness of their outline bore striking resemblance to the picturesque and ever-varying Gothic.

Although the style was developed in England, Holly considered Queen Anne an excellent vernacular style for this country, combining the picturesque qualities of the Gothic style with such domestic necessities as sash windows and ordinary doorways.

Queen Anne became the great picturesque style of the end of the nineteenth century. Its irregular form, made up of a roof with different-sized gables, dormers, high chimneys, towers and turrets; walls hollowed out for recessed balconies and bulging with bays; and porches and verandas that often wrapped around the ground floor, were thought to sum up all that was gracious in home design.

Ideally, the large Queen Anne possessed a "living hall," a two-storied, galleried space featuring the stairway and a large fireplace alcove with seats. The urban rowhouse and the cottage, however, lacked space both for this amenity and for the wraparound porch. The typical Queen Anne country villa had a corner tower; in the urban house the corner tower was often pulled back into the main block of the house or dispensed with altogether. Country suburban cottages sometimes retained an abbreviated candle-snuffer tower.

## Characteristics

- A horizontal emphasis, sometimes combined with a corner tower.
- Irregular plans and elevations. Even in the narrow town house the rooms are more open to each other and more irregularly shaped than in other styles.
- Surfaces are covered with a variety of tactile patterns: horizontal lap siding, a variety of shaped shingles and spoolwork, and foliated plasterwork in panels and friezes. Fishscale shingles were most popular because they mimicked the pattern of English wall tiling.
- Tall chimneys, often with molded terra-cotta decorative panels.
- Generous use of art glass in parlor, dining room and stairwell windows.

*Queen Anne bay window detail*

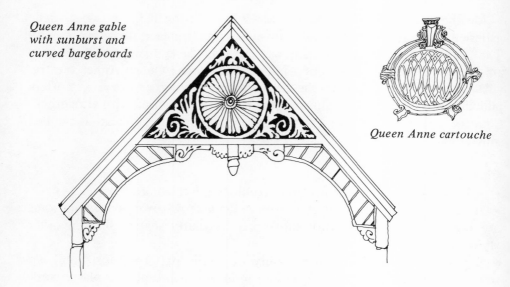

*Queen Anne gable with sunburst and curved bargeboards*

*Queen Anne cartouche*

The exteriors of Queen Anne houses on the West Coast were often painted white, particularly as the style merged with the Colonial Revival. The white was not necessarily a "dead white," as the arbiters of taste in the 1880s termed it, and the trim and expressed framing members might still be painted in dark colors. In some areas the shingles were left natural as they were in many New England examples. But the vibrant polychromy of the 1880s began to be replaced with more subdued color schemes. Queen Anne interiors were similarly lightened. Wallpapers, for example, began to have light backgrounds and delicate floral patterns. Woodwork was increasingly off-white and ornate frieze papers vanished.

## GOTHIC REVIVAL: 1850 to 1865
In this book the term Gothic Revival is limited to what is today called the Carpenter-Gothic cottage, a style strongly resembling the designs of Alexander J. Davis, published by Alexander Jackson Downing in his most popular pattern books.

### Characteristics
• High-peaked roof with central cross gable, also narrow and high-peaked.
• Bargeboards masking the eaves, carved in running vine or icicle patterns.
• Central hall plan.
• Front porch usually supported with "split columns" made of beveled wood members nailed on either side of wood blocks.
• Exterior color generally light.

## CLASSICAL REVIVAL: 1850 to 1865

By the early 1890s in California the Queen Anne style began to calm down and acquire a more regular silhouette. This trend increased toward the turn of the century. The style also began to incorporate more and more Classical detail. Most of the typical examples of this style lie outside the Victorian era in the period around 1900 to 1915.

### Characteristics
- Squared overall forms with hip or gambrel roofs.
- Classical detail.
- Exteriors painted in light colors.

## ELIZABETHAN OR OLD ENGLISH: c. 1885 to 1890

A sub-style of the Queen Anne that features high-peaked gabled roofs with patterned bargeboards often ending in a voluted or foliated form. The house standardly has an L-shaped plan with the cross gables stepped out toward the peak of the gable like the medieval half-timbered house. Heavy consoles or brackets support the gable projections. The facade often has simulated half-timbering with rough-dash stucco panels and carved or molded floriate panels in between, again in imitation of the medieval, half-timbered house. Other surface detail is like "Eastlake" ornament: geometric patterns and elaborate, bold spoolwork on porches and in galleries and balustrades.

## EDWARDIAN: late 1880s to 1915

Although named after Edward VII, who reigned from 1901 to 1910, this local term was given to multiple-family dwellings built as early as 1895 and as late as 1915. Edwardian buildings are two or three stories high with flat roofs and shallow cornices made up of small, flat brackets with rows of molding underneath, usually dentils and egg and dart. The bay windows are the three-sided slanted variety, although buildings on corner lots often have a round corner bay. Some Edwardians have exterior stairs forming a series of balconies in the center of the front of the building; apartments in this type of Edwardian were called "Romeo" or "Romeo and Juliet" apartments because of the balconies, and because the small size of the units made them appropriate for newlyweds but too small once the first baby arrived.

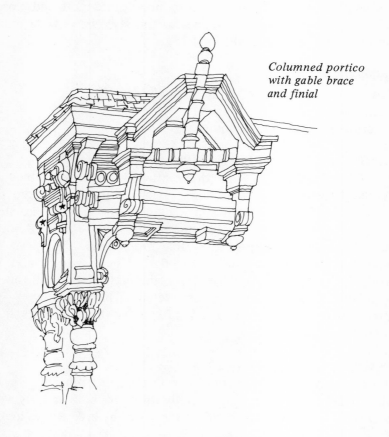

*Columned portico
with gable brace
and finial*

# GLOSSARY

**Architrave** The lowest of the three main parts of an entablature; originally a beam resting on the tops of supporting columns. This term is also used for a door or window frame with moldings.

**Art glass** Ornamental and colored glass used in art objects and for decorative windows.

**Baluster** A small post forming part of a row supporting a handrail.

**Balustrade** A row of balusters.

**Bandsaw** A continuous blade on two wheels, used to cut wood into curved or irregular shapes. Brackets, shingles, dentils and other pieces of trim are cut on the bandsaw.

**Bargeboard** An ornamented, usually flat board placed against the side of a gable to hide the ends of the horizontal roof timbers.

206

**Belt cornice** A horizontal decorative element, usually consisting of shingles or ornamental plaster, running across the middle of a house (in between stories).

**Bow window** An early name for a bay window.

**Brace** An arrangement of turned wood members found in gables of roofs and porches, and underneath rectangular bay windows. Though it appears to help support a structure, it is often only decorative.

**Bracket** An angled support or pseudo-support placed under roof eaves and cornices, porch columns, door and window hoods.

**Broken pediment** A pediment in which the top of the triangle appears broken; at the top it is usually cut out in a circular shape.

**Candle-snuffer tower** A hollow, conical roof placed over porches and on false roof forms to suggest the form of a tower.

**Canted bay** A rectangular bay window set at an angle in the corner of a house.

**Capital** The top part of a column or pilaster.

**Cartouche** A convex surface, often oval in shape and ornamented in some fashion or made of ornamental material; usually framed with ornament.

**Chamfered** Beveled on the edges or ends; also grooved or fluted.

**Colonnette** A miniature column, usually very tall and thin.

**Channel rustic siding** Wooden house siding with angled, or rusticated, edges.

**Column** A vertical support. The five Classical orders of columns are Doric, Ionic, Corinthian, Tuscan and Composite.

**Console** A bracket, usually S-shaped, under a window hood or door hood.

**Cornice** A horizontal projecting molding at the top of a building.

**Course** A continuous layer of material on a building.

**Cove or coved** Concave in shape.

**Cove ceiling** A concave surface between a wall and ceiling.

**Crocket** A curved ornament with a knob-like top.

**Cupola** A small dome on a roof.

**Corner cover** A decorative treatment at the corner of a house. Also called a corner board.

**Dentils** A molding of small toothlike squares.

**Dormer window** A gabled window projecting from the side of a sloping roof.

**Eave** The bottom edge of a roof.

**Egg and dart molding** A molding of alternating egg shapes and darts or arrows.

**Entablature** A horizontal element spanning the columns of a Greek portico or temple and usually composed of a cornice, frieze and architrave. The term is also used to refer to a horizontal element running across the top of a house.

**Facade** The front, or face, of a building.

**False front** A high front, or parapet, hiding a gabled roof.

**False gable** A gable with no structure behind it.

**Finial** A terminal ornament often found at the apex of a tower or a gable.

**Fishscale shingle** A shingle with curved edges, resembling the scale of a fish.

**Five-sided bay** A three-windowed slanted bay projected from the facade of a house by narrow side walls.

**Fluting** Long narrow grooves in a column or pilaster.

**French cap** A pseudo-mansard roof topping a false front.

**Frieze** A horizontal ornamented band under the cornice of a building or on other parts of a house, such as over a window or running around a tower.

**Gable** The triangular portion at the end of a building formed by the two sides of a sloping roof. Gables are also formed by other sloping roof areas, such as those over windows.

**Gabled roof** A sloping roof that forms a gable at either end.

**Gambrel roof** A roof with a double slope, like a leg bent at the knee.

**Hip roof** A roof that slopes in on all four sides like a pyramid; it may or may not have a flat top.

**Hood** A molding projecting over the top of a window or door. A hood may be flat, segmented or triangular.

**Keystone** The wedge-shaped stone at the top of an arch locking the other stones together.

**Lathe** A machine that rotates a piece of wood against various cutting tools to shape it into rounded contours. Details made on a lathe were often called "turned" or "turnings." Newel posts, balusters and finials were all turned on a lathe.

**Lap siding** Siding cut to overlap, often so that the surface of the siding is flush.

**Mansard roof** A roof with a steep slope on each of its four sides and either a flat top or a second slope not as steep as the first.

**Misguided improvement** An alteration of a Victorian house (particularly the facade) not in keeping with its Victorian character.

**Modillion** A square block placed in rows under a cornice. Originally the end of a supporting rafter, in Victorian houses it was purely ornamental.

**Moon gate** A half-moon arch used over a porch entrance or as a frame for an upper-story balcony; originally a type of garden gate used in Oriental gardens. Also called a horseshoe or "Moorish" arch.

**Mullion** A major vertical bar dividing a window.

**Muntin** One of the minor bars holding windowpanes inside the sash.

**Newel post** The main post at the top or bottom of a flight of stairs.

**Oriel bay** A bay window, especially on a second floor, usually appearing to be supported by a large bracket.

**Palladian window** A window with a central arch and rectangular sections on either side; also called a Venetian window.

**Panel molding** A horizontal band of framed panels.

**Parapet** A low wall. This term is used to refer to the part of a false front that conceals the gabled roof behind.

**Pediment** A triangular section of molding above porticoes, windows and doors. Classically a low-pitched gable on a columned temple.

**Picturesque** When used to describe architecture this term implies a house characterized by a variety of forms and textures; the overall effect is assymetrical and irregular.

**Pilaster** A pseudo-column projecting only slightly from the face of a wall.

**Plat** A street plan for a town.

**Portico** A roofed porch, supported by columns or brackets.

**Quoin** An ornamental wooden block placed in vertical rows at the corners of a building; classically a stone corner block used to strengthen the structure of a building.

**Rectangular bay** A bay window with corners meeting at right angles.

**Round headed window** An arched window.

**Roundel** A circular panel, window or niche.

**Routed** Hollowed out or furrowed.

**Rowhouse** One of a row of houses having a uniform structure and appearance.

**Rustication** Large blocks of stone with angled (rusticated) edges, creating deep grooves between the blocks. Wood may be cut to simulate this effect.

**Scroll saw** Also called a jig saw, this is a thin blade used to cut out interior patterns in a piece of wood. Pierced-work on

brackets and in window shields are made with a scroll saw.

**Segmented hood or segmental arch** A window or door hood in the shape of a segment of a circle.

**Slanted bay** A three-sided bay window with two slanted sides.

**Soffit** The underside of any architectural element.

**Squeezed pediment** A pediment in which the triangular section is quite small and appears to be squeezed in from the sides.

**Stop bracket** A bracket at the corner of a roof; so called because it ends the facade entablature.

**Swell or swelled bay** A bay window projecting from the face of a house in a flattened curve.

**Triangular bay** A bay window with two slanting sides meeting to form a triangle projecting from the house facade.

**Turret** A small windowless tower.

**Venetian window** See Palladian window.

**Voluted** Ornamented with a spiral scroll.

**Window shield** A flat, triangular piece of wood at the top corner of a window; used in pairs, often with an incised design.

**Witch's cap** A shingled conical tower roof.

# VICTORIAN PRESERVATION DIRECTORY

This directory is intended as an aid to those who wish to know more about Victorian houses and to assist in their preservation. The organizations listed here are either directly involved with or have information about Victorian buildings. Some are directly concerned with preservation while others are research and study centers.

**San Francisco**
Alamo Square Association
821 Grove Street
San Francisco 94117

Foundation for San Francisco's
   Architectural Heritage, Inc.
2007 Franklin Street
San Francisco 94109

San Francisco Archives and History Room
Main Library
Civic Center
San Francisco 94102

Victorian Alliance
4143 23rd Street
San Francisco 94114

**EAST BAY**

**Alameda**
Alameda Architectural and
   Historical Survey
Department of City Planning,
   Advance Planning Section
Alameda City Hall
Santa Clara Avenue and Oak Street
Alameda 94501

Alameda Historical Society
George Gunn, Curator
Alameda Public Library
2264 Santa Clara Avenue
Alameda 94501

The Alameda Victorian Preservation
   Society
Lloyd Hurwitz, President
3517 Oleander Avenue
Alameda 94501

**Oakland**
Department of City Planning
Chris Buckley, Associate Planner
Oakland City Hall
14th and Washington Streets
Oakland 94606

(The Planning Department will soon release a book titled, *REHAB RIGHT,* by Helaine Kaplan and Blair Prentice, Associate Planners. The book is free to Oakland residents and available to others for a sum from the State Office of Historic Preservation.)

Oakland Landmarks Commission
Carlos Anglin, Secretary
Oakland City Hall
14th and Washington Streets
Oakland 94606

California Room
Oakland Public Library
125 14th Street
Oakland 94606

Camron-Stanford House
Elizabeth Cohen, Director
Lake Merritt
1418 Lakeside Drive
Oakland 94606

**Piedmont**
Piedmont Historical Society
358 Hillside Avenue
Piedmont 94610

**Berkeley**
BAHA Architectural and Historical
  Survey
Leslie Emmington, Director
Anthony Bruce, State Coordinator
Berkeley City Hall
2180 Milvia Street
Berkeley 94707

Berkeley Architectural Heritage
  Association
P.O. Box 7066, Landscape Station
Berkeley 94707

## MARIN COUNTY

**San Rafael**
Marin County Historical Society
Elsie P. Mazzini, Director
1125 B Street
San Rafael 94901

San Rafael Cultural Commission
Andrew Snyder, Director
Dollar House
1408 Mission Street
San Rafael 94901

**Sausalito**
Sausalito Historical Society
Jack Tracy, Director
Sausalito Public Library
420 Litho Street
Sausalito 94965

**Belevedere**
Belevedere-Tiburon Landmarks Society
P.O. Box 134
Belevedere-Tiburon 94920

**San Anselmo**
San Anselmo Historical Commission
Mr. Van der Bilt
San Anselmo Public Library
110 Tunstead Avenue
San Anselmo 94960

## PENINSULA

**San Mateo**
San Mateo Historical Association
College of San Mateo
1700 Hillsdale Boulevard
San Mateo 94402

Palo Alto Historical Society
1685 Mariposa Avenue
Palo Alto 94306

**Cupertino**
California History Center
21250 Stevens Creek Boulevard
Cupertino 95014

Cupertino Historical Society
P.O. Box 88
Cupertino 95014

**Los Gatos**
Los Gatos Museum and Heritage Guild
4 Tait Avenue
Los Gatos 95030

Los Gatos Preservation Society
P.O. Box 1904
Los Gatos 95030

**Saratoga**
Saratoga Historical Foundation
P.O. Box 172
Saratoga 95070

**Santa Clara**
Santa Clara County Historical Heritage
   Commission
Ann Hines, Chairperson
1167 Plum Avenue
Sunnyvale 94087

Santa Clara Historical Society
523 Flannery Street
Santa Clara 95051

**San Jose**
San Jose Historical Museum
Donald de Mers, Director of Kelley Park
635 Phelan Avenue
San Jose 95112

San Jose Victorian Preservation Society
111 West St. John Street, Suite 700
San Jose 95113

San Jose Historical Landmarks
   Commission
801 North First Street
San Jose 95110

**Statewide Organizations**
State Office of Historic Preservation
P.O. Box 2390
Sacramento 95811

Californians for Preservation Action
P.O. Box 2169
Sacramento 95810

California Heritage Council
Room 351
680 Beach Street
San Francisco 94109

California Historical Society
2090 Jackson Street
San Francisco 94109

**National Organizations**
National Trust for Historic Preservation
Western Regional Office
681 Market Street
San Francisco, CA 94103

The Victorian Society in America
The Atheneum
East Washington Square
Philadelphia, PA 19106

## FOOTNOTES TO "VICTORIAN HOME BUILDING IN SAN FRANCISCO"

1. *California Architect and Building News* (hereafter called CABN), December 1880, p. 114.
2. *San Francisco Chronicle,* June 19, 1887, p. 13.
3. "Artistic Homes of California," *San Francisco Newsletter,* March 1887.
4. George Wolfe, "Our Architecture . . .," *San Francisco Morning Call,* December 4, 1887, p. 1.
5. "A Bay-Window," *Sloan's Architectural Review and Builders Journal,* November 1868, pp. 318-22.
6. Francis Goodwin, *Domestic Architecture* (London: H. G. Bohn, 1850).
7. Anne Bloomfield, "The Real Estate Associates." A paper to be published in the *Journal of the Society of Architectural Historians.*
8. CABN, April 1882, p. 53.
9. Frank M. Pixley, *San Francisco Argonaut,* May 7, 1881, p. 9.
10. CABN, April 1885, p. 69.
11. W. N. Lockington, "A Chapter on Architecture," *Overland Monthly,* September 1875, p. 283.
12. *San Francisco Chronicle,* June 19, 1887, p. 13.
13. CABN, September 1884, pp. 157-58.
14. Rossiter and Wright, *Modern House Painting,* 1883.
15. Newton J. Tharp, "What Bad There Is and What Good There Might Be in Inexpensive Architecture," *Overland Monthly,* December 1900, p. 536.
16. CABN, May 1886, p. 67.
17. CABN, May 1886, p. 68.
18. *San Francisco Call,* February 14, 1882, p. 5.
19. CABN, September 1880.
20. CABN, March 1891, p. 1.
21. Newton J. Tharp, op. cit. pp. 536-37.
22. CABN, April 1883, p. 54.
23. Lockington, loc. cit.
24. *San Francisco Morning Call,* April 21, 1887, p. 1.

## BIBLIOGRAPHY

### The Victorian Era in the United States

Gillon, Edmund V., Jr., and Clay Lancaster. *Victorian Houses: A Treasury of Lesser-Known Examples.* New York: Dover Paperback, 1973.

Girouard, Mark. *Sweetness and Light: The Queen Anne Movement, 1860-1900.* Oxford: Oxford University Press, 1977.

Maass, John. *Gingerbread Age: A View of Victorian America.* New York: Bramhall House, 1965.

————. *The Victorian Home In America.* New York: Hawthorn Books, 1972.

Mumford, Lewis. *The Brown Decades: A Study of the Arts in America, 1865-1895.* New York: Dover Paperback, 1955.

Saylor, Henry H. *Dictionary of Architecture.* New York: John Wiley and Sons, 1962.

Seale, William E. *The Tasteful Interlude: American Interiors through the Camera's Eye, 1860-1917.* New York: Praeger Publishers, 1975.

## San Francisco History

Hansen, Gladys, ed. *San Francisco Almanac.* San Francisco: Chronicle Books, 1975.

Lewis, Oscar. *Bay Window Bohemia.* New York: Doubleday, 1956

———. *San Francisco: From Mission to Metropolis.* Berkeley: Howell North, 1966.

Lotchin, Roger W. *San Francisco 1849-1856: From Hamlet to City.* Oxford: Oxford University Press, 1974.

Muscatine, Doris. *Old San Francisco: The Biography of a City.* New York: Putnam, 1975.

Watkins, T.H., and R.R. Olmstead. *Mirror of the Dream: An Illustrated History of San Francisco.* San Francisco: Scrimshaw Press, 1976.

## Victorian Architecture in San Francisco

Baird, Joseph, Jr. *Time's Wondrous Changes: San Francisco Architecture, 1776-1915.* San Francisco: California Historical Society, 1962.

Beebe, Lucius, and Charles Clegg. *San Francisco's Golden Era.* Berkeley: Howell North, 1960.

The Junior League of San Francisco. *Here Today.* San Francisco: Chronicle Books, 1968.

Kirker, Harold. *California's Architectural Frontier: Style and Tradition in the Nineteenth Century.* Layton, Utah: Peregrine Smith, 1973.

Olwell, Carol, and Judith Waldhorn. *A Gift to the Street.* San Francisco: Antelope Island Press, 1976.

## Victorian Restoration and Revival

Church, Ella Rodman. *How to Furnish a Home.* New York: Appleton's Home Books, 1881.

McKenna, H. Dickson. *A House in the City: A Guide to Buying and Renovating Old Rowhouses.* New York: Van Nostrand Reinhold, 1971.

Shoppell, Robert. *How to Build, Furnish and Decorate.* New York: Cooperative Building Plan Association, 1883.

Stanforth, Dierdre, and Martha Stamm. *Buying and Renovating a House in the City.* New York: Alfred A. Knopf, 1972.

———, and Louis Reens. *Restored America.* New York: Praeger Publishers, 1975.

Stephen, George. *Remodeling Old Houses Without Destroying Their Character.* New York: Alfred A. Knopf, 1973.

## INDEX

218

## SAN FRANCISCO STREET INDEX

*Numbers in parentheses are page numbers. Page numbers in italics refer to photographs and illustrations.*

Clayton Street  401-07, 409-11 (94).

Clinton Park  226-37 (14).

Cole Street  500, 508-16 (94). 705-43, 708-22 (93).

Collingwood Street  197, 284-90 (79).

Connecticut Street  415, 474, 512-16, 520-22, 524-26 (42).

Cottage Row  1-6 (112).

Day Street  207 *(29)*.

Delmar Street  116, 124, 130, 151, 155-59, 168 (93).

Diamond Street  649 (74). 826-44, 831, 905, 918, 940-46, 1001-07 (73). 1007 *(75)*. 1015-19 (73). 1019 *(74)*.

Divisadero Street  280 (92). 500, 501-07 (99). 905 (102). 924, 1045 (103). 1924, 2100, 2101, 2110-14 (109). 2131, 2197, 2201, 2221, 2229-31 (108)

Dolores Street  263 *(8)*. 979, 1000, 1001, 1006, 1010, 1027, 1037, 1041, 1070, 1074, 1080, 1083 (65). 1090 (65-66).

Douglass Street  109, 180, 250 (79).

Duboce Street  449, 477 (85).

Eddy Street  1830-34, 1840 (103).

Elizabeth Street  608, 610, 780-88 (74).

Ellis Street  1900 block (103).

Eureka Street  118-22, 282-86 (79). 572 (74).

Fair Oaks Street  8, 11, 14, 31, 68, 72, 77, 90, 108-10, 112 (61). 116 *(60,* 61). 118, 119, 175 (61). 200, 204, 210, 212 (65). 214, 217, 258, 260, 261, 283 (64). 332, 384, 387, 394, 433-47, 446-64, 451, 455, 463 (66).

Fell Street  870 (99).

Fillmore Street  133 (86). 722, 730 (100). 833-35 (101).

Florida Street  905-17, 918-44, 1031-41, 1059-61 (46).

Folsom Boulevard  2417, 2442 (47). 2533 (49). 2906-08 (50). 2914-34 (50-51). 2976 (50).

Franklin Street  1701 (26, 118). 2007 *(119,* 120).

Fulton Street  821-31, 841, 859 (101). 881-93 (26, 101). 915, 921 (101). 1198 (26, 102). 1214-60, 1255 (102).

Green Street  1713 *(23)*.

Greenwich Street  2845 *(16)*.

Golden Gate Avenue  1400-12, 1482, 1513-31, 1671, 1690 (103).

Gough Street  2000, 2004 (118). 2414-24 (120).

Grove Street  745-77, 813, 815, 817-21 (100). 824 (26, 100). 825, 834 (100). 926 (99-100). 940, 957, 975 (99).

Guerrero Street  102 (26). 120-26 (14). 801 (54). 811 *(55)*. 821 (54). 827 (54, *56)*. 845 (54). 860, 862 (56). 900, 915, 948, 966, 986, 988 (58). 1035 (61, *64)*. 1074, 1076, 1086, 1126-48 (61). 1169-77 (63). 1180, 1188 (64). 1201, 1227, 1233, 1241, 1253, 1256, 1257, 1259-65, 1274, 1286, 1317, 1320-26, 1325 (63). 1327, 1335, 1355, 1366, 1400, 1403, 1413-17 (62).

Haight Street  37-63, 100, 176, 185 (87). 198 (86). 319, 323, 391 (87). 395, 414, 588, 596, 605-09, 606, 626, 673 (88). 751, 758, 807-33, 847, 858 (89). 952, 1080, 1081, 1128, 1190 (92).

Hampshire Street  1168-70 (46).

Hancock Street  129, 142, 173, 177 (80).

Harrison Street  2517-29, 2661, 2710-12 (47).

**San Jose Avenue** 200, 210, 216, 220 (61). 248-54, 271-75, 325, 330, 380 (62).

**Scott Street** 9-51, 79, 93, 95 (89). 301-63, 348 (*12,* 99), 513 (99). 814-18, 1200 block (103). 1806-10, 1901, 2100 (109). 2203, 2207 (110).

**Shotwell Street** 618, 646, 650, 658, 680, 701-09, 715 (49), 733 (*48,* 49). 754, 760, 910, 926 (49). 985, 1014, 1016, 1020, 1070 (50). 1100, 1106, 1112, 1150, 1164 (51).

**Shrader Street** 411-15, 414 (94). 510, 524 (93).

**South Van Ness Avenue** 1106-26, 1136-42, 1150-60, 1170-86, 1201 (49). 1380, 1381 (51).

**Steiner Street** 601 (99). 635-39, 710-20, 814, 818, 850 (99). 908, 910 (102). 1057 (103). 2030, 2204-08, 2231, 2242-44, 2251, 2302 (112).

**Tennessee Street** 1002-14, 1036-42, 1045-49, 1060, 1100 block (41).

**Treat Avenue** 770 *(21).* 725 (47). 811 (26, 47). 1200, 1204, 1232 (50).

**Union Street** 2040 *(25).* 2460 (20).

**Valencia Street** 929-45, 953-57, 958 (57). 1049, 1057 (59). 1500 (62).

**Vallejo Street** 2053, 2059, 2065, 2121-27 (120).

**Vicksburg Street** 2, 8-20 (69). 27, 69, 75, 132, 160, 228, 309 (70).

**Waller Street** 210, 224, 234, 243, 252, 261, 269 (86). 515-33, 539, 563, 579, 591, 601, 607-39, 643, 667, 673-79 (88).

**Washington Street** 2269-95, 2355, 2405-61 (117). 2502-06 (112). 2527 (*6,* 112). 2548, 2560, 2561 (112). 3020 (108). 3021, 3022, 3024-26, 3074 (107).

**Webster Street** 81-97 (86). 709, 717 (100). 735-55 (101). 1717, 1737 (114). 1900 (27, 115). 1931 (116). 2209-35, 2239-53, 2311, 2315-21 (117).

**Wisconsin Street** 760 (42).

**York Street** 910, 917-35, 939, 956, 968-82, 1082 (46). 1328-46 (27).

**14th Street** 851-75, 879, 888 (85).

**15th Street** 2229, 2235 (84).

**17th Street** 3863 (81).

**18th Street** 4000-36, 4040, 4052 (81). 4407-09 (79).

**19th Street** 1243 (42). 4033, 4051, 4065, 4135 (80).

**20th Street** 1527, 1745 (42). 3441-45, 3466-76 (49). 3625, 3635, 3643, 3647, 3651, 3672 (54). 3919 *(18).* 4100-38, 4119-41, 4150 (78). 4324, 4327-31 (79). 4331 *(30).* 4417, 4421 (79).

**21st Street** 2773-75 (46). 3233, 3239 (52). 3243 (*26,* 52). 3320-24 (58). 3325 (57). 3329, 3333, 3339, 3345, 3364, 3367-75 (58). 3816-56 (78, *80).* 3833, 3847-55 (77).

**22nd Street** 2403-07 (46). 3126 (49). 3322, 3327-47, 3342-48, 3350-54, 3434-38 (60). 3702-06, 3711-15, 3733-45, 3749-77, 3817-71, 3900-42 (77).

**23rd Street** 2603, 2758-70 (46). 2972-76 (47). 3261, 3326, 3330, 3336 (51). 3339, 3350, 3356-64, 3370 (52). 3503-11 (61). 3679 (65). 3767 (69). 3827-41 (70). 3901 (71). 3968, 4020-22, 4045-53 (72). 4069, 4073-77, 4078, 4200, 4226, 4231-51, 4250, 4270-93 (75).

**24th Street** 3149 (50). 3845, 3896 (70). 3968 (72). 4073-77 (74).

**25th Street** 3166 (50).

**26th Street** 3729-43 (66).

# BIOGRAPHICAL NOTES

**JUDITH LYNCH WALDHORN** is co-author of *A Gift to the Streets,* an immensely popular work on San Francisco Victorians. She has taught Victorian architecture at Stanford University and San Francisco State University and published a number of articles on the subject in magazines. Ms. Waldhorn has two master's degrees from the University of California at Berkeley—one in urban planning and one in journalism.

**SALLY WOODBRIDGE** is the author of *Bay Area Houses* and co-author of *A Guide to the Architecture of San Francisco and Northern California.* She is a member of the board of Directors of the Society of Architectural Historians and West Coast Contributing Editor of *Progressive Architecture.* Ms. Woodbridge is a graduate of Duke University and is presently a PhD candidate at the Department of Architecture at the University of California, Berkeley.

**WENDY WHEELER** is a well-known San Francisco artist who studied in Florence and received her bachelor of fine arts degree from Syracuse University. She is best known for her line drawings, which have been widely published in books and magazines. But she is also active as a fine artist whose paintings and drawings have been exhibited in museums and art galleries from Florence to San Francisco.